THE CONISTON TIGERS

Seventy Years of
Mountain Adventure

A. Harry Griffin

"It's the simple things that matter –
snowflakes floating down on a quiet day,
harebells among the rocks overlooking a pool,
the heather on the fellsides, the water-ousel cheerily singing in the
beck no matter how bad the weather,
or the buzzards soaring."

– *the late Timothy Tyson: Grasmere cobbler, philosopher,
mountaineer and irrepressible tarn bather, in his eighties.*

Published by Sigma Leisure – an imprint of
Sigma Press, 1 South Oak Lane, Wilmslow, Cheshire SK9 6AR, England.

British Library Cataloguing in Publication Data
A CIP record for this book is available from the British Library.

ISBN: 1-85058-752-3

Typesetting and Design by: Sigma Press, Wilmslow, Cheshire.

Cover Design: MFP Design & Print

Cover photographs: main picture – Jim Porter leading Black Wall on Dow Crag in 1936 *(Tommy Tyson)*; colour photographs, from left – Dow Crag and Goats Hause in winter from Brown Pike, on the Dow Crag ridge; Langdale Pikes from Blake Rigg; approaching Wasdale *(all by Bob Allen)*.

Printed by: MFP Design & Print

Dedication

In loving memory of my
wonderful son Robin who
lived for mountains and hills,
and of Violet who persuaded
me to write the book.

By the same author:

Inside the Real Lakeland

In Mountain Lakeland

Pageant of Lakeland

The Roof of England

Still the Real Lakeland

Long Days in The Hills

A Lakeland Notebook

A Year in The Fells

Freeman of The Hills

Adventuring in Lakeland

A Lakeland Mountain Diary

Foreword

– by Sir Christian Bonington CBE

This is a very special book. It tells the story of Harry Griffin, a climber and perceptive writer, and the seventy years he has spent climbing on the crags and wandering over the hills of the Lake District. In doing so he has bridged the pre- and post-war development of climbing.

He paints wonderfully evocative pictures of his introduction to rock climbing in the late '20s, with nailed boots and hemp rope, when there were no such things as double ropes, slings, nuts, harnesses or other safety devices and the rule that the leader 'mustn't fall' was paramount.

Its strength, however, is the way in which Harry has brought to life many of the great characters of Lakeland climbing and his own love of the Lake District hills. Nowhere is this more strikingly portrayed than in the *Country Diary* column which he has written for *The Guardian* for almost fifty years, and selections from which intersperse the chapters.

His is a unique autobiography which is also a living history of modern Lakeland climbing.

Chris Bonington

A. Harry Griffin: an appreciation

Alan Rusbridger – Editor, The Guardian

This is the book which thousands of people have been willing Harry Griffin to write, especially those who follow his adventures and reflections in the *The Guardian*'s Country Diary on alternate Mondays.

Although a modest and little-trumpeted part of the paper, the column is read with a passionate intensity and *The Coniston Tigers* shows why. Every Country Diary column reflects the parallel passion of the writers, born of a vision (in Harry's case, that little boy from Barrow with his blue jersey and scrambling-grazed knees) and honed by the journalist's discipline of getting it all into a few hundred words – or, as the compositor would say, blanking else.

As well as being the official Father of the Diarists, Harry has an intensity all of his own which was well-illustrated when Denis Thorpe and Martin Wainwright interviewed him for the *The Guardian* to mark his 40th year as a Country Diarist. After the usual hike in a blizzard (relishing extreme discomfort recurs predictably throughout this book), Harry became absorbed in anecdotage in front of the blazing log fire of the Queen's Head in Troutbeck. Luckily, beer consumption was still young when smoke and the smell of burning anorak engulfed the great man, although he refused to claim expenses for his charred mountain-wear, saying that the conflagration was his own fault.

Readers will find several other occasions in the *Tigers* when Harry sets himself on fire, either through absorption in the heavenly world of the Lakes or because the alternative to some lethal petrol-stove might have been freezing to death. The dramas are appropriate metaphorically because Harry's writing also sets people alight, kindling the love of the Lakes and climbing which giants like George Basterfield and the Whitings of Wastwater fanned in him.

One of the pleasures of *The Coniston Tigers* (as of all Harry's writing) is the way such people are honoured and given their place in the beloved landscape of the fells. It is not just Blencathra and Catstycam – sonorous names – which make Harry Griffin's Lake District so appealing, but the chance to meet characters like the cave-dwelling Professor of Adventure, Millican Dalton, and the German doctor who never dried after swimming in mountain tarns because he held that the pure water would make its way back through his skin like sweat in reverse.

It might seem clubbish to refer again in conclusion to *The Guardian* connection, because the most whiskery of *Telegraph* readers or the raciest tabloid buyer will equally enjoy this book. But both Harry and the Lake District have a special place in the heart of our paper, whose staff in the great days of Manchester and C.P. Scott were constantly out on Cumbria's hills and lakes. As he movingly describes, Harry lost a staunch companion and fellow climber when his son Robin died tragically young. *The Guardian* too lost a son prematurely when its editor Ted Scott, the son of C.P. and a man both much-loved and of great potential, drowned in Windermere after his yacht capsized on 22 April 1932.

Those were the days when Arthur Ransome was a *Guardian* star, and I hope Harry won't mind if I attempt to match his skill at choosing an apt quotation to summarise the effect of *The Coniston Tigers* and the Griffin Country Diaries. The children of *Swallows and Amazons* nick-named a hilly bluff overlooking their lake 'Darien' because as good young Keats students they knew the conclusion of *On First Looking Into Chapman's Homer* where the poet feels

'...like some watcher of the skies
When a new planet swims into his ken;
    Or like stout Cortez when with eagle eyes
He star'd at the Pacific – and all his men
    Look'd at each other with a wild surmise –
Silent, upon a peak in Darien.'

That is the gift Harry Griffin has given to generations of readers whose only quibble might be with his distinctively old-fashioned byline – A. Harry Griffin. He is not *a* Harry Griffin, he is *The* Harry Griffin and *The Coniston Tigers* shows again why.

Alan Rusbridger – Editor, The Guardian

Preface

Eight years before the start of the Second World War, when the Lake District was a much quieter, more secluded place than it is today, nine young men converted a wooden garage near the shore of Coniston Water into a sleeping hut, and formed themselves into a climbing club – the Coniston Tigers. For years, every weekend, until long after the war, they explored the climbs on Dow Crag, behind the hut, Gimmer Crag in Langdale, the Wasdale crags and, each winter, the Scottish snows. This is their story, written by one of the original nine, and also, for added flavour, some of his own memories of seventy years' climbing, skiing and walking in Lakeland, Scotland, the Alps, the Rockies and, once, in the foothills of the Himalayas. The writer is only a very ordinary mountaineer compared with those far more able climbers who write tales of great ascents and epic dramas in the mountains. Indeed, almost all the Tigers were only average cragsmen. Between us, we managed to put up a number of first ascents and had plenty of excitements but, although we called ourselves the Coniston Tigers, suggesting we were capable of great things, we were not really hard men, and hardly in the forefront of Lake District climbing at that time. But, looking back on those early days, the handful of us still alive are sure they were the best years of our lives.

Until overtaken by age or infirmity we all simply lived for the fells and the crags, and have always, down the years, cherished our love of high places or, when rocks became too demanding, just lovely, quiet places. In my own case, in old age, it is the hills – often, nowadays, only little hills – and the magic of the changing seasons that keep me alive. The book came to be written in this way. My second wife, Violet, who, sadly, passed away suddenly after we had been married only a few months, was always interested in my stories and photographs of the Tigers and the hut, and often tried to persuade me to put them in a book. "Otherwise," she would say, "all these old tales and memories of climbing before the war will be lost for ever." Believing I had finished with writing books, and not, at my age, wanting the work involved, I was most reluctant to embark on the project, but for weeks she kept pressing me. And then, only a few days before she died – completely unexpectedly - she managed to extract a promise from me that I would write the book. I'm afraid it has taken me seven years to carry out her wishes – six years trying to find the drive and inspiration to make a start, and another year to write it – after first mastering the complexities of word processing rather late in life.

Reading through the manuscript I realise I haven't written nearly enough about the exploits of *all* the Tigers but, relying only on my hazy memories of up to seventy years ago, with all our hut records lost long ago, there's little more I could relate. So, I've tried to make up for this lack of balance by writing at length about some of my later companions. But I can't make any excuse for the considerable space given to my own modest adventures, except that a certain amount of garrulity is inevitable in what I suppose is a sort of mountain autobiography. Looking back, it's been an interesting and rewarding mountain life. And I'm sure I couldn't have lasted into my late eighties, and enjoyed so many pleasures and excitements, without mountains. As Geoffrey Winthrop Young, the climber-poet sang:

"Only a hill but all of life to me
Up there, between the sunset and the sea."

A. Harry Griffin

Acknowledgments

I must first thank Chris Bonington for his splendid Foreword. It is a great honour for a very ordinary mountaineer to be noticed in this way by the country's most distinguished climber. My sincere thanks also to Alan Rusbridger, Editor of *The Guardian* for his very generous appreciation of my writing efforts.

Several of the photographs (including those of the Tigers in Scotland and the fine picture of Jim Porter leading Black Wall on Dow Crag) are from the collection of the late Tommy Tyson (kindly loaned by his son, Mr Irwin G Tyson). A few photographs have been loaned by Jim Porter and the photograph of myself on North Wall, Dow Crag was taken by Jack Atkinson. The classic photograph of Siegfried Herford on the first ascent of the Flake Crack, Central Buttress, Scafell Crag was given to me, many years ago, by his partner on the climb, the late George S. Sansom. Tony Greenbank took the photograph of Jim Birkett. Other photographs are from my own collection.

Mrs Betty Wainwright has kindly welcomed my use of the drawing of Dow Crag, which her late husband specially drew for me about forty years ago. The pen-and-ink drawings scattered throughout the book are also by the late Alfred Wainwright who, nearly forty years ago, handed me the rough proofs and gave me permission to reproduce them in my first books, *Inside the Real Lakeland* (1961) and *In Mountain Lakeland* (1963). This permission was gratefully acknowledged in both these books and the acknowledgment is repeated here. Mr Wainwright also specially drew for me, at my request, a detailed endpaper map of the Lake District for use in my first book. This, also, I am delighted to use again.

Several people have encouraged or helped me with the book. Especially, Mrs Jean Ellis steered me through the initial intricacies of word processing; Tony Greenbank provided constant encouragement and practical help; Bob Allen, a fine colour photographer, has been most generous with assistance; and two of the remaining Tigers, Jim Porter and Jack Atkinson, have clarified fading memories of nearly seventy years ago.

Country Diary extracts

The little pieces in italics separating the chapters have been selected at random from my contributions, during almost fifty years,
to the "Country Diary" in *The Guardian* to add some Lake District
colour to the book.

AHG. Kendal, Cumbria

Contents

A MAP OF *LAKELAND*

drawn by
a.wainwright.

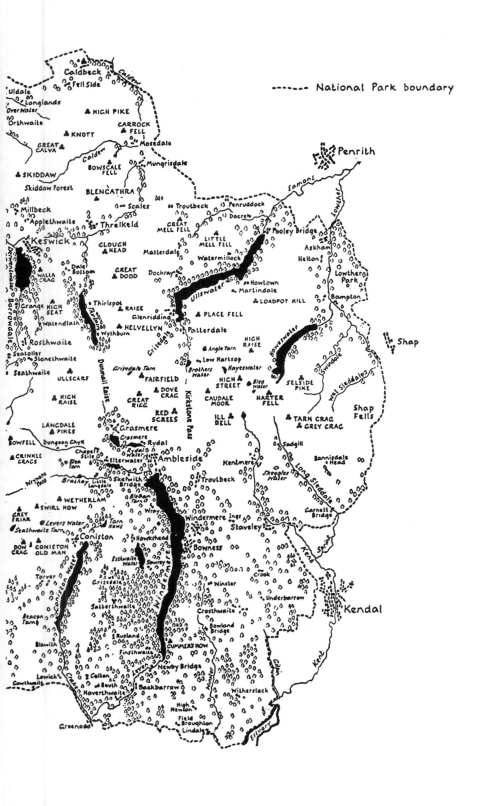

------- National Park boundary

Dow Crag (Alfred Wainwright)

A Winter Transformation

There are days in the fell country, just now and again, when the magic of the scenery leaves you breathless. It may be the sight of mists suddenly swept from a summit with the dale leaping upwards at you like a coloured slide coming into focus, or perhaps you turn a corner on a rocky ridge and see all heaven reflected in a mountain pool. But these are hill days and it is rare indeed that the motorist or the walker in the dale can catch the sort of fairytale beauty we saw the other day. It was the kind of winter's morning that Windermere folk know so well – a blanket of mist over the lake and across the lower fells, but the promise of clear skies later. I drove northwards through the gloom with dipped headlights and a firm resolve not to touch the brakes on such an icy highway.

Over the Raise it was little better, with sheep looming out of the greyness an added hazard, while the Thirlmere shore road was treacherous as an ice-rink. I knew, though, that the transformation would come, for there had been the makings of a clear morning in Kendal, and I had a fair idea it might arrive somewhere near St John's in the Vale; it so often does. What I had completely under-estimated was the splendour of the likely miracle. I expected to drive out of the mists and see brown sunlit fells; instead, the grey curtain was suddenly torn aside to reveal, unbelievably high up in the bluest sky, all the glory of the Alps. Maybe it was only the roof-tree of Blencathra plastered in new snow, but that morning, with the rest of the fell country seemingly buried in fog, and the dazzling white ridges sparkling through one hole torn in the blue sky, it could have been the Wetterhorn at dawn or, very nearly, with a little imagination, the Brenva face of Mont Blanc.

February 1968

1

Early Adventuring

The snow lay deeper on the fells than we had ever seen it before – several feet deep, soft, powdery and all-enveloping – and the cold was the most biting we had ever known, almost searing our flesh. It was snowing hard, great curtains of driven snow sweeping across the fellsides, and, mixed with the snow, hurled about the sky by a boisterous wind, were torrents of hailstones that brought tiny flecks of blood on to unprotected faces. A handful of us were making an ascent of Coniston Old Man nearly seventy years ago – half a dozen young men in clinker-nailed boots, wearing untidy old clothes, balaclava helmets and motorcycle goggles and using long, wooden-shafted ice axes. The weather, we had decided, meant that rock-climbing was out of the question and the snow was far too soft and unconsolidated, and, indeed, avalanche-prone, for an ascent of one of the gullies on Dow Crag. So, we were on a mere walk from our weekend headquarters – our own wooden hut, a converted garage, behind the tall-chimneyed Coniston Old Hall on the shore of Coniston Water. For a change, the Coniston Tigers were having an "off day". This day, at the beginning of the 1930s, is one of my earliest memories of our youthful climbing group, the rather boastfully-named Coniston Tigers, although by then we were already a fairly well-established gang of enthusiastic devotees of the crags.

Sitting in my study this morning, looking out across the rooftops of Kendal, I can still recall incidents of that day so long ago more clearly than I can remember some of the things I was doing last year. Time plays tricks on the elderly and memories of the days of one's youth, when we were enjoying life to the full, with no doubts or worries about the future, are sometimes easily brought back by a faded photograph, a familiar corner in the hills or even a scent or smell. For example, the fragrant smell of woodsmoke always wings me back to dear old Dunnerdale, and especially to one of the farms there. It was there, nearly seventy-five years ago, that I consumed a huge Lakeland "tea" in a vast, stone-floored kitchen after the ascent of my very first hill, the splendidly-rocky Stickle Pike.

And in much the same way, whenever I am coping nowadays with blizzards or soft snow or bad visibility or near-exhaustion in winter, I am immediately swept back, in memory, to that exciting day on the Old Man with the Tigers all those years ago. I have had, since then, many far more desperate or frightening times on ice-climbs, times when I have vowed that if I ever got up I would never climb again. But this winter walk up the Old Man has left a more permanent impression upon me than have any of the technically far more demanding adventures. Probably because this was the first time we had had to struggle against really atrocious conditions.

It was the extraordinary depth of the snow that is my most vivid memory of that exciting day. We had never been out in snow anything like that deep before, although we were already accustomed to far longer and much more severe winters than we get today. The snow blanketed everything – the quarry workings, the spoil heaps, the workmen's huts, the machinery, the rock outcrops and little crags and, of course, the tracks and the quarry road which was supposed to be our chosen route. We must have walked up the steep hill from what was then the railway station to the fell gate as I can clearly remember trudging through thigh-deep snow past the cottages above the Sun Hotel. Here one of us took a photograph of the expedition – the last to be taken, because of the wild conditions, until our return. For much of the way, as we trudged and floundered up the mountain, we were struggling with snow nearly up to our waists, taking turns in front to fight our way through, and just picking what seemed the most promising way up the steepening slopes. There was no question of following a particular route: we might just as well have been in the dark for all we could glean of the way ahead. We all knew the mountain well enough for we often went over the top at the end of a day's climbing on Dow Crag, but there was just nothing to be seen except the swirling snow and a few feet of white-out soaring up into the mist. Even now I can recall the exhaustion from struggling through the deep snow and almost feel the pain of the driven hailstones on my face.

At times, as we floundered about, slipping and sliding and

roundly cursing the conditions, each of us must have privately wondered whether we were going to get up, but nobody suggested turning back. Despite the misery and discomfort we were quietly enjoying the battle, even though, with nothing whatever to guide us, we had little or no idea where we were. But I clearly remember turning a corner round a bit of crag plastered with icicles, and there, just ahead, was Low Water, piled high with snow-draped ice-floes and looking exactly like a photograph of the Antarctic. (I still recall this moment every time I pass the place today.) Now, at last, we knew where we were, below the steepest and craggiest part of the mountain, and could make a rough guess about the direction in which the summit lay. Clearly, under the conditions, we couldn't make a bee-line for the top, even if we could have seen it, because of the crags we knew were in the way, so we decided to turn left, gaining height gently before making for the summit.

There was no sign of the blizzard abating. The snow continued to bucket down relentlessly, as thick as the artificial snow in the early Charlie Chaplin films, and the gale hurled the clouds and, occasionally, the bursts of hail across the sky. Our old tweeds – there were no anoraks or waterproofs in those days – were freezing on our bodies and we could see nothing at all. And so we trudged on in silence, each one keeping his thoughts to himself, until suddenly, without any warning or sound, the leader just disappeared from sight. A second later he was followed by the next man and then the rest of us. What had happened? We hadn't fallen down a crag or an unseen crevasse. We had simply stumbled, one after the other, through the broken roof of one of the quarrymen's stone huts, landing safely enough, although shaken and a little confused, in several feet of snow that nearly filled the tiny building. None of us knew of the hut nor, of course, could we have seen it since everything on the fellside was covered by enormous drifts of snow, but the line of our upward traverse had taken us across the top of it until we dropped through the roof. We could now make a guess about the possible depth of the snow. We dusted ourselves down, trampled down the snow a bit to make a floor and munched our frozen sandwiches in the darkness, thankful that, for a few minutes at least, we had shelter from the storm.

Eventually, rested and fed, we crawled out through the hole in the roof and back into the maelstrom, set our faces to the snow slope and prepared to set off again into the blizzard. Immediately we found ourselves at cross-purposes. Some preferred a line to the left, others more to the right, someone else straight ahead, but none of us knew where we were or in which direction the summit lay. It was then that my brother Leslie, the youngest in the party, came into his own. Glancing at a tattered Bartholomew map he had been carrying in his jacket pocket he mysteriously produced a tiny Boy Scout's compass, twiddled it about over the map, and then announced with impressive certainty and pointing with his arm, "The summit's that way." I don't think any of the others were carrying maps; I know I wasn't. After all, we were only going up the Old Man. And none of us, apart from Les, had a compass. He led us to the summit.

There was no huge, purpose-built cairn and wind-shelter on top of Coniston Old Man in those days – just a big pile of stones. But the snow was so deep that day that the cairn was hardly notice-able; it was just a slight bump in the great white carpet that covered the top. It was difficult to estimate the depth of the snow, and we didn't hang around to work it out, for the blizzard, and especially the fury of the wind, was way beyond our experience. All we wanted was to get down out of the storm as quickly as possible. Later, we thought the snow must have been anything from six to ten feet deep on the summit and very much deeper in the drifts on the slopes.

We decided to make for Goats Hause and then descend by way of Goats Water, but we found it almost impossible to make prog-ress against the gale – even downhill. In this battle down the steep snow slopes, sheeted in ice for much of the way, as we tried to keep in balance with our axes, several of us had items of clothing torn off by the fury of the wind and swept away, no doubt into the next valley. Among these items were a pair of goggles, a scarf or two and, I seem to recall, a motorcycle helmet. Of course, we never saw them again. But we carried on, fighting every yard of the way down to the col, and then, turning left, past Goats Water. Here the gale was hurling the spindrift from the white-topped waves far up the buttresses of Dow Crag – a remarkable sight I have never seen repeated since in anything like so dramatic a fashion, despite hun-dreds of visits to the crag.

Lower down the fellside conditions gradually improved. The snow was not so deep, the clouds lifted to some extent and, towards the end of the short winter's day, the blizzard eventually blew itself out. But the biting cold gripped the white landscape even more savagely, and had we not been struggling so hard, with-out pause, for so many hours, our bodies would have been frozen through. As it was, we were young, strong and healthy and as, at dusk, we trudged through the snow down the lane to our hut on the shore of the lake, we felt glowing and fit and satisfied that we had had a wonderful day.

We opened the door of the hut, lit our prized Tilley lamp and the old combustion stove and then helped each other, in turn, out of our outer garments – old jackets, corduroy breeches and cut-down so-called "waterproofs". We couldn't undress ourselves unaided for our clothes had all frozen into solid shapes like suits of armour. But eventually, after a struggle, we managed to get them all off. And then we stood all our clothes in a line, propped up against the side of the hut, solid as sheets of tin – and photo-graphed them. It had been a good day – probably the first time that the half-dozen of us had been involved in an adventure together – the very first proper adventure of the Coniston Tigers, although it was some time later before we thought of the name for our little gang.

But I must go back much earlier to begin my memories of seventy years on the fells and crags, ignoring all other experiences and excitements of a long life, including participation in a world war. The Lake District was a much quieter, far less crowded place in the late 1920s, when I started climbing. Outside holiday times it was almost a secluded paradise. What wonderful, spacious days they were: carefree, youthful days on uncrowded crags, long, long before even the threat of war. There were few motor cars, the much narrower roads being almost deserted at times, and no caravan sites, camping sites, car parks, public conveniences or litter bins that I can remember. Grassy, uneroded tracks, hardly noticeable in places, wound gently over the fells; farmers drove to market on Saturday mornings in two-wheeled horse-drawn gigs; and four-in-hands were still going over the passes.

Compared with today's sweeping motorways and manicured highways the Lakeland roads in those days were little more than rough lanes, often poorly surfaced. I remember cycling down the Cumberland side of Dunmail Raise on one occasion in the twen-ties, probably doing the 100-mile round trip from Barrow to Keswick and back. It was so bumpy and uneven that, in an unguarded moment, I hit a stone and went over the handlebars, landing in knee-scraping gravel that did considerable painful damage to flesh not yet protected by long trousers. Driving over Wrynose and Hardknott passes a few years later was something of an adventure, too, for the road was then no better than a river bed, and even the twisting hill road over Birker Moor was quite a sport-ing route in those days. There were no tractors on the farms at that time; the farmers did their ploughing with horses and a fine sight it was, too, with the gulls flying around the newly-turned furrows and the rich, dark loam arrow-straight against the stubble. In the autumn came the haymaking, the harvest fields laboriously cut by hand and the horses leading the piled hay down the lane in the evening.

There were no double-decker buses in Lakeland then and any danger on the roads was less likely to be caused by cars and coaches than by wandering sheep straying out of unfenced fields or the open fells on to the highway. Most visitors came to the area by train, and charabancs, as we called coaches in those days, were rarely seen. Many of the present-day hotels and boarding houses were private residences then, although I remember the "Old England" at Bowness had considerable renown as a honeymoon hotel. Keswick and Ambleside were fairly quiet places, even on Saturday nights in summer, and I can think of only two cafés in each of these two towns before the war compared with the many there are today.

In those distant days you could sit on top of Pillar Rock, as I did many times, and look down the long length of Ennerdale without seeing a single tree: nothing but bare fellsides and the Liza winding through the shingle far below. The mass afforestation of this west Lakeland valley, one of the biggest changes ever wrought on any Lakeland dale in my lifetime, had not yet started. Mardale Green near Haweswater was not to be drowned for several years and the hamlet was still a peaceful, old-world oasis nestling among the fells. Regrettably, I never visited the old Dun Bull Inn there as these valleys in the far eastern fells were a little outside our usual stamping ground. However, I can remember looking down on the dale from the shoulder of Harter Fell more than once and admiring the neat, level fields, scattered farmsteads, the winding lanes between old stone walls and the little church just below The Rigg, before it was planted with trees.

There were no youth hostels or climbing huts in Lakeland when I started climbing. The Robertson Lamb hut in Langdale was opened by the Wayfarers' Club in 1930, our own (Coniston Tigers) hut in Coniston around 1931, and the K Fellfarers hut at Seathwaite in Borrowdale in 1934. These, so far as I am aware, were the first climbing huts in Lakeland, so our little, unofficial club was in the very forefront of this big development in the climbing world. Caravans, as we know them today, were just not around in those early days and very little camping was done. Climbers – and other visitors – were almost entirely confined to hotels or farmhouses.

About this time Millican Dalton, the self-styled Professor of

Adventure, whom I knew well, was living in his cave on Castle Crag in Borrowdale during the summer months and had his home-made raft on Derwentwater. He used to take parties on the crags and I often bumped into him in Rosthwaite, stocking up with his groceries at Plaskett's shop and loading the bags on to his old bicycle, which he would push down the lane. You could always tell when Millican was in residence by the plume of smoke from his fire rising up through the trees on Castle Crag at dusk. On all the crags in Lakeland in those distant days there were fewer than 300 classified rock-climbs. Twenty years ago there were far more than 3000; today I could not begin to guess at the number, which leaps ahead every year. That is some measure of the growth of climbing within my lifetime.

There were no "hikers" in those days. The word had not been invented and the masses had not yet "discovered" the hills. I suppose there must have been "weekends" in those days but there was

Borrowdale from the top of Central Gully on Great End

certainly no mass exodus into the countryside, especially the Lake
District, as there is today. Winter was always a quiet time in the
dales and the district seemed to go to sleep. The country was in
depression, ten years or so after the end of the First World War,
with widespread unemployment and hard times, but my climbing
friends and I – the Coniston Tigers – were more fortunate than
many for we were all in work, just at the start of our careers. There
might not have been a lot of money about in those days but most
things were cheap enough. Bed and breakfast at the Crown Hotel,
Coniston was then six shillings and sixpence – full board for the
week was three guineas and baths were free! The rubber plimsolls
we used on the hard climbs – our only climbing gear apart from
boots and rope – only cost ten pence a pair at Woolworth's. If we
had ever stopped to think about it – although I doubt that we ever
did – I think we would have felt secure enough. There were no big
clouds on the horizon and life, for better-placed youngsters like us,
at least, seemed very good indeed. After all, very few people in
England at that time had even heard of Adolph Hitler.

My younger brother Leslie and I lived with our parents in
Barrow-in-Furness, a shipbuilding town with broad, tree-lined
main streets on the edge of the sea. It always seemed very windy
and bracing, with plenty of fresh air. As youngsters we were well
used to looking at hills. Black Combe was perhaps ten miles away
as the crow flies, but on a clear day it sometimes seemed at no distance at all – a great hump of a mountain filling half the sky so that
we felt we almost lived in its shadow. And, not far from our home,
from the golf club at Hawcoat, on a hill above the town, we could
look across at the Coniston fells – lovely, familiar shapes that have
been in the forefront of my memory for more than seventy years.
Today, sitting in my study on the rooftops, I have just drawn, on a
sheet of A4 paper, the outline of these well-remembered hills to
make sure I still know every wrinkle. Indeed, I'm quite sure I could
still draw, without looking at a map, the whole 360-degree panorama of the Lakeland fells and Yorkshire hills that I used to see
every day from my previous home just inside the national park. I
have since moved into the town but the memory is undiminished,
so familiar have these high places become in a long lifetime.
    At home in Barrow we youngsters believed that Black Combe
was an extinct volcano and that the crags we could see behind the
"black combe" were the rim of the crater. It was a bad sign, we
thought, when we could see these crags very clearly and pick out

the lines of the ravines, the bracken and the heather and even the farms at the foot of the fell: it would probably rain the next day. Sometimes we couldn't see the mountain for days, or even weeks, because of mist or rain, but there were better days when the sun shone on its snows, clearly revealing the "crater" of the "volcano", or when the shadows of the clouds raced across its broad, sunlit summit. When we looked across the Duddon estuary from the shore at the north end of Walney Island or from the sandhills not far from our home it sometimes seemed as if you could row over to Black Combe in half an hour. On other days, from high points above the town, we traced the coastline around the Duddon estuary and across the foot of the mountain, and watched the smoke of the trains as they chugged along past Green Road.

Black Combe was, of course, our first mountain – if you can so describe a hill that falls thirty feet short of the magic contour of 2000 feet. It had always been a mountain to us. Leslie and I were staying with our parents for a week's holiday in the inn at The Green, a little hamlet two or three miles away from the foot of the fell. The full board and lodging for the four of us for the week probably cost about ten pounds. We explored the area thoroughly, ate huge meals, tried our hands at Cumberland and Westmorland wrestling with the local lads on the green in the evenings, and eventually persuaded our father to take us up Black Combe. Left to our own devices we would have been up the hill long before then but this was forbidden by our parents who thought – probably correctly, for we were an adventurous pair – that we would get into trouble.

Not that Dad was any great shakes as a mountain guide. He'd never been up there before – nor up any other mountain, so far as I am aware, up to that time. He had no idea of the route, had no map or compass and none of us had boots or waterproofs. Anoraks hadn't yet been invented. But we could see the great bulk of the mountain looming over us and, after a couple of miles of road walking, we climbed over a wall and started up.

Although I've since been up Black Combe, by all the recognised routes, many times, I've never been able to decide which way we went up all those years ago. It certainly wasn't by the most popular route – from Whicham Church – for that would have involved several more miles of road walking than the couple of miles or so that I remember. And I don't think it was from Beckside for that starts up a lane whereas we went straight up the fellside. We must have taken a line far to the left or west of Whitecombe Beck and made straight for where we judged the summit might be, avoiding the "crater" below its ring of crags which we didn't even see. All I can remember is that it seemed a long, steep plod with many ups and downs. We undoubtedly learned our first mountaineering lesson that day: that there are, nearly always, several false summits before the real one.

From the top we looked at the Lake District mountains, far away to the north-east, and didn't find them all that interesting. We knew the Coniston fells, anyway, for we could see them every day, if we wanted, from the road above our house. We didn't know that Black Combe was a famous summit and that Wordsworth had been up there and had said it was the best viewpoint in England. (Actually, he had written that it was the most extensive "unobstructed" view in Britain.) What really interested us was the view in the opposite direction, on the seaward side. That was the view of Barrow-in-Furness, our home town, with the shipyard and the big cranes, the bridge over the Channel, and Walney Island, and all the villages around, stretched out, nearly two thousand feet below our feet, as if on a map. This really excited us, the first time we had looked down from a great height, and that was what made our day – not the famed view of the Lakeland hills. And, after more than seventy years, it is the only part of the day that I can clearly recall.

But although Black Combe could be described as my first mountain, I had already been taken, a year or two earlier, up my very first Lake District hill – if you discount all the really little hills around our home. This was Stickle Pike (1231ft), the delightful, pointed, rocky summit that sticks up so proudly at the southern end of the Dunnerdale fells. I was about 12 years old at the time, still in short trousers, an undistinguished pupil at the grammar school. Trying to recall that first proper day in the hills I am helped somewhat by a faded, yellowing photograph that shows a huddle of schoolboys on the top of the Pike with me somewhere in the middle. We are all wearing our school caps of blue, with a gold ring round the crown and a badge in front; blue blazers with the school badge on the pocket; short trousers and low shoes. I believe we were members of the school's junior mountaineering or fell-walking club. Nowadays, such school clubs have their own transport and their members are kitted out with boots, rucksacks, anoraks and even climbing equipment, but we had none of these things. "Outdoor pursuits" or "leisure activities" had not even been conceived and were many years away: it was unusual for school parties to be taken into the hills or, indeed, anywhere else. I seem to remember one or two of us having school satchels or simple cloth haversacks, made by our mothers, on our backs, but this was the full extent of the party's equipment.

We went by the early morning workmen's train from Barrow to Foxfield and from there walked all the way through Broughton and Broughton Mills to the top of Stickle Pike and back – between ten and twelve miles. In charge of the party was Mr H.M. Sawtell, our geography master, and I will always be grateful to him for thus introducing me to the hills and first opening my eyes to their beauty. Before we left for the scramble to the summit he gathered us round him and issued two orders. "Don't, whatever you do," he said, "drink from the streams; this will spoil your wind." He continued, "Never roll boulders down the fellside." And ever since that far-off summer's day in 1923 I've always obeyed his second, very sensible, command and consistently ignored his first – even after Chernobyl. Drinking the icy-cold water of fast-flowing becks has always been one of the joys of an outing in the fells. We finished off that first real hill-day wolfing down a huge meal of scones and cakes in a cool, farmhouse kitchen before trudging down the lanes back to Foxfield Station.

But my very special memory of that day – apart from the lovely, spiky summit – has always been the wonderful scent of woodsmoke, sniffed perhaps from some cottage chimney as we tramped back down the valley in the evening. And, indeed, whenever I smell woodsmoke today I am back in a flash to those earliest days in the thickly wooded country east of the Duddon where, perhaps, my love for the hills began.

A Child's Mountain

Old men with walking sticks, young children in gym shoes and even babies cocooned in fathers' rucksacks were on top of Catbells the other day in their dozens, wandering along the lazy ridge to High Spy. It was a perfect day for idling on the tops – warm and sunny, barely a breath of wind and matchless views to far horizons. The last drifts of snow were still clinging to the cornices above the north face of Helvellyn and later, from High Spy, we saw the last white handkerchiefs of winter on Great Gable. Catbells has always seemed to me a family hill for enthusiasts of all ages, but mostly for children. It was, I recall, my daughter's first "mountain", ticked off at the age of two and a half, half a century ago. It's a pretty name for a child's mountain – the hill where Beatrix Potter's Mrs Tiggy-Winkle had some of her adventures, finally disappearing through a door somewhere Newlands way. And from the top, this bright afternoon, Keswick looked a fairy town in a magic landscape, and Derwentwater, spread out below us, ringed with wooded fells, dotted with enchanted islands and white yachts becalmed like floating butterflies, an exciting place for youthful adventure. There was so much to see and admire: the lovely, unspoiled Vale of Newlands and every step of the routes up Robinson and Hindscarth; the crumpled ram's horn shape of the summit of Causey Pike and its exciting ridge; the crowded woods and crags of Borrowdale with seventy years of adventurous memories; and, straight ahead, a glimpse of the highest land in England. Two jet aircraft streaked, in a sudden crash of sound, through the Jaws of Borrowdale and a pair of ravens performed aerobatics for us high above our perch on High Spy. We came down by Hause Gate, past the memorial seat for Hugh Walpole who lived in the lovely house on the lower slopes of the fell, today carpeted with daffodils. Each morning, after breakfast, he would cross the lawn to his big library over the garage and write quickly, often describing scenes he could see from his windows. Many of his heroes strode these grassy slopes or ran up through the bracken and the heather to watch the sun setting behind Grasmoor.

May 1988

Chapter Two

Discovering the Hills

S eated at my desk by an attic window that looks out over the roofs of Kendal and across to the 1000ft summit of Benson Knott, I am, in my eighty-eighth year, trying to bring back memories of rock-climbing in the Lake District, Scotland and other mountain areas up to seventy years ago. A few of these memories are as vivid and clear as if they had happened last week; others, as obscure and hazy as the morning mists hanging over Windermere. Most, probably, have gone forever.

A few old snaps, some youthful scribblings and scraps from a mountain diary, most of it from the post-war years, help a little but there are huge gaps of many years – besides six years' army service, far from crags – and little pattern to the memories. I can clearly recall my very first climbs in almost photographic detail and, before then, my first hills, but after that events are so blurred that memories of scores, even hundreds, of mountain days have, sadly, disappeared. But to find a thread on which to hang these memories I must try, shutting my eyes to the view of a sunlit fellside out of the window, to peer even further back into earliest days, long before the fells and the rocks became so important. Perhaps then I will be able to see how it all started – this almost childish urge to climb, this abiding love for mountain beauty.

The very first thing in my life that I remember is being in the cellar of a house in Liverpool, staying with relatives, while Zeppelins were bombing the city in the First World War. Perhaps there was only one Zeppelin, and I've never been sure whether or not it dropped any bombs, or whether all the noise was simply our anti-aircraft fire. I can remember the searchlights and the excitement, picture the great airship caught in the beams and hear the thud of the bombs, but perhaps this is no more than childish imagination. We were in the sitting room of the house when it happened and I ran to the front door to look out at all the excitement, but was immediately told to come back indoors. It was then that we all trooped down to the cellar, much to my disgust, so missing the rest of the attack – apart from the noise. I might have been four or five years old.

I can also remember being taught the elements of knitting in an infants' school and knitting little squares of woollen cloth. These, we were told, would be joined together and made into socks for the soldiers in the trenches. But none of these things has anything to do with the Lake District or climbing.

My first clear memory of the Lake District is being called down from a crab-apple tree for a walk over a gorse-entangled, limestone-wrinkled shoulder of fell and, from the summit, being shown the blue shape of the hills. That was more than eighty years ago and I was a small boy in a blue jersey. I was told the names of some of the hills but soon forgot them. All I wanted to do was to get back to climbing the crab-apple tree, pick the mushrooms we had noticed on the way up the fell and, later, try to find some crabs in the pools on the beach. We were on holiday at a farm somewhere in the Kent's Bank area and perhaps the limestone hill was Hampsfell. We were often around the Kent estuary in those days, having travelled by train from Barrow. Indeed, there is a photograph somewhere of me, aged about two years or less, in a pram on Arnside promenade, being pushed along by my mother wearing a large feathered hat and a voluminous dress.

This memory of climbing that crab-apple tree reminds me that tree climbing was to become almost a way of life for my younger brother Leslie and myself a little later. We had our "own" trees in Sowerby Woods, not far from our home in Barrow, and devised different ways of climbing them and sliding down on ropes – probably "borrowed" clothes lines. Proper abseiling didn't come until several years later when I had begun rock-climbing, but this was generations before abseiling became a sort of new sport on its own, a firm favourite with youngsters on "leisure pursuits" courses. (Curiously, it is invariably wrongly pronounced on television and radio nowadays as "absailing".) We abseiled from climbs when it was necessary and not as a game: it was all part of climbing. And as this was long before karabiners and slings or fancy harnesses, we did it the old-fashioned way, with the rope round the back and up the thigh, which on a long abseil could be rather painful.

Like most children in the days before television, and even radio, when you had to make your own entertainment we were quite adventurous – exploring forbidden caves, deserted mines and quarries and getting into all the usual scrapes. We used to make rafts of logs and paddle them across one of the docks where ocean liners or warships were being built, and when we were quite young tried our hands at skating on one of the frozen reservoirs near the town. The winters were much more severe in those days than they are today so we had many opportunities for practice and, after a time, became reasonably adept. Indeed, many years later, on my honeymoon in Aviemore in 1937, I was so keen on skating that I drove all the way to Perth with my bride Mollie for some instruction at the ice rink there on how to do loops. Ice-skating, in fact, became a favourite winter pursuit until I "discovered" skiing at the end of the Second World War. Many, many times I rode on my bicycle from Barrow to Tarn Hows, Rydal Water, or wherever else there might be skating in Lakeland, and, after a day on the ice, rode back home in the dark. One year – I think it was 1929 – I cycled all the way from Barrow to Lakeside to skate on Windermere which was frozen right across for its full length, with ice up to a foot thick. There were scores, possibly hundreds, of cars parked on the ice, as well as braziers to keep you warm, refreshment stalls and dense crowds of people. The railway had organised special excursions from towns and cities as far away as London for the "ice carnival" and it was all very exciting for a youngster. I remember I skated for two or three miles northwards up the lake on superb black ice. After the first few hundred yards the ice was completely unmarked as there were no other skaters that far up the lake. I then skated back to the Lakeside crowds before cycling back home.

Many years later, after the Second World War, I remember a superb Christmas Day on Tarn Hows when the sun blazed down from dawn to dusk on beautiful black ice framed by snowbound fields and fells, with Wetherlam soaring up behind the woods like an Alpine giant. There were dozens of people on the ice – children with their Christmas scarves and hats and parents with old-fashioned skates brought down from the attic – and I've rarely seen a happier scene. Mollie and I never bothered to take off our skates at lunchtime but just walked in them on to a convenient island where we ate our turkey sandwiches, washed down with a bottle of Christmas wine, before getting back on to the ice for our "threes" and "loops". We don't get Christmases like that nowadays.

Going back to much earlier days when Les and I were given our first bicycles – for passing the eleven-plus examination to the Grammar School – we found these greatly increased the possibilities for youthful adventure. We could now go further and further into more and more exciting places. First we explored all the local fells such as Kirkby Moors, the coast road to Bardsea and Piel Island but soon we were riding into the Lake District at weekends. We would leave our bikes at farms or behind hedges and then – at first, I'm afraid, without maps – walk into the fells, completely new, exciting country. At the start we had only our ordinary shoes but we very soon acquired cheap "army surplus" boots and hammered studs into the soles. We had no waterproofs or anoraks and hadn't yet got our first rucksacks so it was with this very basic equipment that we started to explore the hills. As I remember, it must often have been in the rain for we were always coming home wet through. But soon we were getting used to the twenty-odd miles cycle ride from home to Torver or Coniston, a strenuous day walking the fells, and then the long ride back home, usually in the dark.

More often than not I was on my own in the early days: it was a year or two before Leslie, who was two years younger than me, became a regular companion. I well recall one particularly enjoyable day when I went out alone. I was studying for some school exam at the time and needed a change. For some reason, I wanted to bathe in Beacon Tarn in the Blawith Fells, south of Torver, which I'd heard about but never seen. I found the tarn, enjoyed my bathe, as always, without a costume, climbed the hill at the back of the tarn and looked, due north at the Coniston fells, perhaps four miles away but looking much closer that bright, sunny afternoon. I can easily picture the wonderful panorama I saw all those years ago for I've been back to Beacon Fell many, many times since just to look at the view – Walna Scar, the shadowed steeps of Brown Pike and Buck Pike, the great, dark cliff of Dow Crag and the sweep of Coniston Old Man, full in the westering sun. These hills of my youth were the ones that I was to come to know better than any others and they must have inspired me that day. Instead of cycling home straight away, I rode round the toe of Coniston Water to High Nibthwaite and scrambled up a steep, slippery fellside to a minor summit on the lower slopes of Top o' Selside. This was a magnificent viewpoint for the length of the lake and the mountains behind and, feeling proud of myself, I built a tall cairn, four or five feet high, from the boulders lying around. It was the first and only summit cairn I have ever built. Cycling back down the road towards Greenodd and, ultimately, home, I stopped for a moment and admired it – plain to see for miles. It was there for a year or two, until it fell down or was pushed over.

Gradually, I was learning more about the hills and going further afield. Soon the Langdale fells – the Pikes, Crinkle Crags and Bowfell – were visited and then Fairfield, Helvellyn and the eastern fells. By now Leslie was often with me and I recall one day in these quieter hills when we saw our first red deer and fell ponies.

The north face of Fairfield

The deer were suddenly encountered high on the ridge of High Street and then bounding nimbly down the steep fellside towards Riggindale, and the fell ponies were quietly grazing above Hayeswater.

Another memory of the eastern fells at that time is of watching men of the Ordnance Survey building a triangulation column on one of the summits. Every time I'm in the area nowadays I try to remember which summit it was but can never be sure: it could be any one of several. The men had tents on the summit and several ponies were grazing the grass nearby. Presumably they were for carrying up the sand and cement. The men all looked incredibly brown and fit. We chatted with them for a few minutes and then, boy-like, I immediately decided that this was what I wanted to do with my life: to work for the Ordnance Survey, up in the mountains all day long, in sunshine or in snow. A wonderful life perhaps, but nothing came of these boyhood dreams and I'm sure, even before the days of aerial photography and computers, it was never quite the idyllic existence I imagined.

An especially clear memory is of our first close-up views of the Wasdale hills. We had seen Great Gable and its neighbours from afar on many occasions and must also have seen them, although without identifying them, from Black Combe but we had never been to Wasdale Head, which we understood was the very heart of the sanctuary. And we were quite sure the hills around Wasdale were the finest hills of all. So one day the two of us, Leslie and I, set off for the Promised Land. We had a small, cheap tent, a couple of blankets apiece, a heavy groundsheet, a dangerous petrol stove in a tin, a big packet of Quaker Oats, a lot of bread and some candles. The loads, carried in old-fashioned knapsacks, were bulky and heavy and our shoulders unaccustomed to the work. Undoubtedly, the blankets were the biggest trouble but we had no sleeping bags and had probably never even heard there were such things. But our spirits were high, and we had no doubts we would reach our goal.

We went by train to Foxfield and walked the rest of the way, mostly in the rain, to Broughton-in-Furness, through Dunnerdale to Ulpha and then over Birker Moor to Eskdale. Here we established a base camp, first near Stanley Force where we had a swim, and then in a field below The Hows farmstead at Boot. Two clear memories of that wet walk come winging back over the years. The first is of enquiring the price of bed and breakfast at the inn at High

Cross beyond Broughton and being staggered to learn it was six shillings. Why we were considering abandoning our tent so early in the expedition I can't remember. It was raining hard but we were well used to Lakeland weather by that time and this can't have been the reason. At all events we decided the price demanded was well beyond our pockets and cruelly extortionate, and so on we trudged into the downpour. The second memory is of brewing tea a couple of miles further on in the lee of a tumbledown wall near the Duddon, and in the process setting fire to one of the confounded blankets.

The camp in Eskdale was not a great success. It rained most of the time and we spent half the nights holding down our miserable tent against what seemed like gale-force winds. After a time, too, our diet of tea, porridge, sausages and bread fried on a bit of tin with lard bought from Sim's store in Boot became a trifle unappetising. But this was only a staging post and we put up with the problems, even the frequent plagues of midges that we tried to clear out of the tent by recklessly lighting handfuls of grass inside it. Then one morning, at last, came a glorious day and we set out over Burnmoor in the sunshine to look at the real mountains. When we came to Burnmoor Tarn we sat on the shore eating our soggy sandwiches and then, shouldering our heavy knapsacks again, trudged up the rise ahead.

Suddenly, we forgot our aching shoulders, our chafed ankles and toes, and the discomforts of camping on empty stomachs, for the green trough of Wasdale had opened up below our feet and the most noble ring of mountains in England rose up to greet us. These were the hills we had come so far to see and they did not disappoint us. They looked shapelier than our own familiar Coniston and Langdale fells and yet more massive and rugged. There seemed something especially exciting about the way they were grouped together around the patchwork fields of Wasdale Head. As we watched the cloud shadows racing across the rocky slopes of Yewbarrow and Gable I think we both realised that these and their companion hills were the best mountains we had ever seen. We felt, too, that this lonely dale-head between the lake and the track over the Sty was a most wonderful, almost magical place. And today, a long lifetime later, I still think this corner, in many ways, the very best of Lakeland.

It was on this same holiday, a few days later, that we enjoyed one of the most remarkable mountain-top views that could ever be experienced in this country. On our way to Wasdale, walking over Burnmoor, we had noticed the rather dreary slopes on our right and, looking at the map, discovered this was Scafell. To both of us this was most disappointing for we had assumed that Scafell and the Pikes, the highest mountains in England, would be impressive, rocky places. At that time we had yet to see the other side of Scafell with its great crag, and the soaring buttresses of Scafell Pike. But, despite our disappointment with the appearance of Scafell from this side, we decided to spend a night on top of it and watch the sunrise from the summit.

And so, a couple of days later, we left our Eskdale camp in the evening, after our usual, unexciting meal, and took to the slopes. We didn't find the modern track, by way of Eel Tarn and Stony Tarn, to Slight Side, but went across the moor towards Burnmoor Tarn again and then struck up the steep slopes beyond Great How. There were no guidebooks in those days – none that we knew of, anyway – and our map didn't seem very helpful. But at least we knew the way across Burnmoor and had already identified the dull slopes of Broad Tongue as likely to lead to the top of Scafell.

It was a tiring, trackless trudge and, as night came on, it was difficult to see the way, so, just below the ridge, near a cluster of rocks, we decided to stop and see if we could get some sleep. By this time it had become very cold and we huddled together against the rocks, pulling on every scrap of clothing, and tried, with little success, to keep warm. The time seemed to crawl along terribly slowly. Round about midnight we got out the petrol stove and managed to brew some cups of tea without setting fire to ourselves – which had happened before – and soon after that managed to doze off, between fits of shivering, for an hour or two.

It was not yet dawn when we awoke but a strange light seemed to have come over the fells. We puzzled about this at first and then realised what it was – morning mists, like cotton wool, creeping up all around us. We shouldered our knapsacks, scrambled up to the ridge, and could then see that the white sea of mist covered all the valleys with just the tops of the highest fells sticking through it, like little islands. We had never seen anything like this before. Fully awake now, we strode on to the summit of Scafell and, as we gained height, saw the dawn coming up somewhere in the eastern fells, way beyond Langdale. Soon the summit rocks were flooded in the brightest sunlight. The sea of cotton wool quickly melted away and the valleys began to open up below our feet.

With the highest summit we had yet reached entirely to ourselves, amid growing excitement, we began to study the view, realising at once that we had never experienced this sort of clarity before. The Lowland hills of Scotland and, beyond, much higher mountains, were dazzlingly clear, and across the blue, dancing waters of the Irish Sea there was the Isle of Man, looking almost close enough to be within swimming range. This was no great surprise for we had seen the Isle of Man from the tops on several previous occasions, but this time, behind the island and mostly to its left, we could see quite plainly a huge, mountainous mass that could not be anything other than Ireland. Entranced, we moved across the summit for a couple of hundred yards so that we could get a better view to the south. And there, on the farthest horizon, beyond the very rim of the sea, we could make out the tops of distant mountains, not clouds, just discernible in the clear morning air. These, we decided, must be the mountains of Snowdonia, and having done considerable research into the matter in the intervening years, I've found no reason to change our opinion. So that, from the summit of Scafell although not from exactly the same place, under absolutely perfect conditions, it may be possible to see the mountains of England, Scotland, Ireland and Wales.

A few years ago I received fairly convincing evidence that we had, indeed, seen Scotland, Ireland and Wales from the summit of Scafell in the 1920s. Reading in one of my books of our view of four countries from Scafell, a correspondent in Hertfordshire wrote to tell me of his own experience one November day in 1967. With a friend he had been crossing the Carneddau in North Wales, and from the summit of Carnedd Llewelyn they had had what he described as "the view of a lifetime". He wrote to me, "We could see Ireland, the Isle of Man, the whole of Wales spread out like a map with the Bristol Channel glinting beyond, and, to the north, we saw two or three peaks sticking up out of the sea – very small but absolutely clear – and my friend said that one of them was Scafell. It was 11.30 in the morning, crystal-clear air, frosty and the first snows of the Welsh winter down to about 3350 feet." So I'm pretty sure that just after dawn on that exciting morning in the 1920s my brother and I really did see Snowdonia from the top of Scafell.

About forty years later, from exactly the same place, I enjoyed the same view of cotton-wool clouds covering the whole of Lakeland when the ceiling of white mist was at about 3000 feet. The only islands sticking up above the cloud that day were the topmost rocks of Scafell itself where I was standing; the upper rocks of

Scafell Pinnacle, a little distance away; and, a mile away, the summit of Scafell Pike, the highest point in England, with half a dozen tiny figures like black matchsticks grouped about the cairn. But although the cotton-wool blanket over the whole of Lakeland was much the same as in our boyhood view, it never lifted this time while I was on top. I waited in vain for half an hour in the hope that I would see across the seas as we had done all those years earlier.

Soon after this time in the 1920s, now well into our teens, we felt we knew most of the Lakeland fells fairly well and wanted something a bit more adventurous. Already we were scrambling about on bits of rock wherever they were encountered, and also tackling some of the gills and waterfalls. We knew nothing about rock-climbing at this time and didn't know any climbers, but soon we were seeking out steep places and using them for "practice". Among these places were the crumbling walls of Piel Castle on Piel Island, reached by getting the boatman at Roa Island, a cycle ride from Barrow, to row us across the channel. We didn't know then that the monks of Furness Abbey, near our home, had used the castle as a lookout for pirates and raiders from the sea or that Lambert Simnel had landed there in 1486 for his foolhardy attempt on the English throne. And we were not interested in the fact that there were virtually unrestricted drinking hours at the rough-looking pub on the island: we were not into beer drinking yet. It was just that there were plenty of hand and footholds on the castle walls, and it was exciting to get to the top and sit on the crumbling stones looking out to sea. I'm sure we slipped off now and again but there were no injuries that I can recall. We also tried out the red sandstone walls of Furness Abbey, only about a mile from our home – long before the official preservation of the ruins put an end to vandalism of this sort.

Another of our early "crags", before we started proper climbing, was an ironstone outcrop on the lower slopes of The Hoad at Ulverston which I have heard became a practice ground for local climbers many years later: it certainly hadn't been "discovered" before our adventures there. Wearing ordinary low shoes, not plimsolls, with soles made, I seem to remember, from some material called Uskide, Les and I worked out routes up, down and across the crag, often getting ourselves into exciting situations, but never coming to any harm. The hardest route on the outcrop, up The Nose, as we called the exposed prow at the top, gave us the most trouble. After many attempts Leslie managed to climb it first and then, for shame's sake, I had to do it. It took several assaults before I succeeded and, looking back all those years, I think it was a bold lead for boys with our lack of experience. My very last "lead", at the age of 78 years, was a v. diff. on Grey Crag in Buttermere: I don't think I could have led The Nose then and I certainly couldn't climb it now – or probably even get off the ground at its foot. Of course, Les and I didn't have a rope.

In sixty years of rock-climbing I was fortunate enough to avoid serious injury on the crags but my first climbing fall happened before I had started "proper" climbing. My father, brother Les and myself were walking from Woodland to the Coniston fells and, somewhere on the slopes of Caw, we boys decided, as boys do, to race each other to some nearby summit. Les was getting ahead of me so, to gain ground by cutting off a corner, I foolishly began scrambling up a convenient, small crag. Lacking experience, I rushed up as quickly as I could, grabbing the holds instead of testing them, and soon one of the holds suddenly came away and down I went, smashing into the rocks, to the bottom. I probably fell only between fifteen and twenty feet but it knocked me about a bit – a damaged ankle and plenty of cuts and abrasions, with quite a few splashes of blood.

I was bandaged up, probably with handkerchiefs, and then, strangely, we decided to continue our journey with me supported on each side by my father and brother to take the pressure off the damaged ankle. It would have been far easier and wiser to have gone back to Woodland or even to Broughton but, stupidly, we carried on with me hobbling, in some discomfort, along the steepening fellsides. On we went to the Walna Scar track, over the top of Dow Crag – without my noticing the cliffs – down to Goats Hause, up over Coniston Old Man and down through the quarries to the railway station. I believe I passed out for a time, either on the platform or in the train.

But this early accident didn't put me off climbing – very much the reverse. As soon as I had recovered, and the damaged ankle took a few weeks to heal, I was desperately eager to learn about climbing. During my convalescence I had suddenly become quite besotted with this strange game that few people had even heard about at the time. Climbing was almost completely unknown to the general public in the late 1920s. Mallory and Irvine had been lost on Everest only a few years earlier and we had been told about it at school. Climbers were regarded as a strange breed, quite mad people, who played about on rocks and mountains and, now and again, got themselves killed. You didn't see climbers in the fells, there was no television to picture their antics, no climbing magazines, no climbing equipment shops, no lectures, films or slide shows and no "outdoor pursuits". The whole business of climbing – if they ever thought about it – was a complete mystery to most people. What was the rope for? Did they throw it up to catch on a rock and then swarm up it? Nobody seemed to know. To most people climbing must have seemed a strange game played out on dangerous cliffs, probably by crazy people from the universities. None of us since leaving school, and certainly not before then, had ever seen a climber or anybody with a rope. Although we lived on the edge of the Lake District and were adventurous youngsters it was right out of our world.

Two things changed all this for me in my late teens, probably around the time of my convalescence after the fall on Caw. My father's family, all born and bred on the edge of the sea, was involved and interested in ships and seafaring. Two uncles were in shipbuilding and had taken part in trials of ships built in Barrow – once, to Chile – while a third uncle was a Merchant Navy engineer officer. The talk at their homes, while I listened with all the wonderment of youth, was mostly about the sea and ships and voyages to the ends of the earth, especially to the Antarctic. Their hero, and he became mine, was Sir Ernest Shackleton – not so much because he had nearly reached the South Pole, but because of his ocean voyage in an open boat, and his crossing of the mountains of South Georgia to save his crew. What a man, I thought. So I went to the Barrow Public Library, sought out all the books on Shackleton and Antarctic exploration and devoured them.

But it so happened that the shelves containing the Antarctica books were next to shelves of books about mountaineering and rock-climbing, and very quickly my reading habits changed from Scott, Amundsen, Cherry-Garrard and the rest to the likes of Owen Glynne Jones and the Abraham brothers. Not only did I read every book about climbing by the pioneers of the sport that I could lay my hands on but I discovered, on a lower shelf, all the annual Journals of the Fell and Rock Climbing Club. These were crammed full with enticing articles and photographs about climbing and climbers, right up to that time. I couldn't take these books out of the library but every hour I could spare I would go there, take the chosen volume to a convenient desk and devour every word. At that time I had never been on a proper climb nor, indeed, had I seen one, but very soon I had found out quite a lot about the game and what it was all about.

And then came the second factor that was to lead me into climbing. I had cycled to Coniston on my own – a regular trip from Barrow for me at the time – climbed the Old Man and started wandering down the slope above Goats Water. At that time I hadn't been aware of the great cliff of Dow Crag or even seen it, for although we had walked along the top when I had damaged my ankle, I hadn't then been in the mood to admire the scenery. But this time it was different. As I wandered down the grassy slopes suddenly the whole crag, its great buttresses and gullies full in the sunshine, came into view and, spellbound, I sat down to take it all in. This was the crag, I remembered from my reading, where they did all the climbing and then, as I peered across the combe, I saw tiny specks moving down the screes below the crag and, here and there, a flash of colour on the buttresses. These, clearly, were climbers, apparently completely at home on this great cliff! There and then I decided, and to this day I can clearly recall making the decision, "This is what I want to do. I'm going to become a climber."

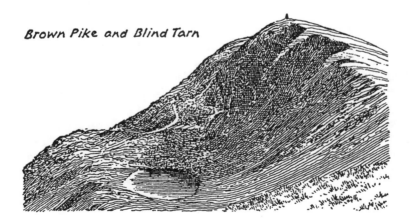

Brown Pike and Blind Tarn

Return to Dow Crag

The other day, which was warm with a pleasant breeze on the
tops, I went back to Dow Crag where I had started my
rock-climbing seventy years earlier. But we weren't climbing this
time – just walking over the top from Walna Scar to try to catch
something of the remembered flavour of those more adventurous
days in the late 1920s. On the way up the fell we visited a secret
place where weeks earlier we had sadly scattered the ashes of my
only son, a fine mountaineer and staunch companion. The
modest ascent from the pass seemed more demanding than it
used to be but the splendour of the view kept me going, for there
are few ridges in Lakeland more rewarding than this one. The
long length of Dunnerdale, perhaps the least-spoiled valley in the
district, stretched out far below and, straight ahead, the Scafells,
the highest land in England, with every tiny detail etched sharp
against the sky. From the top of one of the gullies on Dow Crag I
looked down and watched two climbers on Trident Route, a
well-remembered climb. They were the only climbers we saw all
day. Years ago there would have been dozens of them; perhaps
climbers prefer quarries and climbing walls to crags nowadays.
But, scrambling about the summit and walking along the ridge
were scores of people – from grannies (and at least one
great-grandmother) to small children (including two babies in
rucksacks) and several dogs. Other noticed changes were the
grossly eroded, stony tracks where there used to be grass, the
growing profusion of unnecessary cairns and, above the fell-gate,
more parked cars than I had ever seen there before. Mountain
bikers on Walna Scar pass and pony riders on the lower slopes
added to the variety, while in the air there were silent
parascenders and noisily-buzzing microlights and, away to the
south, a couple of balloons inching northwards, no doubt from
Holker Hall. Big changes indeed, for years ago this used to be
largely climbers' territory. Happily, the beauty of the hills that
had drawn us all our lives remained unchanged.

September 1998

Chapter Three

Learning the Ropes

But how was I to go about becoming a climber? I'd no idea how to get involved in "proper" climbing, as distinct from the scrambling and pottering about on rocks with which I was already familiar. The first thing, it seemed to me, might be to get hold of some properly nailed boots. I knew that climbers wore boots edged with nails called clinkers for I'd seen them in photographs in the Fell and Rock journals. But how could I get my old ex-army boots fitted with these special nails? There were no shops selling climbing equipment in Barrow – nor anywhere else, to my knowledge – and I didn't know anybody in the town who climbed. Perhaps, indeed, there were no climbers in Barrow. Then I remembered references in the journals to a climber called George Basterfield who I seemed to remember came from Barrow. The name seemed vaguely familiar, I thought, and then I realised why: he was the Mayor of Barrow-in-Furness. There was only one thing to do. I had to see him as quickly as possible and get him to tell me how to get my boots nailed.

So I went along to Barrow Town Hall, a most imposing red sandstone building in the town centre, and asked to see the Mayor. The official, curious, no doubt, about what business a callow youth could possibly have with His Worship, asked me the reason for my request and I told him, "I want to ask him about nailing climbing boots." "That's all right then," said the official, clearly knowing all about the Mayor's extra-mural activities. "Come this way." I was ushered into the Mayor's Parlour.

George Basterfield was at that time (1929) the President of the Fell and Rock Climbing Club – although I didn't know it then – and a very distinguished climber. Six or seven years earlier he had taken part, with H.S. Gross leading, in the first ascents of the three very severe "Eliminate" routes on Dow Crag and the girdle traverse of the crag, four of the most demanding routes in the Lake District. In 1926 he had written the climbing guide to Great Langdale and he had also been active with first ascents in other areas, notably on Boat Howe, Kirkfell. At the time of my visit he was still climbing to a high standard. In the field of local politics he was to become one of the town's most distinguished citizens and a Freeman of the Borough, with schools and other buildings named after him. He was also something of a poet, a philosopher, an imaginative writer with an ear for a good melody and an excellent dialect speaker. But when I went into the Parlour I knew none of these things. The Mayor was seated at the head of a long, brightly polished table – a big, burly man with a bald head, spectacles and a kindly look on his face. Nothing at all as I had imagined a climber might look – more like a friendly bishop.

"Take a seat," he said. "What can I do for you?" And that was the start of my introduction to "proper" climbing and my first meeting with a wonderful man to whom I owe a great deal – not only in rock-climbing, but also for expanding my love for hill country and all its delights. I told him my problem, how to get my old boots nailed for climbing, and he gave me the answer right away. "Go to George Stephens with your boots." he said. "He's got a place at the back of the Black Bull in Coniston. Anybody will tell you where it is. Tell him I've sent you, and he'll do the job." We then chatted for a few minutes about the different types of nailing and then he asked me, in a friendly way, what I had climbed. I had to confess my complete lack of experience.

And then he came out with a most remarkable offer that almost left me speechless. "Tell you what," he said, "I'm going up to Dow this Sunday. Meet me at Torver, and I'll take you up a couple of climbs. Bring along some rubbers." I stammered out my thanks, and we shook hands as I left but, of course, I didn't then realise that this short chat was to change or, at least, shape my life. For it was George's generosity to a complete stranger, thirty to forty years his junior, that propelled me into climbing and focussed much of the rest of my life on mountains and mountain adventure. I owe this kindly, thoughtful man many hundreds of matchless mountain days, climbing friendships that have lasted a lifetime, an acquaintance with many distinguished men and women, and a way of life that has brought me much happiness and, occasionally, high adventure.

I could hardly wait until the following Sunday. A few months earlier I had started work as a trainee journalist on the local paper, but I'm sure I thought much more about the weekend excitement ahead than about my job. When the day came I went along to the railway station in my roughly studded ex-army boots, carrying a pair of rubber plimsolls, and travelled to Torver, changing at Foxfield en route. I couldn't see George Basterfield on the platform at Torver but assumed, with the optimism of youth, that he had gone on ahead. Sure enough, after I had gone a mile or so up the lane, I caught up with him, striding along in his big, clinker-nailed boots with a rucksack on his back.

We went through Banishead quarry which, along with the rest of the route from Torver, I was seeing for the first of what were to be hundreds of times. And it was here that George gave me the first of many lessons about the countryside – a few words on Lakeland rock and the minerals that might be found in it. "That's copper," he said, pointing out a vein, "and these specks here are garnets." And so he continued as we ambled slowly up the fellside: little talks on the harebells sprouting through the grass, the special characteristics of the quietly grazing Herdwick sheep and the little stone memorial to Charmer, the Coniston foxhound killed in a fall from Dow Crag in 1911. There seemed nothing that George didn't know about the area.

Then, somewhere near the big quartz cairn on the way to Goats Water, he suddenly stopped in his tracks, looked down at the trampled, muddied soil of the path at his feet, and announced, mysteriously, "A.T. Hargreaves and Billy Clegg are on the crag today." The great crag was straight ahead but I couldn't see any movement or sign of figures on the cliff. Then George pointed to the track at his feet and the nail marks in the mud. "Those are their nails," he explained, and then told me all about it. Albert Hargreaves, one of the top climbers of the day, had invented a new type of edge-nail – not unlike a tricouni but of quite distinctive shape – and the impressions made by these nails, worn by both climbers, were clearly different from the other nail marks in the soil. It all smacked of magic to me.

We walked up to the crag and I was introduced, high up on the screes, to The Cave. Over the years, I was to come to know every hole and corner of it as intimately as any room at home. This was where we congregated on our way to the crag, as generations of climbers before and after us have done, to rest, change into rubbers, eat our sandwiches or shelter from the rain, telling our jokes and stories as we did so. Reaching the foot of the crag and having changed into rubbers since my old, nail-less boots were hardly up to the job, George fastened me to the end of the rope with a bowline knot, carefully showing me exactly how to tie it. In the seventy years that have passed since that wonderful day, I have never forgotten how to do it. He then told me how to pay out the rope – round the shoulder in those days; it was many years later before the waist method began to be used – and started climbing, remarkably quickly and neatly for such a bulky man.

The route, he explained, was Woodhouse's B. It was a "difficult" which meant it wasn't very hard, and we were going to do the variation start. Our rope was Beale's "Alpine Club" rope with a red strand running through it and it was made of hemp which, as I was to discover later, made it heavy and rather unmanageable when wet. As George was leading the second pitch, to the left of the large pinnacle, he was hailed by two climbers down on the screes and asked why on earth he was on Woodhouse's, a comparatively lowly climb. And George, to his eternal credit, instead of saying he was climbing with a novice, shouted down, "Because it's a bloody good climb." The climbers turned out to be Hargreaves and Clegg, whose nail-prints George had spotted on the way up to the crag. Later we joined up with them on a descent of Great Gully and chatted together for some time.

Already, right at the very start of my first day's climbing, I was hob-nobbing with the great: George Basterfield, President of the prestigious Fell and Rock Climbing Club and a renowned leader and guide-book writer; A.T. Hargreaves, one of the leading climbers in the country and later author of both the Scafell and Dow Crag guides; and William Clegg, another fine climber who was later to write the second guide to the Langdale climbs, following George's first.

My first climb went easily enough, despite my excitement, although the last steep, little pitch, just below Easy Terrace, seemed rather strenuous. On my second outing with George, which, miraculously, occurred just a week or two later, he made me lead this rather awkward move and thereafter I never had any trouble with it. Although, months later, as I will subsequently recall, I had a very frightening adventure at this very place, that, at least, taught me a very important lesson.

Some years ago, looking through old climbing guides, I noticed that by the time of the 1968 guide to Dow Crag, Woodhouse's B had been upgraded from "difficult" to "very difficult (hard)". This might have been because of the damage we had done to the holds on the steep wall of the third pitch by many ascents in our clinker-nailed boots; either erasing them altogether or rendering them smooth or polished. Remembering the number of times we had been up and down this route in all weathers, including rain, snow and ice, as well as at least one descent in the dark, and once roping down a rescued sheep, it was satisfying to know that the climb was judged to be more difficult than we had thought.

On my first climbing day George and I carried on along Easy Terrace and then climbed down Easter Gully. On the way down I was shown all the great climbs around the amphitheatre, including the intimidating-looking Black Wall. I was enormously thrilled by the tremendous rock architecture, the frighteningly steep walls and the great soaring cracks and chimneys, and wondered whether I would ever be able to climb any of them. Everything seemed so exciting: the actual feel of the rough rock, the thrill of stepping up on small holds or balancing across a wall, and the stimulating exposure of being so high above the screes. And it all seemed so safe with George ahead of me, or, in descent, behind me, taking in the rope over his shoulder and quietly telling me what to do if I hesitated. We went down to the foot of the crag to eat our sandwiches and George showed me the spring coming out of the rock near the foot of Intermediate Gully which I have since used for most of a lifetime. He then said, "You did all right on Woodhouse's but I'd like to try you out on a bit of exposure. We'll do Arête, Chimney and Crack next."

And so, on my first day's climbing, I did my first "severe" and enjoyed every moment of it. The slightly awkward move at the top of the first pitch went easily enough, but then most things went well with George, whether he was leading or, to encourage me, acting as the perfect second, quietly explaining every move in advance. When we were going up the long final crack George suggested as I was climbing that I should stop, look down between my legs at the screes and the tarn far below, and quietly savour the experience. Again, nothing frightening with George up above, but just the joy of climbing up a very steep place, with a lot of fresh air below, and trying to do it as neatly as possible. We came down off the top of the climb into Great Gully, where we encountered Hargreaves and Clegg. Together, with me in most exalted company, we descended the cave pitch. It had all been a wonderfully satisfying day. I had learnt many things. Everything had gone well. The climbing had exceeded all my expectations. It was great to be alive.

That wonderful first day's climbing with George opened up a completely new world. All at once climbing seemed almost the only thing that mattered. Work was no longer exciting, or, sometimes, even interesting. Other activities seemed mundane. Even classical music and my piano playing which I had been increasingly practising, without getting much better, for years was not now so inspiring. Life was now all about existing to the weekends when I could go climbing again. Every weekend, Saturday or Sunday, I would take myself off to Torver – sometimes by train, but more often on my bicycle. I would walk up to Dow Crag and hang about around the foot of the crag until – if I was lucky – somebody took pity on me and invited me on to their rope. I don't think I actually pestered people into taking me on a climb, but I'm sure I must sometimes have been a bit of a nuisance.

Several times I was fortunate enough to be invited to tie on to the ropes of people doing the easier routes and very soon I acquired a rough, working knowledge of the crag and, perhaps, some slight competence about the game – at least in the lower grades. After all these years I'm sorry I can remember the name of only one of these very kind people – probably because she took me up climbs on two or three occasions. She was Mrs Blanche Eden-Smith, who had been the great H.M. (Harry) Kelly's partner on many famous first ascents, including that of Moss Ghyll Grooves on Scafell in 1926. I remember her with gratitude as a nimble, boyish figure, very friendly and helpful to a novice. She introduced me, I remember, to several of her friends, and whenever we met she was always interested in my progress.

When I wasn't fortunate enough to be invited on to a climb I started to potter about the easier parts of the crag on my own – it might have been these unskilful scramblings that persuaded people to take me in hand. In fact, rarely a weekend went by when I didn't get in some climbing of one sort or another. It was on one of these early visits that I acquired my first rope – sixty feet of a hundred-foot rope belonging to a senior climber. It had been severed by a falling stone in Great Gully. I happened to be around at the time and was made a present of the larger half of the rope, possibly because the senior climber felt sorry for my rope-less state. Perhaps I asked him for it. But this short rope was all I possessed for some time, which is why my copy of George Bower's red-backed guide to "Doe Crags" – the spelling at that time – was annotated in ink by me, "Climbs possible with sixty-feet rope". The battered guide is in front of me now, a vivid reminder of happy days sixty to seventy years ago. I see that I had listed nineteen climbs on the crag as suitable for my short length of rope. In the graded list of climbs from "easy" to "very severe" I notice I had marked with an ink dot all the climbs on the crag that I had done, with a ring round the dots when I had led them.

One day when I was leaving the crag after pottering about on my own I met a young climber, a year or two older than myself, who was also on his own. We chatted on our way down the fellside together, seemed to get on with each other very well, and arranged to meet later for a day's climbing. This was the start of my friendship with Bryan Tyson, an established climber who had already taken part in two or three first ascents. One of these was Asterisk, the hard severe on Gimmer Crag that finishes just below the start of Kipling Groove. The leader on this first ascent in 1928 – about a year before our meeting – had been H.S. Gross, who had first led the three Eliminates on Dow Crag and the girdle traverse of the cliff. In all cases the second had been George Basterfield, and it might have been our joint friendship with George that brought Bryan and I together, following this first meeting.

Bryan was a good-looking, well-spoken lad who lived at Hawkshead Hill and worked in a bank in Ambleside. He was the first real friend, apart from George Basterfield, I had made in climbing and I treasured his friendship for many years – until his death, at an early age, some time after the war. Bryan, as I say, was a well-spoken lad and it was, therefore, something of a surprise to discover, years later that he had a local reputation for telling stories in a broad Westmorland dialect. After the war I became a member of the Ambleside Society for the Prosecution of Felons and Other Offenders Against the Laws, a sort of annual dining club dating back to the days before police were invented. Bryan, too, seemed to be a member or, at least, he often appeared at the dinner to relate a long string of funny stories in a beautifully exaggerated dalesman's accent that had us all rolling in the aisles. For years I'd had no idea of this delightful side to his character.

Through Bryan I met Dick Mackereth, a tall, rather imposing climber from Ulverston, and the three of us climbed together, as a team, for some time. G.H. Mackereth was always called Dick and was a businessman in Ulverston. He was a member of a well-known family in the district, and several years older than us. At that time I had no transport, apart from my bicycle, and I used to travel from my home in Barrow to Ulverston on the bus, go to Dick's house and be transported in his car to Torver or Coniston,

probably picking up Bryan en route. I don't think I properly realised my good fortune at the time, but my friendship with these
older climbers and their ready acceptance of, and generosity to, a
comparative youngster, still little more than a novice, certainly
opened up my climbing experience. With transport available we
travelled to Langdale to climb, as well as Coniston, and even, now
and again, to Wasdale.

It was not long after these early days, rich with climbing experience, that the Coniston Tigers were formed, but before then Bryan,

The south-east face of Gimmer Crag,

Dick and I had had certain adventures on Dow Crag. For me the first of these excitements was on Woodhouse's B Route, my very first climb, which, over the years I have probably climbed more often than any other route and in all seasons. One wet day the three of us were on the crag with three girls, but whether they had been taken to the crag by Dick or Bryan, or whether we had met them there by chance, I can't now remember. All I can clearly recall is that I was told, as very much the junior of the party, that I had to take one of them up Woodhouse's. Either Dick or Bryan explained to me that she was quite a competent climber, having, in fact, recently climbed the Matterhorn, but that she hadn't had much experience with Lakeland rock. Dick and Bryan then disappeared with the other two girls. What they climbed, or whether, indeed, they climbed anything, I can't say.

However, as instructed, I tied my girl on to the rope and we set off up the climb in the rain. We were both wearing clinker-nailed boots – mine nailed by George Stephens of Coniston on George Basterfield's recommendation. Since my first day's climbing in rubbers I had done a fair amount of climbing in nails: indeed, we usually climbed in nails, reserving our rubbers for the harder climbs. It was rather miserable on the climb in the rain, with the rope getting heavier, and more and more unmanageable, all the time. The girl was rather slow but I don't recall any serious difficulty until the last pitch – the strenuous pull over a steep little overhang that I had found awkward on my very first climb. When I had pulled over the top of this final pitch I was wet through and impatient to get the thing over and down off the crag. I scrambled up a few feet to a rock corner, jammed myself firmly in with my feet braced against a rock, and, without bothering to belay, shouted down to my second to come on.

I had explained carefully how to climb the pitch: to get as high as possible up the corner before reaching for a good hold with the right hand. But, time after time, she almost reached the hold – I could just see her fingers stretching up – and then she would slip back. It was quite exhausting, urging her on in the rain, easing her back down the pitch after each attempt, and getting more soaked and more irritable all the time, but it must have been far worse for her. Then, fast losing my patience, I persuaded her to make one last attempt and, almost sobbing, she started up once again, her fingers reaching for the hold.

"Come on, you're nearly there," I shouted down. Suddenly, there was a tremendous tug at my waist and I was plucked out of

my rock corner like a cork from a bottle and dragged, quite help-
less, towards the edge of the cliff. There was no time to be afraid of
the drop of hundreds of feet immediately below, or for my past life,
very short until then, to pass before me. Everything happened in a
flash and my only reaction was of self-preservation – at all costs, to
stop myself from being pulled over the edge. Even now, I can
remember hauling on the rope with all my strength as I shot across
the rocks on my back. And then, miraculously, two things happened in the same mini-second: my boots, as I was being dragged
forward, suddenly jammed against a rock at the edge of the drop,
and, providentially, my second landed on her feet at the foot of the
pitch. I had been pulled downwards perhaps about fifteen feet and
she had fallen the same distance. We had both, amazingly,
escaped unscathed from my very serious negligence in not properly belaying at the top of the pitch.

Very frightened now, but murmuring a little prayer of thankful-
ness, I crept back carefully to the rock corner and tied on an
extremely safe belay so that I could hold anything. And I then did
what I should have done twenty minutes earlier at the start of her
difficulties – sent her round an easier way to the right, avoiding the
awkward move, an escape route I had only just remembered.
When we joined up at the top of the climb I never told the girl I had
been pulled off my stance. She was probably so relieved to get up
safely that her fall down the pitch was an incident that could be
forgotten. I never saw her again and I can't now remember her
name or what she looked like. If she is still alive today she will be a
very old lady indeed – up to ten years older than I am. I'm so sorry
that, entirely due to my unforgivable negligence, I nearly killed
her. But the near-accident taught me two very important lessons
that I hope I never forgot: never neglect proper belaying and never
allow over-confidence at the end of a climb to cloud your judge-
ment. Many accidents happen at the end of a climb.

Other memories of Dow Crag days with Bryan and Dick are not
quite so shaming. In particular, I remember how we laid siege to
what we eventually named Tiger Traverse – the steeply sloping
slab that starts about forty feet to the left of Murray's Route, the
splendid severe on B Buttress. We had shown this slab to George
Bower, one of the famous climbers of the day, with many first
ascents to his credit, who was also George Basterfield's son-in-law.
He immediately dismissed it as a possible route. "Only a tiger
could get up that," he announced decisively, but Dick and Bryan

must have thought differently for they told me we were going to attempt its first ascent.

It shows how naive and ignorant of climbing jargon I must have then been for I thought George Bower was referring to actual tigers scrambling up the rock. I didn't realise the word "tiger" was then being used to describe the high-altitude porters being employed by Bauer and others in their attempts on Kangchenjunga, and also on the early Everest expeditions. Later it became a word to describe the most daring and resourceful of climbers.

Anyway, we mounted our attack – at least Dick and Bryan did – while, perched at the top of the third pitch of Murray's Route, I held the rope for them. When they were satisfied the route would go, after each had had several attempts, they announced that we were going to climb the pitch. Dick led it splendidly, Bryan followed easily enough and then I went up, caressing the holds for the first time. You start from the top of a vertical flake and then launch on to poor, sloping holds on the wall, traversing diagonally to the right and upwards. It was the sort of climbing I was enjoying at that time – neat balance moves on small holds. I seemed more at home with this sort of climbing than strenuous struggles up overhangs. It was the first time I had been involved in a first ascent and an important stage in my climbing career. The date was September 20th, 1931. I was just twenty years of age.

Two or three weeks later I led my brother Leslie on the second ascent of the route which, many years later, was incorporated into a variation of the original Murray's Route – the very severe Murray's Direct. Our Tiger Traverse variation had been classified as very severe right from the start and, I understand, is still treated with some respect.

The very next Sunday, September 27th, 1931, the exploratory instincts of Dick and Bryan having been whetted by the ascent of Tiger Traverse, they were at it again. With the air of conspirators, they confided to me that they had had their eyes on another possible first ascent to the left of Easy Gully for some time. It was a nasty-looking crack they had already named, with good reason as it turned out, Blasphemy Crack and they intended doing it right away. So we all crossed the screes to the foot of the climb and Bryan started up, eventually reaching a thread belay below the final, steepest section of the crack. He then brought Dick up to the stance and, thus safeguarded, started up the very strenuous second pitch. I could see, and hear, the struggles and the imprecations, and they went on for a long time. Eventually Bryan pulled himself out over the top and it was my turn. By then it had started to rain and I skated about in my rubbers on the wet rock for some time, without making much progress. Then the shower became a heavy downpour and it was obvious I wasn't going to get up in rubbers so I climbed down, with some difficulty, and changed into nailed boots. At that time I had not learned the trick of putting socks over plimsolls to provide better friction on wet rock.

Anyway, I progressed clumsily up the now-streaming rock in my boots until, about halfway up, on a smooth slab, the difficulties became too much for my limited technique and I came on the rope, swinging across the face. By that time Bryan and Dick were wet through and beginning to complain and I was rapidly losing interest in the route, so I was unceremoniously lowered to the foot of the climb and we called it a day. In all the later years of my climbing on Dow I never again attempted Blasphemy Crack – one of the few routes on the crag, apart from recent additions, I have not climbed. And strangely, for they were a formidable pair, this was the last new route on which Dick and Bryan were involved. At that time, however, we were not especially interested in finding new routes, being quite satisfied with the wealth of climbs on all the crags we still had to do.

This also happened to be the last time that I fell on a rock-climb, although there must have been occasions when I was glad of a tight rope. But we were always falling off boulders, especially the Pudding Stone in Boulder Valley, where once, I remember, an awkward fall put one of my ankles out of action for weeks. Many years afterwards, when on leave in Kashmir during the war, I had a bad fall, but this was on snow and ice, not rock.

This business of falling on climbs in the early 1930s – or, rather, avoiding falls – may need a little amplification. We were brought up on the strict maxim that the leader must never fall under any circumstances, and seconds were not really expected to slip either. If one did, he usually kept quiet about it. How very different the situation is today when the protection on a climb can be so secure that desperate things can be attempted, and leaders can fall with impunity – and frequently do. But we couldn't afford to fall, with long run-outs on hemp ropes, and no protection whatever. These hemp ropes, heavy and difficult to manage when wet, did not have the elasticity of nylon and often on the hardest routes we used only half-width line, to lessen the pull or drag. In this way, with less weight pulling from behind, we felt more comfortable, although we realised that in the event of a fall the rope was only half the strength of the normal rope. This meant that when leading with line you had to be twice as careful as usual, and never take the slightest chance.

And, remember, we had no double ropes, slings, nuts, harnesses or other appliances for added safety nor, of course, sticky boots or chalk-bags to ease the climbing. You just ran out the length of rope needed for the pitch – even if it came to eighty or a hundred feet – and as you progressed up the climb, you became increasingly aware of how far you were above your second. Consequently, when leading, we did a lot of "yo-yoing" on a hard pitch, climbing up a few feet, and then, doubtful about the next move, climbing down again until, after several attempts, you had worked it out. I know I did. With a lot of rope out below you couldn't risk a desperate move. Climbers nowadays, with protection perhaps a few feet away, can take more risks. This is one reason why standards are so much higher nowadays.

For all these reasons we must have done quite a lot of climbing down, and this can't have done us any harm. But, despite our always-cautious approach we probably completed climbs much quicker than would be the case today, for there was never any fiddling about with the nuts and bits of wire that hadn't even been thought of in those days. With just the rope and our nails or rubbers, climbing was a far less complicated business in the 1930s, but, perhaps, even more fun. You had to rely completely on your companion or companions in those days: your life could, literally, be in their hands. This why climbing friendships can last for a lifetime – and why I will never forget the Coniston Tigers.

A Rocky Corner

A circle with a radius of about one mile centred somewhere near the head of Wasdale's Mosedale and not far below the Pillar-Scoat Fell ridge would, I believe, embrace more crag and rough mountain country than any other area of similar size in England. It would include Pillar Rock, the biggest cliff in the country, and all its outlying crags; the sharp prow of Steeple and the rocky coves that overlook the Liza; and also the impressive face of Red Pike flanking Mosedale. This last, if you have plenty of imagination, might be likened to a miniature south-west face of Everest guarding the Western Cwm. There is a mountaineering route through the Red Pike cliffs not mentioned in any climbing guide and any number of variations waiting to be made by elderly climbers past their best or adventurous fell walkers, for this wild corrie, only two miles from Wasdale Head, is largely unexplored country. As steep as you want, still unscratched and trackless, here is a cool, shadowed corner where you can escape the heat and the crowds on a summer day and get all the exercise you need. I saw it the other day in a different setting with clouds on the summits and mists swirling about the crags, but this only heightened the interest for a solitary scrambler, providing just that extra flavour of adventure. Indeed, the sudden sight from the ridge of the billowing vapours suddenly swept from below my feet to reveal the Liza and the forest, 2000 feet below the beetling mountain wall, was an exciting interlude. The starry saxifrage grows undisturbed near the rowans in the Blackem Head gorge below the Scoat Fell col, for not one in a hundred of the Black Sail walkers turn aside to explore this steep, lonely corner.

June 1981

Chapter Four

Memories of Wasdale

Although Dow Crag and, to a lesser extent, Gimmer Crag and the other Langdale cliffs were our principal haunts at this time, I had already been introduced to the Wasdale severes by George Basterfield. I seem to recall George promising to take me to Wasdale Head "some weekend soon" at the end of that exciting first day's climbing on Dow so it would have probably been 1929 when I first visited "the heart of the sanctuary". Certainly, it was before we formed the Coniston Tigers. Over the next few years we went together to Wasdale several times and the memory of all these visits has fused together into a pleasant blur of youthful happiness and adventure. In recollection, everything was wonderful, with no harsh notes, discomfort or fear. To a sensitive youngster like myself it was almost unbelievably exciting. To be holiday-making at Wasdale Head, the birthplace and centre of British rock-climbing, with one of the best climbers in England as my companion and guide was an experience way beyond all my hopes and dreams.

But although my memories of these delightful visits are now blurred together I can still recall many revealing pictures of that very first visit seventy years ago. We travelled together by train from Barrow to Seascale. George had with him a big box of groceries, mostly oranges and grapefruits, for John and Sally Whiting at the Wastwater Hotel, as it was called in those days. George was in business as a grocer in Barrow at the time, although he was to retire early, to give more time for climbing, a few years later. I can't remember how long the holiday lasted on this first visit but the later visits were always for at least a week or longer. At Seascale we were met by the hotel car and driven in style, along the shore of Wastwater and up the dale, to the front door of the hotel, to be warmly welcomed by the Whitings. It was the first time I had been close to the lake, underneath the imposing rampart of The Screes, and I was most impressed by the majesty of the scene.

George was an old and trusted friend of the establishment and as I was under his wing, so to speak, I was made most welcome as well. I'm sure I was charged a very reduced rate for my board and lodging, being a young lad and a friend of George, and maybe my guide and companion was generously accommodated. Indeed, after dinner that first evening, and on many subsequent evenings as well, I was invited, with George, to take coffee with the Whitings in what was called "the office" but was, in fact, their pleasantly appointed drawing room. This was a rare honour, indeed. None of the other visitors, so far as I could find out, were treated in this way during our visits.

This was, of course, my first visit to the hotel and, indeed, to Wasdale Head. All I had done up to that time had been to look down into the dale from some of the surrounding tops. I had seen the walled fields, the farms, the church and probably the white-washed hotel from above and I had a picture of the hamlet in my mind, but nothing more. For me, it was the most wonderful place in the world, the place I had read so much about in the books of Owen Glynne Jones and the Abrahams and in the Fell and Rock journals.

The first thing that struck me as I went through the front door into the narrow hall was the strong smell of what turned out to be dubbin. Dozens, perhaps scores, of nailed boots, shiny from the recent application of the stuff, were littered about the floor and on the long seat at the side. Then, at the end of the hall, draped on what might have been a hatstand, were several coiled climbing ropes, a large number of long-shafted ice axes and, I seem to remember, one or two fell-poles, relics of an age only a generation or so earlier. It was very obviously a climbers' hotel, and I'm sure that if non-climbers had arrived they would have felt very much out of things – I can't recall seeing any non-climbers around. You sat, in the dining and breakfast room, under the overpowering gaze of the redoubtable Will Ritson, the original proprietor of the hotel and notable story-teller, looking out from a very large, old-fashioned photograph that dominated one end of the room. At the other end of the room – we ate, in those days, on each side of one long dining table – was a glass case containing an ancient, stuffed fox and there were rather grimy, old-fashioned, glass cruets on the table cloth.

But to me, the most interesting feature of the dining room, even more fascinating than old Will Ritson, was the collection of scores of photographs of rock-climbs and snow and ice-climbs, most of them in Lakeland, completely covering the walls of the room. Included in the pictures were photographs of mountaineers, sometimes in groups, most of them famous climbers, dating from the very beginnings of the sport to the "tigers" of the day. And when you came down to breakfast you might easily find yourself sitting next to one of the men in the photographs – a famous climber, perhaps, just back from a fortnight in the Alps or an expert on the gabbro rocks of Skye.

At the top of the stairs to the bedrooms there was an old, dark, oak chest, full, I discovered later, of discarded or lost articles of clothing which were readily available to all and sundry, as replacement wear for damaged, lost or forgotten gear. Thus you could quickly and easily, at no cost whatever, replenish your climbing wardrobe with anything you might need from an extra sweater to better-fitting trousers or a cleaner or less-darned pair of socks. Over the years I used it several times and probably some of my own discarded garments went into the chest.

The Whitings ran the hotel in their own individualistic way and primarily, so far as I could see, for the climbing fraternity which, in those days, consisted largely of the professional classes. There always seemed to be two or three professors, doctors, lawyers, businessmen and the like staying there. If you didn't "belong" you couldn't drink in the smoke-room but were condemned to the "chauffeurs' room" at the back of the hotel. I remember once when I was staying in the hotel a few years later, I was asked by a man I had met camping near Ritson's Force whether I could smuggle him out a Fell and Rock journal from the bookcase in the hotel. He wanted something to read in his tent at night and although he was a member of the club, indeed, I discovered later, a distinguished member, the Whitings would not allow him into the front part of the hotel, where the books were kept, because he wasn't staying there. As a mere camper and non-resident he was confined to the "chauffeurs' room" and could stray no further. I was a new member of the club by that time and managed to smuggle him out a journal without being detected. The man was H.G. Knight, a top-class climber who had taken part, with H.M. Kelly and others, in a number of important first ascents, including the splendid, very severe Grooved Wall on Pillar Rock.

Although the Whitings ran the hotel in a rather autocratic fashion – in a sense almost selecting their own clientele by discouraging those they did not favour – I never had anything but kindness from both of them. This was also the case with Edith Long, a sister-in-law of J.R. Whiting, who helped to run the hotel. On more than one occasion Mrs Whiting repaired my clothes when I had torn them climbing, and for years I was especially proud of my knee breeches, with a black patch on one knee and a light-coloured patch on the other, both skilfully applied by her. On another occasion I was foolish enough to get myself badly sunburned on my back and shoulders through climbing on the Napes in broiling heat and without a shirt. Edie – Edith Long – was most concerned. She treated me with calamine lotion and loaned me a silk scarf for protection.

Wastwater Screes

Going back to my very first visit to the Wastwater Hotel, I clearly remember waking up early the following morning and lying in bed listening to the sound of the Mosedale Beck sliding along past the rear of the hotel. To me it seemed a thrilling sound, full of the promise of happy and exciting days to come. Here I was in Wasdale Head, to me the most wonderful place in England, and sleeping in the famous hotel, the very birthplace of climbing. Furthermore, it was the beginning of my first holiday on the great crags all around the dale about which I had read so much, but hadn't even seen. Next came breakfast in the long dining room, with all sorts of interesting people for company, although whether they were interested in talking to a comparative novice youngster I rather doubt. Over the years I climbed with George on the Napes, on Scafell, on Pillar Rock and in other places so we could have tackled any of these on that first day – probably the Napes or Kern Knotts. I'm sure we had a wonderful day; all the days at that time, no matter what the weather, were wonderful.

The famous billiard table on and around which climbers performed all manner of feats of strength or agility, including "billiard-fives" and the billiard-table traverse done with feet on the walls, was not in use by this time, and the elegant drawing-room, with its chintz-covered chairs, came rather later. In my day the important room, both before and after dinner, was the smoke-room, not far from the dubbined boots and ropes in the entrance hall. To this small, crowded snuggery we would all repair, not especially to smoke but to talk, and how those climbers could talk! And, although it seems almost unbelievable now, sometimes we would sing. I probably sat on the floor to make more room but the rest of the company would comprise several serious, mostly middle-aged or even elderly, professional men of apparent distinction. And there they were, relaxing after a hard day on the crags and a hearty meal, by telling unbelievably tall mountain stories, or joining in the choruses of climbing songs. The senior member would perhaps beat time with the poker from the fire, or bang out the beat on the fire tongs.

I would sit, usually literally, at their feet, drinking it all in and not daring to say very much in case I said the wrong thing. Many were distinguished climbers of whom I had read in books or journals, all were cragsmen of ability and they all seemed to me pretty learned and important. One of the professors staying in the hotel was said to complete the fiendishly difficult "Torquemada" crossword puzzle in *The Observer*, without reference books, after breakfast every Sunday morning, before setting off on his climb.

One evening after dinner they sent me off to go up and down Scafell Pike. They had been discussing mountain distances and times – there had just been an early attempt on the Lakeland 24-hour fell record – and, probably because I had ventured an unwise opinion, they suggested I should show them what I could do. They were probably glad to get rid of me for an hour or two. I forget the challenge – some ridiculously short time – but I said I would have a go, and off I went, at the double, for Brown Tongue. For two or three hours I toiled up and down the Pike, running most of the way down, and managed to get in before it was really dark, pretty well exhausted. I'm sure I failed in the challenge, whatever it was, but I was congratulated on my effort and given a large glass of lemonade.

There was one picture among the scores on the walls of the dining room that both frightened and fascinated me. It was an Abraham photograph of the upper part of Eagle's Nest Direct on the Napes showing a climber, dressed in old-fashioned tweeds and wearing nailed boots, poised on what looked like the edge of space, high up on the ridge. His position looked precarious in the extreme for the footholds appeared very small, smooth and downward sloping, while the climber seemed very lonely and a long way up. Even so, he appeared remarkably relaxed and composed and I greatly admired his sangfroid. But I strongly doubted whether I would ever be able to get up the same place without dying of fright.

On one of my early visits to the Wastwater Hotel I was fortunate enough to be introduced to the climber in the Abraham picture of Eagle's Nest Direct – Mr A.E. Field. He was then an old man but still erect and alert and enthusiastic about the crags, and we chatted about climbing for some time. He had been a professor at one of the universities and had climbed a great deal with the legendary Owen Glynne Jones – also prominently pictured in the hotel dining room. Indeed, they had been together on the first ascent of the redoubtable Walker's Gully on Pillar Rock, and with them on this famous occasion in 1899 had been the ubiquitous George Abraham. Years after my first visit to the Wastwater Hotel, when I had become a member of the Fell and Rock Climbing Club, I came to know both the Abraham brothers, George and Ashley, who were prominent in the club. And I especially recall spending a fascinating afternoon with George Abraham in his Keswick home, listening to his stories of early Lakeland climbing and climbers. It so happened I had climbed Walla Crag Gully in Borrowdale a few weeks earlier and I mentioned this to George, knowing he had been the first to climb it, leading his younger brother Ashley, in 1892. This, in fact, had been the very first route to be climbed in Borrowdale.

When George heard I had been in Walla Crag Gully his eyes twinkled and he asked me, "Is the old root still there on the first pitch?" I told him it was, nearly worn away but still a necessary foothold to get up the first few feet of the climb. George Abraham would then have been about 90 years of age. It was a few years before his death in 1965, and he was recalling an experience seventy years earlier! To have known A.E. Field and George

The author leading North Wall, Dow Crag in the early 1930s.

Stickle Pike – my first hill, 1923.
The picture shows the summit party with
me in the middle and H.M. Sawtell on
the right.

George Basterfield

Left to right: unknown, Jack Diamond, Archie Stammers, Tommy Tyson,
Jim Porter.

Leslie (on right) and I leaving Skye after an early visit.

George Basterfield, centre, with rope. In Hollow Stones, Scafell.

George Basterfield in the snow,
early 1930s.

Myself leading Trident Route,
Dow Crag in the early 1930s.

Abraham, two of the three pioneers of a famous climb, Walker's Gully, of 100 years ago makes me feel even older than I am, but also quite proud and rather humble.

On a visit to the former Wastwater Hotel in 1997 I noticed that the photograph of Will Ritson had been removed from the dining room and had been replaced by a large picture of George and Ashley Abraham, the former, much as I remembered him. I was sorry that Auld Will had been deposed, if only to another room, but, at least, the Abrahams had been better climbers, and had done a great deal for Wasdale and the hotel.

I first climbed Eagle's Nest Direct either on this first visit to Wasdale or on the next one. George Basterfield was with me and, always anxious to encourage youngsters, insisted I should lead it. Everything went well but, then, it was difficult to do anything wrong with George behind you on the rope. I remember that when I reached the parallel cracks he told me the exact sequence of hand and footholds, and the whole thing went quite easily. Even now, seventy years later, I can recall the sequence as he explained it in his quiet but authoritative voice. And, once I was on the ridge, his voice came up calmly and clearly from below, "Now step up easily. Don't try to pull. Just use your hands for balance. There's nothing to it." And with George behind me, there wasn't.

But I was in rubber plimsolls on a warm, sunny day – vastly different from the first ascent, in nailed boots, on a cold April day in 1892. The intimidating, unknown ridge was to become the most difficult climb in England up to that time. Even today it rates a very severe grade. Once, in Borrowdale, just before the war, I met the leader of that most important first ascent of more than a hundred years ago. Godfrey Allan Solly was a solemn-looking, rather austere gentleman with a big white beard. He was about eighty years old at that time, but still climbing. Solly was a distinguished member of the Fell and Rock, and also of the Scottish Mountaineering Club, having also been involved in several important early ascents in Scotland. I believe the famous, slightly ponderous command, "Silence while the leader is advancing," is attributed to Solly. Certainly, he possessed exactly the required gravitas for such a remark.

On one of my early visits to the hotel George Basterfield introduced me to the new, resplendent drawing room, complete with piano. There was nobody else about and George idly caressed the keys, trying to pick out a tune. He was a poet, but hardly a musician and certainly no pianist. However, he clearly had music in his head for these tunes he was picking out for me were the basis of the music for his very atmospheric "Songs of a Cragsman". I especially remember him working out the melodies for "The Dale of the Yew" and "Eternal Hills". In front of me now, as I write, is an early signed copy from George of these songs, without the music, dated 1931, and also a copy of the same poems, this time set to music and orchestrated by Oliver Knapton. This latter is dated July 1936, and signed to me, "With the compliments of Geo. B". My old friend had carefully worked out the tunes for the orchestrator, who had produced the most professional score. I often play his mountain songs on the piano to bring back the old days.

Outside the hotel, in the inn-yard, was the Stable Door (or Barn Door) Traverse – quite a gymnastic feat. You had to climb up the rough slabs on the right-hand side of the wall and then make a delicate traverse, on very poor holds, into the open door about ten feet above the ground. Above the open door, in white paint, was a sign "Post Horses", a memory of earlier days. Of course, in the days of my early visits there wasn't a climbers' shop and self-catering apartments as there are today, but I do recall a tiny rock garden in a corner of what is now the residents' car park in front of the hotel. This little garden had been laid out with tender care by George Basterfield and filled with mountain plants, including harebells, thyme and grass of Parnassus, he had brought down off the fells.

Thus my introduction to Wasdale Head and the Wastwater Hotel. George took me on my first climbs there: the Needle and the Napes ridges, Kern Knotts, Eagle's Nest, some routes on Scafell's Pinnacle Face and several trips to Pillar Rock. Afterwards he often handed me over to other people or, occasionally, I found my own companions. For example, I remember a splendid day with a man called Macfarlane, who was another of the university professors. By leading through on all the climbs we rattled through most of the ridges on the Napes in one day (Arrowhead, Buzzard Wall, Cutlass, Scimitar, Sabre and Rainbow included) and I remember how comparatively easily they all went. Up to that time I'd not tested myself on anything really hard.

To introduce me to Kern Knotts George first took me up the Chimney, and then the Crack, which I found rather hard, especially the smooth wall to its right. Immediately afterwards he told me to go down to the foot of Kern Knotts and, flicking a rope down Innominate Crack, instructed me to climb that. This seemed more the sort of climbing I could best manage, balancing up on small holds and, on this first visit, I certainly found Innominate easier than the Crack. Later visits, when I have been leading, have reinforced this early opinion and Kern Knotts Crack never became a favourite climb of mine, even in rubbers.

On one of my early visits to Wasdale – it could have been this first visit – I was introduced to a new type of bathing. A group of us had been climbing on Scafell and on the way back to the hotel we all had a dip in a delightful pool in Lingmell Beck, not far from Down-in-the-Dale. Naturally, we had no costumes and I never used a costume in hundreds of dips into becks and tarns on the fells. When we came out of the pool one of the company, a German doctor, told us it was a waste of time drying ourselves. Far better and healthier, he said, to pull our clothes on to our wet bodies as soon as we came out of the water, and then trot or walk quickly to keep ourselves warm. We all did this, experiencing no inconvenience whatever, and found our clothes remained perfectly dry. Thereafter, I always dispensed with the services of a towel after dips on the fells. I would pull my clothes on to my wet body, and never felt any ill effects. But I was never convinced by the German doctor's claim that by not drying oneself the surplus water somehow went back into the body and restored it.

One of the most interesting characters I met during these early visits to Wasdale Head was C.F. Holland, who had taken part, with Herford and Sansom, in the first ascent of Central Buttress on Scafell Crag. He had also written the first climbing guide to Scafell in 1924 and had been on the first ascents, with H.M. Kelly, of Sodom and Gomorrah on Pillar Rock in 1919, and many other fine climbs. It was Holland who had first suggested the rather dramatic names for these two climbs "under the stress of a slight contretemps on Route 2 which might have ended in disaster", but the more prosaic names of Routes 1 and 2 were entered in the logbook. Many years later, in more permissive times, the original names were restored.

Holland was a shortish man with chiselled, rather piratical features and a reputation for preserving his sangfroid – and sometimes his pipe – when falling off climbs. H.R.C. Carr, who had climbed with Holland, once described his grin as "reminding one of a famous gargoyle on Notre Dame" and his laugh as one "that became more and more Rabelaisian after the second or third pint". And this is more or less how I remember him. He was a schoolmaster and later, during the Second World War, when he must have been a good age, served in the Commandos and as an army mountain instructor.

I remember one very wet and wild day, with the clouds very low on the fells, George Basterfield, Holland and I set off from the hotel to climb on Pillar Rock. We did that sort of thing in those days – setting off to climb in bad weather. You just lowered the standard of your climbs a grade or two. On top of Black Sail we were crouching in a rock corner, trying to get a bit of shelter so that we could eat our sandwiches, when we heard some noise among the rocks and scree. Looking up, we were surprised to see a man with a bicycle on his back emerge through the cloud and rain a few feet away. And we were even more surprised when he addressed us in a broad Lancashire accent, "Excuse me. Am I on't reiight road to Whitehaven?" Holland was the first of us to recover from the surprise. "Keep straight on," he said, pointing down the steep, rocky track into the murk. "You can't miss it."

We did two or three of the Jordan climbs on the Rock in the rain that day. As we walked down the fellside, back to Wasdale Head, Holland told me, very seriously and sincerely, how the great Siegfried Herford, who first led Central Buttress in April 1914, had "returned" to the area at the moment of his death in France during the First World War. Holland had no doubt about it: his old friend had come back to the crags for a moment to say goodbye. He (Holland) had been walking down from Scafell Crag and, somewhere near Hollow Stones, he had met Herford, whom he thought was in France. They had walked down together, chatting, as friends do. A few days later Holland learned that Herford had been killed in France at about the time when he sincerely believed they had walked down the fellside together. I'm quite sure Holland was completely convinced that Herford had come back to see his old friend. He told the story without embarrassment and didn't suggest an explanation. George had heard the story before and knew that you couldn't talk Holland out of it.

These days of my early visits to Pillar Rock were some time before the mass afforestation of Ennerdale, and from the top there wasn't a tree to be seen. Today, this once-lonely dale is packed with hundreds of thousands, no doubt, millions, of densely crowded conifers, with traffic virtually excluded. It is a dramatic and hardly welcome transformation. There were no restrictions in those happy days nearly seventy years ago, but you rarely met other climbers up there. On top of the Rock you had a feeling you were in a very special place: indeed, not so many years earlier you could leave your card in an old tin box up there to record your visit.

One day when I was getting ready to join George Basterfield on another trip to our beloved Wasdale I received a postcard from him, written in an unfamiliar, spidery hand. The card explained: "I'm writing this with my left hand as I've had a bit of an accident. Sorry to say I won't be able to go with you to Wasdale this time, but George Sansom will be on his own at the hotel, and I've arranged for him to climb with you, instead. Have a good time." My disappointment at being deprived of George's companionship and concern over his accident were mixed with feelings of excitement about this completely unexpected chance to climb with the man who had partnered Herford on the first ascent of Central Buttress on Scafell – at that time, the hardest climb in England.

George's accident had been an unusual one. He had been climbing on Black Crag, Scafell with A.B. Reynolds. Reynolds, who had first led The Crack on Gimmer Crag in 1928, was leading a pitch high up on Black Crag when he came off and fell past George, landing on a ledge below him. Concerned, George shouted down to ask whether Reynolds was all right and was assured that he was. When Reynolds enquired about his second's condition, George answered, "I've lost my bloody thumb." Apparently, in holding Reynold's sudden fall George's rope had wrapped itself round a thumb and the tremendous jerk had wrenched off the end of it. I can't now remember the length of George's convalescence, but I know that before very long he was back climbing again, despite his serious injury.

Meanwhile, as a direct result of this unfortunate accident, I was having my climbing holiday with George Sansom. I had never met him before but, as a keen student of climbing history, knew quite a lot about him. One of these bits of knowledge was that every time Sansom came to Wasdale from his home in the south of England he would first climb Hopkinson's Gully on Scafell which he and Herford had first climbed in 1912. This was partly for sentimental reasons and partly to assess his form. He would usually climb this, a hard severe, on his own, and I believe had already done so on this holiday before we met.

George Sansom was a neat, rather short man, very sunburned when we met, and exuding an atmosphere of quiet efficiency. He moved incredibly slowly up steep slopes like Gavel Neese, believing you should always arrive at the foot of your climb breathing completely normally, but he was the quickest and neatest climber

I have known. He smoked a cherry-wood pipe when he was in the hills, and at the start of a climb would chew barley sugar, getting as much of it as possible on his fingers. The resultant stickiness, he claimed, helped him in the use of smooth, sloping handholds – a technique he demonstrated on Napes Needle and other places. George Basterfield, on the other hand, was a great believer in the efficacy of grapefruit in the same context. He was always sucking grapefruit on the crags; no wonder he used to bring dozens of them to Wasdale.

With my new, very fit companion we rattled off many of the climbs on the Napes and Kern Knotts, but I don't remember climbing with him on Scafell – the scene of so many of his triumphs. I recall we did Napes Needle together. By that time, I had led this famous climb, probably more than once, but with Sansom in the lead it seemed almost a new experience. He went up incredibly quickly, almost dancing up the rock, and on the descent almost slid down the Wasdale Crack. In a way, he didn't seem to use the holds so much as caress them. There was never any question of pulling up on anything, just stepping up neatly. I learned many important lessons about neat climbing that day and, indeed, on all the days we climbed together.

Then one day he announced we were going to Pillar Rock, already a favourite climbing ground of mine. I wish I could remember everything we talked about on that long walk to the Rock and back all those years ago. Certainly he enthused about Scafell and the great climbs he and Herford had done there before the war, and he told me about Herford, Holland and all his other climbing friends, but I can't now recall the details. I remember we also chatted about climbing techniques and the way to use different types of holds. This was many years before the development of hand-jamming techniques but he was certainly interested in the technical, engineering side of the sport. When we reached the Rock, on a bright, sunny day, by way of the High Level Route, we walked along Green Ledge and Sansom announced we were going to do North-West Climb, a very severe. I'd already done Eagle's Nest Direct and Innominate Crack by this time but North-West was certainly one of my first very severes and I remember nearly every moment of the climb.

With Sansom in the lead, climbing quickly and neatly, my impressions, looking back over the years, are that it seemed steep and exposed, particularly in its upper reaches, but relatively straightforward, and by no means frightening. In fact, I managed it so well that two or three weeks later I was able to lead my brother Leslie up it. This new-found assurance was entirely due to the confidence George Sansom had given me. In a rather different way he was almost as wonderful a teacher as George Basterfield. And the two Georges were almost equally devoted to Wasdale: the finest valley in Lakeland, in their opinion. Sansom seldom climbed anywhere else in the area.

A year or two later, in 1933, I was elected a member of the Fell and Rock Climbing Club, my proposer, of course, being George Basterfield and my seconder, George Sansom. I could not have been more fortunate in my sponsors. Sansom, who lived in the south of England, would have been in his mid-forties when we had this holiday together. We kept in touch by letter, occasionally, over the years, and he read some of my books and writings. Later I discovered he had had a distinguished First World War record – the war in which his great friend, Herford, had been killed. Regrettably, I never met him again. At Christmas 1973 he wrote to me, in his eighty-sixth year, about his "very happy memories of Lakeland". Certainly, he loved the Wasdale hills, probably above all others. Once he sent me some small prints of photographs taken on his first ascent, with Herford, of Central Buttress. I wish we could have kept up our climbing association, but we were a generation and much of the length of England apart. Herford and Sansom, as climbers, were years ahead of their time, and I feel greatly honoured that I was able to climb with one of them.

One of the characters of Wasdale Head that I well remember from my first visits was the red-bearded old shepherd we all knew as "Owd Joe". He was a scruffy, little man, dressed in dirty, old clothes, with a grinning, toothless face almost completely hidden by his matted beard, and, always carrying a long stick. He had not the slightest respect for anybody, and if he didn't like you he would tell you so. Every so often he would work himself up into a tremendous rage if anything or anybody annoyed him, and even his Herdwicks, which he loved above all living creatures, were not safe from these outbursts. You would often hear him in the farmyard cursing them in his high-pitched, almost unintelligible, dialect and see him fiercely belabouring them with his stick. It was said he could recognise individual Herdwicks better than he could human beings, and he certainly thought them much more interesting.

"Owd Joe" was said to sleep in his clothes in a sort of lean-to, not unlike a hen-cabin, at the back of the hotel. It was also said he had never seen a bus, a train or a lamp-post and, indeed, had rarely left the dale. But on one of the very few occasions he had done so, on a trip to Egremont Crab Fair in the hotel trap, he showed them he was not so simple as they thought. They gave him a shilling to spend and late at night he returned, drunk as a lord, with a wicked grin across his toothless face and two shillings in his pocket. Nobody could find out how he had managed to get drunk and yet double his money, but he might well have won the first prize in the "gurning" contest – awarded to the contestant pulling the ugliest possible face while peering through a horse-collar. He had exactly the right sort of face for the job.

But the real point of the story was that on his return, "Owd Joe" was said to be completely unintelligible, even to his fellow dalesmen; he was mouthing a foreign tongue. They said it was Ice-landic. Puzzled, they brought professors and scholars staying at the hotel to listen to his drunken ramblings and they all came to the same conclusion: "Owd Joe" had lapsed into something defi-nitely Scandinavian. I won't spoil a good story by further enlarge-ment but, of course, there could have been some association with the Vikings who colonised these western dales a thousand years ago. Indeed, it has often been said that a Cumbrian-born dialect speaker could get along with the language in Norway, many of the words being similar.

The last time I saw "Owd Joe", almost a lifetime ago, he was a very sad man, the greatest tragedy in his life having stricken him in his declining years. He had been taken off the fell and relegated to take charge of the ducks. My very last memory of the old rascal is of watching him weaving his way down the lane, shouting at the ducks squawking along ahead of him, and waving and banging his stick. An unforgettable Wasdale character, he is still pictured, I believe, in the bar at the back of the hotel.

Opposite: The first three verses of "Owd Joe O'Wasdale 'Ead" from "Songs of a Cragsman" by George Basterfield

" Owd, JOE O' WASDALE 'EAD."

It's fine to be doin' wid nabbut wot
    When I ga gadderin' sheap,
I gang aboot an caw ont dogs
    Ta laet 'em 'oot ont steäp.
There's chaps as cums ta Wasdle 'ead,
    Fer why I nivver cud tell,
Wid nivver a sheap to coont, mi lads,
    Tha' slidder aboot ont fell,
O wid nivver a sheap ta coont, mi lads,
    Tha' slidder aboot ont fell.

Chorus :
    Hi, hi, git awa' git awa' cum' ere Lassie and Jack,
    Hi, hi, git awa', git awa', cum' ere git awa' back.

These climmin' chaps when tha' ga oot,
    Reet oop tha rocks tha' graep,
There's nobbut yan road oop tha' naas
    Togidder, and teed wi raep
Tha' tuk mi fer a climmer yance
    On Scowfle top yan day,
Ah nivver owivver was I a climmer
    I wark it awe the way.
Ah nivver owivver was I a climmer
    I wark it awe the way.

I watched 'em clim' a rock yan day,
    Reet oop on " Gabble " side,
At last·tha git oop pretty 'igh,
    Wid nivver a spot ta bide ;
An then I laffed ha!, ha, ha, ha !
    By gok I 'ad sum fun,
A blidderin block was t'end ot rock,
    An down tha 'ad ta cum,
O, a blidderin block was t'end ot rock,
    An down tha' 'ad ta cum.

Deserted Fells

On a bright April day when there were said to be more cars in the Lake District than ever before and the popular routes across the fells seemed "wick wi' foak", two of us sat in a rock corner high above the Lingcove Beck and looked out over the wild, tumbled landscape. And, incredibly, there was just nobody to be seen – nobody, so far as we could see, in upper Eskdale or in Moasdale or in Green Hole or on any of the fellsides, and not even the glint of a car windscreen down in Dunnerdale. Here we were, perhaps only half a mile away from one of the best-known mountain tracks in the district on the most crowded day that anybody could remember, and yet we seemed to have the fells absolutely to ourselves. For half an hour we sat peering up each valley in turn and systematically sweeping every square mile of fellside and crag, but not a sign of movement anywhere, except, now and again, a distant grazing sheep and the ravens quartering the sky. And then, as we got up to wander down to the valley, one of us spied tiny moving dots on the snow-covered summit ridge of Scafell, nearly three miles away, and we realised we were not quite alone after all. For those who seek peace and solitude in the hills this, surely, is the saving grace: that on days when the roads and the villages are chock-full of traffic, with cars bumper to bumper over the passes, and noble fells like Helvellyn, Gable and Scafell alive with winding processions of brightly coloured anoraks, you can still find quiet places for yourself by getting off the crowded tracks and exploring new ways across the fells. Hundreds of places, if you know where to look, where you can be alone with your thoughts, the views and the little movements and sounds of the countryside, with rich discoveries round every corner.

April 1979

Chapter Five

Days with the Tigers

Our happy little climbing group, the Coniston Tigers, must have been formed about sixty-eight years ago – probably not long after the first ascent of Tiger Traverse on Dow Crag by Dick Mackereth, Bryan Tyson and myself in September, 1931. Three of the four surviving members, all rather doddery, got together in 1997. After a great deal of peering back through the years, we came to the conclusion that we had acquired our hut and started operating as a club late in 1931 or, at the very latest, early in 1932. And the date is important for it establishes the fact that ours was the second climbing hut to be established in the Lake District – far ahead of all but one of the vastly superior huts of the established clubs.

Even more importantly, these early years of the Coniston Tigers, the 1930s, the years before the start of the Second World War, were the happiest and most exciting years of our lives. They were years that some of us still look back upon with reassuring, rather than aching, nostalgia, a time when we were living life to the full. We had all made satisfactory starts to our careers, there were no problems on the horizon, and we were all extremely fit and climbing to quite a high standard. Most of our weekdays were spent looking forward to the next weekend when we would, as usual, be climbing the crags of Dow, Gimmer or some other conveniently-sited precipice. None of us had much money, and in the beginning only one or two had cars, but we were rich in another way: we had our own climbing hut, a converted wooden garage near the shore of Coniston Water, adjoining the tall-chimneyed Coniston Old Hall.

These permanent headquarters, although basic in the extreme, gave us a big advantage over the other small groups of climbers from the towns and villages scattered around the Lake District who were also beginning their exploration of the crags. Our name, the Coniston Tigers, implied climbing abilities most of us did not really possess. Only one of us could have been fairly described as a "tiger", and he met with a very serious accident two years before the start of the war which, regrettably, put an end to what might well have been an outstanding climbing career.

At the start there were just nine of us in the venture – the original members of the Coniston Tigers. These were: Tommy Tyson, an Ulverston motor engineer and sportsman to whom I had first been introduced by Dick Mackereth a few years earlier; Jack Diamond, an old friend from Grammar School days; Jim Porter from Eskdale; Jim Philips from Dalton; David Birch, another old school friend; George Anderson, Jack Atkinson and Len Brown, all from Barrow; and myself. Some of them were old climbing friends, but at the start I was meeting Jim Porter, Jim Philips, George Anderson and Len Brown for the first time. Other early members included my younger brother Leslie, but he was not in the group at the very start, and George Jones, who might have been a founder member but who left the area after a year or two. George was a solicitor and years later I heard he had become a town clerk somewhere in the south of England. Eventually, I believe, he went to live in Canada.

Other friends used the hut occasionally but were not involved with the project at the very beginning. These included Charlie Smith, who later took over a shop in Coniston to be close to the fells; Jack Blackshaw, a much older man than any of us, whose serious deafness did nothing to quench his enthusiasm for the crags; Archie Stammers who, when he wasn't swarming over mountains was, I believe, the chief clerk at Euston railway station; and Syd Brown. Frequent visitors to the hut in the early days, and companions on the crags, were Dick Mackereth and Bryan Tyson, with whom I had had my first climbing adventures. They are sometimes pictured with original members but I can't remember them staying overnight. Many must have enjoyed the hospitality of the hut during the war but as I was in the army for six years, much of the time abroad, I have no Coniston memories for that period.

The oldest of our original members, in every way our senior member, was Tommy Tyson. He was perhaps ten years or so older than most of us. I had first met him through Dick Mackereth, also in business in Ulverston, and had climbed with him on several occasions. Tommy lived near Ulverston, where he had his motor engineering business. He was a rather stocky countryman with a confident air and friendly manner, who was something of an all-round sportsman. He was fond of fishing in Scotland, which he knew quite well, did a bit of shooting, and was quite devoted to the Lakeland hills. Very soon after we had first met I found myself being transported to Coniston and other climbing centres by Tommy in his Talbot (in the earliest days) and we started climbing together. Perhaps it was through Tommy that I first linked up with the people with the climbing hut, the group that was to become the Coniston Tigers. Tommy was the first one of us to own a motor car – in later years he seemed to have access to several – and was, or so he seemed to us, very much a man of the world. For example, he seemed to know all about exotic drinks, such as liqueurs and brandy, which were quite outside our scene at that time. You could say he was almost an avuncular figure and he put up with our schoolboy pranks with commendable restraint. On one occasion, I recall with regret, we tied a long string on the handle of the door of the shed that contained our toilet arrangements, and when Tommy was inside, engaged on his morning operations, the string was suddenly pulled. The door flew open and there was Tommy, sitting peacefully on the toilet with his trousers down, and half a dozen of us, with our cameras in position, recording the scene. We thought the pictures very good, especially the surprised look on Tommy's face, but it was all very childish and Tommy was not really amused.

Several of us were fairly good storytellers, and when he was on form Tommy often provided riotous entertainment. Our stories were usually slightly dirty stories and sometimes of a scatological flavour, I seem to remember. But the best storyteller of all of us was undoubtedly Dave Birch, who was particularly brilliant when acting out his tale. There was one hilarious story about a man complaining to his tailor about the fitting of his new suit and we never tired of hearing this, calling for it on every possible occasion. Dave's stories gained a special piquancy, especially when he was sitting down, because of some sort of nervous twitch with which he was afflicted. It caused him, quite involuntarily, to shoot out a leg at regular intervals and with great vigour. And these sudden kicks always seemed to occur at exactly the right moment, underlining the denouement like an outsize exclamation mark.

Our best climber was undoubtedly Jim Porter, and he always

seemed to me to be even fitter than the rest of us. One evening when he was living in Eskdale, he rode on his bicycle to Wasdale so that he could "christen" a new rope by soloing a climb with it trailing behind from his waist-loop. The climb he selected was Botterill's Slab, the very severe and delicate route on Scafell Crag. He had never climbed it before and there was nobody about, but he managed it all right, even though darkness was coming on when he was two-thirds of the way up the climb and he had a struggle to find the holds. Jim was the only one of the Tigers to lead Black Wall, the ferocious climb on Dow Crag described in Bower's guide as "exceedingly severe" and probably the hardest route on the crag. When Jim was leading a climb he would often infuriate his second by temporarily abandoning the route and exploring uncharted rocks to the side. Certainly, his ability inclined him to be rather over-confident on rock, and, most unfortunately, this, as you will read later, was eventually to lead to his undoing.

Jack Diamond was our principal organiser and secretary, a man devoted to the mountains and to mountain huts; our ideas man, if you like. Not content with our Coniston hut he eventually sought out and established other huts: one in a derelict cottage in Miners' Row, above the village, and another in an old quarry high up Coniston Old Man above Goats Water. After the war he gave up his insurance job, became a schoolmaster in Coniston, and settled down with his wife, Peggy, in a house at Haws Bank – just above Coniston Old Hall and the hut. I had known Jack longer than any of the others for we had started at Barrow Grammar School together. Soon after I had begun climbing, at the age of 18, I had tried to encourage him to do some routes with me. But, he said, and this was very typical of him, that he intended to tick off all the Lake District summits before he started on the crags, and this he did. Not long after he had done all the tops, having completed his apprenticeship to the fells, he took to the rocks and I believe I took him on his first climbs. He became a very sound climber and later was involved in several worthwhile first ascents.

George Anderson, Jack Atkinson, Len Brown and Dave Birch were all employed in positions of some responsibility at Vickers, the big shipbuilding company in Barrow. Probably George was the best climber among them – a big, strong man of few words who just got on with the job in hand. On rock he was a sound, thoughtful leader and he was a good man on snow, too. He became an engineering manager at the shipyard, highly regarded by all his colleagues. Jack Atkinson, one year behind me at the grammar school, was a chemist and metallurgist and, indeed, taught metallurgy for many years. Len was in one of the offices, in charge of accounts, and, later, I believe, head of the stores department. Dave, a little older than me at school but a close friend, became a cost and works accountant at the shipyard. I seem to remember that George and Jack had done a lot of cycling before taking, first to the hills, and then to the rocks. Len Brown, like myself, had had the advantage of some climbing with the ever-helpful George Basterfield. Jack Atkinson was a fine photographer. Hanging in my dining room is a treasured picture taken by him of me leading Jack Diamond up North Wall on Dow Crag about sixty-five years ago. I am wearing rubbers, floppy knee-breeches, the usual white sweater and a deceptively nonchalant air.

These, then, were the Tigers, a carefree, happy crowd, but you must not imagine that the Coniston Tigers was a climbing club like the Fell and Rock, the Wayfarers, the Heckmondwike Rock-Hoppers or any other club – real or imaginary. Perhaps we weren't a real club at all since we had no rules, no proper subscription and not even a list of members. Maybe you could have called us a gang, a gang of crag-rats if you like. But at least we had our own hut, which I believe was only the second climbing hut to be established in the Lake District. The first, set up in Langdale in 1930, was the Robertson Lamb hut of the Wayfarers' Club. Our little wooden hut, a pretty poky affair in comparison, was bought and set up on its site at the back of Coniston Old Hall the following year or, at the latest, in 1932. It had been, I believe, a garage, with a large door and a good-sized window that gave us an excellent view of Coniston Water and the low, wooded fells behind. In those days, at the beginning of the 1930s, this was a very quiet, secluded area, and apart from the occasional invited visitor we seemed to have the place to ourselves. Nowadays, there is a busy caravan park with adjoining sailing facilities close by. Most weekends we had a dip in Coniston Water from Land's Point, a hundred yards or so from the hut. We would be in the nude, of course, since we never had any bathing costumes. You couldn't do that today – not with propriety, anyway.

The next club hut to be opened in the Lake District after ours was High House at Seathwaite in Borrowdale by K Fellfarers, the out-doors club for the employees of K Shoes in Kendal. This took place on May 5th, 1934. While our hut is no longer in use as a climbing hut, High House still goes on from strength to strength. After these, the first hut of a recognised climbing club to be established in the Lake District was at Brackenclose (Wasdale Head) in 1937. This was the first of the several huts of the Fell and Rock Climbing Club.

So, although the Coniston Tigers were relatively unknown in the climbing world, we were at least in the forefront of the development to establish huts in the climbing areas of Britain. The primitive nature of our headquarters, however, would hardly have satisfied the modern demand for, at least, hot and cold water, showers and the most up-to-date cooking facilities. I can't now remember whether we even had a tap, or just got our water from the farm. What I can clearly recall is that we kept a bucketful of water inside the hut at night and that on many winter mornings we had to break sometimes as much as an inch of ice off the top of it before we could start cooking our breakfast.

We had made the beds, or bunks, ourselves, and judged by today's climbing-hut standards, they were pretty rough: just canvas stretched across a wooden frame. They were not very substantial, either. One night we were all awakened by a tremendous crash to discover that Tommy Tyson, probably the heaviest of the Tigers, had burst through the canvas of his bunk and dropped on to the floor, several feet below. It must have been an even ruder awakening for him.

Of course, we had no sleeping bags; indeed, in the early days, we had not even heard of them. Perhaps they didn't even exist at that time. But we had all brought blankets from our homes, probably those that were too old, tattered or worn for household use or, most likely, stolen from unsuspecting parents. These blankets were kept in an old, black tin trunk at the hut and rarely, if ever, aired. Doubtless many of the ailments that have afflicted some of the Tigers in later life could be traced back to those years of sleeping in damp, fusty blankets. But with the cheerful abandon of youth, we just didn't care, or even give our health a moment's thought. Of course, we had no mattresses either, and foam rubber hadn't yet been invented, but coiled climbing ropes and piles of old newspapers, covered with a blanket, seemed to be good enough padding for healthy, young bodies. I never lost a night's sleep through the discomfort of my bed.

I remember that Jim Porter did, in fact, acquire a sleeping bag several years later. He found it in a rucksack, somewhere high up on the Napes Ridges on Great Gable, and brought it down to the hut. Jim thought that somebody had lost the sleeping bag, of the eiderdown type, perhaps in a fall, or that it had been mislaid or even forgotten. We all thought this a bit strange, but Jim was the very last person who could possibly have been suspected of stealing by finding. I only hope the owner had not carefully concealed

Jim Porter leading Black Wall on Dow Crag in 1936 *(Tommy Tyson)*

Centre – myself (with scarf) and Dick Mackereth. Outer two not identified.
1930 or earlier.

Left to right: Tommy Tyson, myself, Bryan Tyson, George Basterfield,
unknown, unknown. About 1930.

Left to right: unknown, George Anderson, Jack Diamond, Archie Stammers.

Tigers going up the Dow Crag screes for some winter climbing.

Tommy Tyson in the hut.

Jack Diamond at the hut,
Christmas 1939.

Jack Diamond

George Spenceley

the rucksack and its contents for use later, perhaps for sleeping out on the tops!

The other important feature of the interior of the hut – probably the most important feature – was the sturdy, old-fashioned combustion stove. We used to stoke this up with coal or coke until the pipe or chimney was red-hot. The atmosphere in the hut in the evenings, what with the stove and the cooking of our dinners, was usually very warm, and often indescribably fuggy. Even so, in wintertime all this heat was not enough to prevent the thick layer of ice forming on our bucket of water just inside the hut door.

There was a wooden shelf along the side of the hut, underneath the window, and here we did our cooking on three or four rather ancient Primus stoves. Each man cooked for himself and there were some weird and wonderful concoctions. But we did ourselves pretty well – often porridge, bacon and eggs for breakfast, and sausages and mash or chops or stew, with perhaps rice pudding, for the evening meal. We didn't go into pubs at that time – except for our annual dinner, which was the only time when we ate out. Otherwise, life in the hut in the evenings was very quiet and restrained. We were nearly always tired out by our scamperings on the crags. After the meal and the washing-up we usually talked about the events of the day or planned new adventures. Some of us, incredibly, played contract bridge. George Anderson, Jack Atkinson, Len Brown and perhaps Dave Birch were the usual players I seem to remember. You can picture the scene on a winter's evening with two or three playing bridge by the light of our latest acquisition, a Tilley lamp, and the others smoking their pipes over a book or studying maps. I can't remember any of us drinking beer or spirits inside the hut, nor can I remember any hut rule that forbade it. But things might have been different during the war years when I was away, although I doubt it.

We were usually ready to move off to the crags by 9am and often glad to do so, either to get out of the airless hut and the fug or, on winter days, to escape from what sometimes seemed an ice-box with icicles creeping in around the door. There were rats and mice, too, and, once, we found a rat's nest in an old jacket somebody had left hanging in the hut. We walked from the hut to Dow Crag, usually past Heathwaite to the Walna Scar track, and then along the familiar path over the shoulder of the fell to Goats Water and up the screes to The Cave. It was a walk that was to become, for all of us, just as familiar as the roads around our homes.

Often, on arrival at Goats Water, especially if we had not bathed in the lake that morning, the more hardy among us would have a quick dip in the tarn. This ritual bathing, either in Coniston Water or the tarn, became a feature of our weekends. It could be very cold indeed, for these immersions were by no means confined to summer time, but we felt that the job had to be done for the honour of the club. I can't recall that we ever went swimming or bathing in the usual sense. A quick dip lasting perhaps two seconds, rather like a baptism, was all that was required for honour to be satisfied. I shiver nowadays every time I think about it.

With the help of Jim Porter and Jack Atkinson, two of the three other surviving founder members of the Tigers, I have been able to piece together the probable story of how and when the hut came into being. Jim remembers playing football for a church team with a master joiner called Irving Gradwell and hearing that this man and another from Dalton named Jim Philips had a wooden hut at Coniston and wanted to sell it. Whether the hut was then on its site at Coniston Old Hall or whether it was moved there from some other location, none of us can remember. I know that Jim Philips was involved in the original transaction and became a founder member of the club, although I can't remember him doing a lot of climbing. But he had already played his major role in the acquisition of the hut. After most of a long lifetime I also can't now remember how I came to be involved. Tommy Tyson, Jack Diamond and Dave Birch were all old friends so it might have been through one of them. The memory of Jim Porter or Jack Atkinson is that the hut was finally bought from Jim Philips for the tiny sum, even in those days, of £20. I remember all of us – the original nine members – bought shares in the hut, but I can't now recall the sum we paid. A very small figure, I'm sure. Jack Atkinson thinks we also each paid threepence a week into a kitty.

At first, Tommy Tyson, the motor engineer with his own garage business, was probably the only one of us with a car, and we must have relied on his friendly generosity very often when our expeditions began to spread further afield to, say, Langdale and Wasdale. But soon we all began to acquire our own transport, sometimes rather ancient motorcycles. My own introduction to the internal combustion engine was by motorcycle – a 350cc Le Vack model New Hudson with twin upswept exhaust pipes. This machine was bought from a back-street garage in Preston, where I was working for an evening newspaper. It was far too heavy and powerful for a complete beginner like me, and I crashed it ten yards after setting off on my trial run from the garage. Immediately prior to the crash I had been given about two minutes' instruction on how to work the, to me, complicated levers. There was no kick-start, and I was told to run forward with the heavy machine, fiddle with the levers, jump on to the saddle and then, when it fired, twiddle the accelerator. I think it was a lamp-post I hit. The purchase of this first vehicle cost me £12 10 shillings – plus the cost of the repairs!

Soon afterwards I crashed it again on an awkward bend just outside Coniston on the Ambleside road, damaging a knee rather badly, which kept me off the crags for a few weeks. Motorcycling didn't seem to be my scene, so I moved up one bracket and bought an open-top Morris Minor for the considerable sum, to me in those days, of £42. Now, at last, I had the freedom of the open road. Before long, I was driving to Skye and the Scottish Highlands, but more of that later. Of course, none of us had to take driving tests in those days and, probably fortunately for me, I've never had to take one since.

Once we were comfortably established in our new headquarters so close to the crags we began to spread our wings. We worked through the graded list of routes in George Bower's red-backed guide to Dow Crag, explored the Langdale climbs, especially those on Gimmer Crag, got to know the Wasdale cliffs and, now and again, went on night walks. One winter evening in the early 1930s six of us were in the hut, smoking our pipes after a good dinner and yarning before turning in for the night. Outside, a brilliant moon lit up the lake, the fells and the fields like winter sunshine. Suddenly, Tommy had his idea. "Jack," he said. "What about a midnight walk over Gable?"

"And miss Dow tomorrow?" we shouted. But Tommy was not to be so easily swayed. "Oh, we can go there any Sunday. It's a pity to waste such a wonderful night." So, half an hour later, rucksack-laden and booted, Tommy Tyson and Jack Diamond stepped out of the warm hut into the moonlight.

"Wait until you see our photograph of the Needle at midnight, you lazy dogs," they joked, as a draught of cold, night air, blown down from the snows, swept into the hut. "An ounce of Murray's Mellow Mixture (Tommy's favourite brand of tobacco) that you won't take it in the moonlight," I challenged, and the bet was accepted.

They were away twelve hours. We were sleeping soundly by the time they had trudged through Yewdale and past Tilberthwaite to Little Langdale. Over Blea Tarn pass, under the shadow of Langdale Pikes and up Mickleden they tramped, and by two o'clock in the morning they had struggled up Rossett Gill and reached the top. The wind, fresh from its gusty passage across miles of snow-covered hills, was bitterly cold, the moon cast a ghostly light over Gable, Bowfell and the hummocks of Glaramara, and half a dozen stars peeped out from the purple curtain of the night. The crunch of the half-frozen snow under their feet was the only sound until they heard the weird croak of the peregrine high up in the crags of Hanging Knott, above the black pool of Angle Tarn. A swish of his sickle-shaped wings, and he had swept over the pass.

At four o'clock in the morning they took their first breakfast at the foot of Napes Needle. One hundred feet above their heads reared the top block, so neatly balanced on top of the pinnacle, up which they had swarmed on many a summer's afternoon. Ice now clothed its familiar walls, the moon threw fantastic shadows across the face and, on the other side of the dale, snow was lying in the gullies of Great End and the Pikes. The bet was remembered, the camera set, and a half-hour's exposure taken before they climbed up the screes to the summit of Great Gable – for many, the most splendid viewpoint in England. Eventually, their effort and patience were rewarded and they witnessed the dawn of a new day from the summit. Slowly, a watery, winter sun rose over the crags of Great End, clouds disappeared as if afraid of day, a few birds drifted over the pass, puffs of mist crept down from the tops, and bright light filled the dale two thousand feet below.

Tommy and Jack walked back over the tops, the way they had come, well pleased with their midnight trip, with the feeling they had stolen an extra day. A few days later, back in Preston, I received a stout envelope from Tommy and out of it tumbled a photograph of Napes Needle taken at 4.25am. By return, went the packet of Murray's Mellow Mixture – very well deserved, I thought. And Tommy's picture of the Needle by moonlight hung on the wall of my study for very many years until, with age, it began to yellow a little and was kept in a drawer with many other photographs of early days.

Not long afterwards, Jack Diamond and I had a night adventure of our own, although this didn't go quite so carefully to plan as had his trip with Tommy. Our idea was to have a day's climbing on Gable from the Coniston hut, using the same route that Tommy and Jack had taken in the moonlight. The outward journey, although long, went well enough, and after some hours we were uncoiling the rope at the foot of Kern Knotts for our first climb. We then went on to the Napes, where we did several of the ridges. In those days we would think nothing of doing half a dozen climbs in an afternoon. We would usually lead through, and since there were no delays in fixing and removing protection with nuts and wire, as would happen nowadays, we probably climbed more quickly than is the case today. And this despite the very special care the leader always had to take, knowing he must never fall.

And so Jack and I carried on climbing well into the evening, although I forget how many routes we managed. It was a comparatively rare treat to be climbing on these wonderful Gable ridges, and we wanted to make the most of the opportunity. It was summer time, with long days, and it would have been nine o'clock or later before we coiled up the rope after our last climb and trotted down the fellside to Styhead. But we weren't worried. We both had torches, for we hadn't expected we would get back before dark. We both visualised getting back to the hut around midnight.

On the ascent to Esk Hause it began to get quite dark, and, when we began to stumble over boulders we couldn't see, we got out one of the torches. For a time we seemed to make satisfactory progress, but soon this torch faded and then failed altogether. By the time we reached the dark pool of Angle Tarn the second torch was also getting more and more faint. We managed to stumble in the very last of the light to the top of Rossett Gill – by this time we had had to throw away the second torch – but soon realised that our eyes were just not getting accustomed to the darkness. It was going to be a very black night.

We shuffled downwards, unable to see anything at all, although we thought that if we could feel ourselves going downhill, keeping in the same direction, we should be descending the main bed of the gill. But after a while, unable to keep our feet among the rocks and scree, and constantly falling, we decided we would be better off if we did the descent sitting down. After much crashing into rocks and a great deal of bad language, we got out the rope and tied on. We took it in turns to lead, the first man probing with his feet and hands, but every now and again taking a slip down the rocks, and the second man holding him on a short rope and controlling the falls. In this way we slowly descended the gill, taking a few knocks. Every now and again we had a rest, for it was a most exhausting business. The night remained as black as pitch; we could see nothing at all, not even the long length of Mickleden which we knew must be opening up down below. How long we took to descend Rossett Gill I've no idea but we must have done it in record slow time – probably hours.

It was now long after midnight, probably in the early morning hours, and we were still many miles from the hut. Even when we decided we must have reached the foot of the gill there was still no lightening of the sky. We looked for the sheepfold at the head of the dale as a marker, but couldn't find it, although we managed to keep a wavering course, in and out of the beck, down the valley. By now we were both tired out, and the prospect of tackling the miles of road to Coniston in complete darkι ess appalled us. However, as we trudged on we felt, at last, we must be approaching the Dungeon Gill area for we thought we could pick out vague shapes that could be farm buildings. Eventually, we made for one of these and, feeling our way round the walls to try to find a door, we came upon what seemed to be a barn. In a couple of minutes we had burrowed into what might have been straw or hay, and, completely worn out, still in our boots, were fast asleep in seconds.

Hours later we awoke refreshed in broad daylight and discovered we had spent the night with a horse, several chickens and heaven knows what other livestock. Looking outside, we could see that our overnight accommodation had been at Wall End at the foot of Blea Tarn pass, a place that many years later was to provide much-appreciated shelter for impecunious climbers and walkers, although not in this barn. Our morning toilet consisted of a rough wash in the beck, after which we went to the farmhouse door and asked if we could have some breakfast. The farmer, "Daddy" Myers, a good friend of outdoor folk, sat us in a stone-flagged kitchen with an open door through which sheep wandered now and again to take a look at us, and soon we were enjoying bacon and eggs. We thanked the farmer for the overnight accommodation and offered payment for the bed and breakfast, but he wouldn't take anything. Whether, in these days of mass tourism, farmers would be as generous as this, I can't say, but over the years I've often had good reason to be grateful to the farming community of the Lake District. So, feeling refreshed, we strode out along the road for Little Langdale, Tilberthwaite, Coniston and the hut with another little adventure under our belts.

I remember, too, another night escapade – this time on Dow Crag. My brother Leslie and I had been climbing all day and it was getting quite dark when we decided to come down off the crag and leave for the hut. For some reason, we thought the quickest way would be to descend Blizzard Chimney and Easter Gully. Halfway down the chimney we found it was too dark to see the holds, and it seemed to be even darker further down in the now quite-black recesses of the gully. Overhead, however, it looked a little lighter, so we decided to climb back up Blizzard Chimney and descend by the usual route of Easy Terrace, the way we should have taken in the first place.

It proved quite difficult, clawing our way up the fortunately familiar chimney in the growing darkness, feeling for the unseen holds, and by the time we reached the Terrace it was completely dark, and a very black night indeed. So we kept the rope on, as Jack and I had done in Rossett Gill, and proceeded very cautiously, a few inches at a time, on our posteriors. Very soon we realised we had little idea whether or not we were going in the right direction. The Terrace, in effect, is a downward-sloping ledge going across the crag, above the steep cliffs of "B", "C" and "D" Buttresses. But how near the edge of the drop were we? One foot? A yard? We could only guess. So we resorted to what I think was quite a clever ploy. The man in front, as we slowly edged forwards and down-wards on our bottoms, would scratch a few pebbles from the stones on which we were seated and drop them a foot or so to his left. We would then both listen intently. If we heard the pebbles drop immediately we would know we were some little distance, at least, from the edge. If we heard no sound for some time, as the pebbles dropped into space, we would know we were right on the edge and, accordingly, would shuffle on our bottoms a foot or two to the right for safety.

It was a nerve-racking descent in the darkness, but the scrambling pitches approaching the foot of the Terrace went more easily as we felt for the holds, for we knew we must then be well away from the edge of the cliff. Turning left at the base of the Terrace we then had to work along the foot of the buttresses above the screes, feeling our way along the crag. We were now standing up and had taken off the rope, but the problem was to know exactly when to move down the screes to The Cave, where we had left our ruck-sacks and the torches. This was done by remembering the shape and feel of cracks and holds on the first pitches of the climbs, and striking straight down to the right when we thought we were directly above The Cave. Again, everything went well. We were soon in The Cave, and the descent to the hut, in the pitch-darkness but now with the help of the torches, presented no problem. An hour or two later we were tucking into our meal in the familiar fug beside the red-hot stove.

This minor epic is not my only memory of Blizzard Chimney. One day several of us were on the crag when we spotted a crag-fast sheep on one of the buttresses and decided to get it down. Many years later, I was involved in two or three rescues of sheep from other Lakeland crags, but in this case it was somebody else who managed to grab the sheep and tie it on a rope – either George Anderson or Jack Atkinson, or both of them. The plan was to lower it down Blizzard Chimney but the sheep was not prepared to co-operate, clinging to the holds and refusing to be dislodged, no matter how we twiddled with the rope. In the end, I was sent down on another rope, leaving my hands free to prise the animal off the holds and accelerate its descent. The best method seemed to be to get just above the sheep, knock it off its holds so that it was hanging on the rope, then descend a foot or two before repeating the process all the way down the chimney. We then had to get the sheep down the lower reaches of Easter Gully. I remember that as we took off its rope the sheep seemed to give us a nasty glare, and even stamped her foot before scampering down the screes to a patch of grass. Her ingratitude, after all the effort that had gone into her rescue, was a little trying. We thought she had been marooned on the crag for several days.

Meanwhile, the exploration of the crags – mainly Dow and the Langdale cliffs most weekends, and Wasdale or Buttermere at holiday time – continued, summer and winter. Although we had no waterproof clothing and hadn't even heard of anoraks or cagoules, we regularly climbed in the rain, and just carried on up the chosen route in the nailed boots we had used for the walk to the crag. The weather had to be especially foul for us to abandon climbing and go for a fell walk, but on scores of occasions we would round off the day by carrying on over Dow Crag and Coniston Old Man or the Langdale tops after our climbs.

And it was often on these walks down from the crags in the evening that I used to be filled with an almost overpowering sense of wonder and gratitude at the beauty of the scene. The crag might be in shadow but the valley would be filled with sunshine and the shadows lengthening across the turf. Perhaps the lake lay below or, over the fells, there might be a glimpse of the sea. Probably we had had a wonderful day, with several hard climbs successfully completed, and now all this beauty – so much of it, I sometimes thought, that it was impossible to take it all in. And that night, or the next day, we would have to leave it all behind and it would be another long week before we would be back again. Very early in my mountain life I seemed to be grasping the two-fold appeal of the hills: beauty and adventure.

Our clothing for the crags remained largely unchanged during our hut days; mostly old tweed jackets, far too scruffy for ordinary wear, corduroy breeches and, in wintertime, balaclava helmets or motorcycle caps. Later we took to wearing white sweaters on the crags because they showed up better on photographs. Much of our climbing was done in clinker-nailed boots, but for the harder routes we used rubbers, normally black plimsolls with, I remember, a diamond design on the sole. They cost tenpence a pair at Woolworth's and with the amount of climbing we were doing lasted only a few weeks. We always bought them at least one size too small, believing that tiny feet were best for tiny holds. Orthopaedic surgeons have told me since that the many problems I have had with my feet and toes in later life were caused by the years of climbing with this constricting footwear. And the narrow, pointed "P.A." climbing boots that appeared many years later couldn't have helped much, either.

As a nailed-boots climber, I considered the Stubai nail, which had a deep groove cut in the width of the clinker, a big advance in design. It seemed to provide double the grip. We didn't think much of tricouni nails for Lakeland rock – not round the edge of the sole, anyway – and the Hargreaves nail didn't seem to take on in a big way. But as Jim Birkett, probably the best nailed-boots climber in the country, once told me, "It's not the boots or the nails that matter: it's the man in them that counts." He and I climbed together quite often after the war years, and I never ceased to marvel at his technique. We were once climbing together in nails on Dow Crag, probably on one of the easier severes, and I was making an awful meal of things. Jim was very patient, but couldn't understand my clumsiness. He happened to be climbing that day in quarrymen's clogs, with huge horseshoe "caulkers" round the sole, but, of course, found not the slightest difficulty.

When my ex-army boots wore out – I might have exhausted several pairs – I decided to go in for the number one climbing boot of the era – the Robert Lawrie boot. Bob Lawrie, who later had elegant premises in London and built up a European reputation for his mountain equipment, then had a very small boot shop in Burnley,

Lancashire. So I drove down there one day to see him and had quite a job finding the shop. I knew I had come to the right place when I saw in the window of a little shop in a side street the incredible boots in which, in 1931, Dr Raymond Greene, with F.S. Smythe and others, had climbed Kamet in the Himalayas. It was then the highest mountain that had been climbed. Dr Greene, who later took part in the 1933 Everest expedition, was an exceptionally tall man and these boots, displayed in the window of Lawrie's shop, were the biggest I had ever seen. They seemed nearly twice the length of an ordinary pair.

Anyway, I saw Bob Lawrie and he measured me for my boots, which he later nailed to my specification. These boots were certainly the most comfortable climbing boots I have ever owned and I used them for many years. Just after the war, when I was skiing regularly, I got in touch with Bob Lawrie again. He was then in business in London and he was able to acquire for me from Switzerland, through his continental associations, a pair of a special type of skins for ski mountaineering, not then available in this country. Many years later, when Ivan Waller and I were doing a lot of climbing and skiing together, he told me how he and Bob Lawrie had taken part together in the Le Mans 24-hour motor car race in 1940, coming in eleventh.

On the crags, we Coniston Tigers and everybody else climbing at that time used ordinary hemp rope, usually 100 feet long, but nothing else. We had no slings or karabiners until after the war, and, of course, no nuts on bits of wire, sticky boots or chalk bags. The rope was merely tied round the waist with a bowline, no harness at that time, and we paid it out under one shoulder and over the other. Waist belays came many years later. For the harder routes or routes with long run-outs we sometimes used half-thickness line, on the principle that there would be less drag for the leader and it was often easier when tying on belays. The safety factor, with ropes of only half-strength, didn't seem to come into it. We must have borne charmed lives.

I recall one development in mountain gear before the war that impressed me. Graham Macphee, a distinguished climber of the day, and I were climbing on Gable Crag when I noticed he was wearing rather an unusual jacket. Questioned about it, he explained it was really a raincoat, but by a clever arrangement of cords and stitching he had managed to convert it into what, I suppose, was a climbing jacket – a forerunner, perhaps, of the now ubiquitous anorak. To demonstrate he pulled a couple of strings and there he was, dressed in a raincoat, ideal for walking down from the crags in the rain. This seemed a wonderful idea, and I tried to persuade my mother to do something of the same for me with an old coat, but I don't think anything came of it.

Which reminds me, since I am writing about climbing gear, of a story told by an elderly climbing club president, a man of distinction and grave demeanour. He was walking over Esk Hause one day when he came upon two people, a man and his wife, toiling over the pass carrying heavy suitcases. "Excuse me, sir, " said the man to the senior mountaineer. "What is the name of that thing on your back and where might I purchase one?" To which the elderly club president ponderously replied, "The object on my back is a rucksack, and you may buy one in any sports outfitter in most towns and cities." "Thank you very much, sir," said the man. "My wife and I are enjoying a fortnight's holiday in the Lakes, walking over the mountains from place to place, and we are getting a little tired, carrying all our belongings in these suitcases."

Helvellyn from Red Tarn

A Little-Visited Fell

*Inconspicuously wedged between the greater glories of Great
Gable, Great End and Glaramara, the craggy two-thousander
plateau of Seathwaite Fell remains untracked and little visited –
a curiously-neglected height amid over-popular places. But
besides giving the finest view of the long length of Borrowdale and
intimate glimpses of the surrounding tops, Seathwaite Fell can
provide a secluded link with the Esk Hause highway and also has
another distinction. Few, if any, Lake District fells are so
besprinkled with tarns and pools, making its crossing on a hot
summer's evening a perfect delight. The large-scale map shows
six blue blobs, including the well-known Sprinkling Tarn, but on
a recent descent I counted ten pools, and, since I did not comb
the entire fell, there could be a dozen or more of them. Apart from
Sprinkling Tarn, all are unnamed. However, Heaton Cooper, the
Lakeland painter who described this tarn as "the most completely
satisfying" in the fell country, gave the name Sprinkling Crag
Tarn to the next largest – an even more beautiful pool cradled
among the rocks with the bulk of Great Gable filling the view to
the west. I can think of few pleasanter ways of spending a hot,
lazy day in the fells than to bathe in all these tarns in turn; a
costume would be unnecessary since few people pass this way.
My last visit followed a hot, sultry ascent of Grains Gill and a
cool, shadowed climb up Cust's Gully on Great End crags, still
partly packed with snow in June. Seathwaite Fell then seemed the
quick way home and this time I managed only one token bathe.
One person, at least, knows the fell well – the man who keeps the
rainfall records, for some of the gauges that confirm the hamlet of
Seathwaite as the wettest place in England are sited on this
lonely fell.*

June 1975

Chapter Six

Excitements on the Crags

In those happy, sunny days, years before even the threat of war, the Coniston Tigers were by no means the only local climbers regularly disporting themselves on Dow Crag although, quietly to ourselves, we regarded the cliff as "our" crag. Strangers were not exactly viewed with suspicion, but we did want to know who they were. On the other hand, we knew the lads from Kendal, Penrith, Keswick and other local areas for we were always bumping into them on Dow, as well as on Gimmer and the Wasdale crags. Now and then, there might have been a bit of healthy, local rivalry between us, but we all became close friends – friendships that have lasted long lifetimes in some cases.

The Kendal crowd were the ones we knew best. We seemed to share Dow Crag with them more often than with the others. They were, among others: Sid Cross, Roy ("Pedlar") Palmer, Tom Philipson, Stan Bewsher and Bud Fallowfield. Some of them were tough rugby players, and all hard men. Sid, with another youngster called Charlie Tatham, had started climbing at 14 with a clothes line borrowed from one of their mothers, and both had been taken to task by senior climbers for their suicidal lack of technique on quite hard routes. He was to become one of the best climbers in the district, as well as a notable mountain rescue leader, later being honoured with the MBE for his long service in this field.

He had been one of my oldest and closest friends, but, sadly, died in April 1998 at the age of 85. The memorial service in Langdale Church, crowded with mountain folk from all over the country, was a very moving occasion. I can't remember doing much climbing with him in the early days, probably his climbing standards were well above mine, but in later years we often pottered around together, chatting about the old days. Like Bud Fallowfield, Sid became a hotelier, and eventually, the popular landlord of the Old Dungeon Ghyll Hotel in Langdale. Through his drive and personality, it came to be regarded as more or less the headquarters of mountaineering in Lakeland. As a leading hotelier and friend of all of us, Sid became our host at the Coniston Tigers' annual dinner when we moved it to his establishment in the post-war years. Indeed, we later made him an honorary Tiger – the only person we ever honoured in this way.

Sid Cross later began a very strong climbing partnership with A.T. (Albert) Hargreaves, the climber I had met, with Billy Clegg, on my first day's climbing with George Basterfield. Between them, Hargreaves and Cross – sometimes accompanied by their wives, put up a number of first ascents in the Lake District, some of them of the greatest severity. A.T. Hargreaves' death in a ski-mountaineering accident in the Austrian Alps after the war was a great blow to climbing in Britain: he had also been prominent in developments on Scottish crags.

I recall an occasion when "A.T." had the bad luck to break a leg while skating on Goats Water, below Dow Crag. The many climbing friends assisting him down the fellside, myself among them, were greatly heartened by the unexpected appearance, on the shoulder of Coniston Old Man, of a horse and cart. This, I seem to remember, had been coaxed up the fellside by one Billy Fury, a fireman in Coniston, and "A.T." was able to continue his journey down the fellside in the cart and, we hoped, in rather more comfort.

"Pedlar" Palmer, one of the tough rugger men, always seemed immensely fit, walking long distances over the fells to get in a climb. He is still around as I write, in his eighties and looking not much different. With the passing of Sid Cross, "Pedlar" is now, I believe, the only surviving member of the old gang of Kendal climbers I remember before the war. Tom Philipson, Stan Bewsher, Ron Berry and Bud Fallowfield have all passed on. Tom, who was very keen on mountain birds, once, just after the war, lowered me over an overhang on Buckbarrow Crag in Longsleddale to a peregrine's nest that he knew contained eggs. Once I was down at the nest, he got me to mark the eggs with indelible dye to foil any poachers who might have been interested.

This excursion on the right-hand side of the crag might have suggested a possible line up the face to us, for some time later, with my old friend Eric Arnison from Penrith, the three of us put up a new route on the steep slabs and called it Sadgill Wall. None of us, at first, could get up the first pitch, a steep corner, in our nailed boots. As I was the only one with a pair of rubbers in my rucksack, I was pushed into the lead. After a struggle I managed to get up the awkward pitch in rubbers and continued in the lead up the climb, the others skilfully completing the ascent in their nails. We thought it quite a good route, especially the airy exposure of the upper part of the climb. Modern climbers have told me it is, nowadays, considered the best route on the face.

The Penrith contingent in the old days was also a group of hard men and I remember especially, Eric Arnison, Ron Fidler and Tom Savage. Eric, my second on the Buckbarrow climb, was a staunch companion for half a century until his death at 90, a few years ago. He was an active member of the Alpine Club, the oldest man to have climbed Mount Kenya, and, at an age when most climbers had long since hung up their boots, had gone exploring in the unfrequented mountains of Ethiopia. He and I had scores of adventures together on the crags, on skis or just general gallivanting. I still miss his merry, generous company and must return to him in greater detail later.

Among the Keswick climbers were Stanley Watson who became one of the first climbing guides in the Lake District; Dunbar Usher, tragically killed on the crags when still a young man; "Bonk" Holmes and Charlie Cowen, to name just a handful. I would sometimes bump into Stanley Watson in Keswick, alone at his table in Storm's Cafe, having his quiet cup of coffee. Stanley, a fine climber who later had a guest house in Borrowdale, was essentially a quiet man who kept himself to himself – the very last person, you would have thought, to achieve a sort of notoriety, as he did, by doing climbs blindfolded. J.E.B. Wright, another early guide, also made the headlines by doing climbs in "record" time. It must have been good for business.

Many other climbers from around the Lakes were often on Dow and other crags, and local climbers remembered from pre-war days included Charlie Wilson, "Chuck" Hudson, Gilpin Ward and Geoff Barker and several from the universities at vacation time. I especially remember Maurice Linnell, a splendid climber who was involved in some of the first new climbs on Scafell's East Buttress. Linnell, who came from Kendal, was tall and slim and seemed to glide up the screes to the crag much more smoothly than anybody else. He was equally neat on the rock. Strangely, he had been involved in one of the earliest climbs on Buckbarrow Crag, very close to our Sadgill Wall. This climb was done in 1926, twenty-three years before our route, when Linnell must have been just a schoolboy. His early death on Ben Nevis before the war, when doing a winter climb with the great Colin Kirkus, shook the climbing world.

Of course, quite famous climbers, sometimes of a bygone age, could occasionally be seen on Dow Crag. One day Geoffrey Winthrop Young, the distinguished alpinist and poet, who had lost a leg in the First World War, put in an appearance. He had had himself fitted with an extraordinary metal attachment on the end of his "peg" leg which enabled him, no doubt with extreme discomfort and difficulty, to get up to the crag, and he then announced he wanted to do a climb. I watched him do it, but I can't now remember which climb, although I think it was on D Buttress. Perhaps it was either Raven Route or Hawk Route for I seem to recall a steepish wall. George Bower, one of the best Lake District climbers at that time, led the route and there was a third man who helped Winthrop Young get the contraption on to the holds. "G.W.Y." seemed to manage all right, but, then, he'd been coping with rock-climbs in the Alps. He was a very brave and determined man, and a wonderful mountain poet.

Many years later, just after the first ascent of Everest in 1953, I had the pleasure of meeting Winthrop Young at the Outward Bound mountain school in Eskdale, together with Sir Edmund Hillary, the hero of the hour. After his death, I came to know his widow, Eleanor, quite well. She was the daughter of W.C. Slingsby, the famous pioneer of Norwegian mountaineering and, incidentally, Solly's second on the first ascent of Eagle's Nest Direct on the Napes way back in 1892. We would chat at Fell and Rock dinners – she, too, had been a pioneer climber – and her memories went back a very long time. Sometimes, too, she would write to me, in a spidery hand, about the old days, and I remember she kindly gave me permission to use one of her late husband's wonderfully-evocative poems in an early book of mine.

Years earlier than my meeting with Winthrop Young at the Eskdale Outward Bound school, Eric Shipton, an earlier Everest pioneer than Hillary, had been the warden at this school. One day, I went for a walk in the valley with this great mountaineer and, nowadays, legendary figure. Unfortunately, I recall only an off-the-cuff observation he made about Alpine climbing. I was planning a first visit to the Alps at the time and seeking some information about routes. He confided to me, almost dismissively, "It's only walking, snow walking; nothing to it." But I found it rather more difficult than that when I first climbed abroad.

Quite early in our Coniston Tigers days we decided we ought to have a president. Tommy Tyson was the obvious man for the job so he was elected by acclamation, but he must have insisted he would only do the job for a year or two, for we later had a succession of presidents. So far as I can remember the president had only one duty: to invite a guest to our annual dinner and, presumably, to pay for him. After more than sixty years I can't be sure where we had this first annual dinner: it might have been in the Crown Hotel at Coniston or even the Ship Inn. However, I can remember that Tommy's guest was George Wood-Johnson, who had been a member of early expeditions to Kangchenjunga and Everest. Wood-Johnson was a well-known Lake District climber who had gone out to Darjeeling to learn tea planting, study the language and prepare himself for a possible future Everest expedition. He was later working in West Cumberland where Tommy had got to know him. The dinner, of course, proved a great success, with Wood-Johnson regaling us eager youngsters with his tales of Himalayan climbing and other adventures.

Some later dinners must have taken place in the Crown Hotel for I remember Dunbar Usher, the Keswick climber who was later killed in a fall near Scafell, showing us how to mull beer on a shovel held over the drawing room fire there. Dunbar might have been the guest that year of Jack Diamond. But the principal venue for the Tigers' annual dinner soon became the Blacksmith's Arms at Broughton Mills, for by that time we all had some form of transport. The dinner was never a particularly grand affair – not, at any rate, in those early days – for the Blacksmith's Arms didn't run to bone-china dinner services and silver cutlery. We ate on the huge apple-wood dining table, built from one piece of wood, which was still there when I last called, and will always be there, for they'll never be able to get it out of the door. And they brought on the meal in the child's tin bath in which it had been cooked, and placed it ceremoniously on the table. It was usually steak and kidney pie, with a lovely, brown crust, and we just divided it up into ten or twelve portions – whatever the number – and consumed it with relish. Really splendid food for healthy young appetites.

We went to the Blacksmith's several times and I recall the food, the surroundings, the blazing log fires, the always-exciting smell of woodsmoke, the company and the talk with a feeling of sadness that those happy, carefree days can never come again. Whether the annual dinners were held during the war years I can't say, but after the war our dining headquarters became the Old Dungeon Ghyll Hotel in Langdale, with Sid Cross and his wife, Jammy, serving us, with perhaps a little more elegance, equally succulent food.

Most, if not all, of the original members, became president in turn. When I was elevated my guest was, of course, George Basterfield, but we did not have the dinner at the Blacksmith's Arms as it was before we started going there. It might have been at the Crown or even at Mrs Seamany's guest house, which used to be on the corner in Coniston, facing the Black Bull. George sang for his dinner all right that night, going through most of his hilarious dialect stories, including "The Ghost Hare" and "The Girt Lang Thin Gun", and also related, with gusto, some of his climbing memories. It was a grand evening with the lads, but then, they all were.

The farmers at Coniston Old Hall, near the hut, were the Inmans and they provided us with our milk, and perhaps even our water, for I don't remember any tap. Perhaps there was one outside, in the farmyard. The two young sons of the farmer were a little younger than us and were named Barker and Dawson, but we, with excruciating schoolboy humour, always knew them as Barker and Dobson. We never went into the village, never went round the pubs, and the only thing I remember doing outside the hut, apart from our dips in the lake, was, of all things, playing golf. Why we were wasting our time in this way I can't imagine, but one of us must have got hold of a couple of clubs and a golf ball or two and we banged them around the field just outside the hut. We didn't bother with holes but just stuck sticks in the ground that you had to hit with your shot. I don't think any of us were much good.

Up on the crag climbers even younger than us, schoolboys really, occasionally put in an appearance, and I remember two in particular – Stephen George and Bob Newton. Both came from Barrow and I knew Stephen's family, especially his father and his sister Isabel, quite well. Mr George senior had been the art master at the Barrow College of Art that I had attended, and Isabel and I had both been in his "life" class, occasionally drawing or painting from the nude, although the usually elderly models were not particularly enticing. Both Stephen and Isabel began to climb and Stephen, in particular, soon reached a very high standard, although sometimes he was, perhaps, a little over-ambitious. Earlier, when climbing with my brother Leslie, he had had a fall in Easter Gully on Dow Crag that could have been serious, had it not been for Les's stout work with the rope. Incidentally, he had done a very early lead of our Tiger Traverse.

One day Stephen and Bob, by now skilled and determined climbers, decided to attempt Eliminate B, the very severe route embracing the redoubtable pitches of Giant Grim and Central Wall. They were leading through, had inched their way up Giant Grim and were starting to tackle the very delicate crossing of Central Wall, high above the depths of Central Chimney. This is one of the most serious pitches on Dow Crag. Stephen was tied on to the detached pinnacle at the left-hand side of the Wall and Bob was coping with the first couple of moves across the vertical face when, without warning, he slipped on the tiny holds. Instinctively, since Newton was only perhaps a yard away, Stephen reached forward to try to grab him, but failed to do so, and, with the tension on the rope momentarily released, the leader plunged down the almost vertical Chimney.

Some of us, all Tigers, were climbing on C Buttress (on Southern Slabs or Lazarus or both), keeping roughly level with the two as they progressed up their climb so that we could closely observe their movements. We had not yet climbed Eliminate B but hoped to do so after George and Newton had shown the way, perhaps the next weekend. Whether we saw the actual fall or heard a shout I can't remember, but we immediately abandoned our climbs and hurried to see what we could do. Two or three – including George Anderson and Jack Atkinson – traversed into the foot of Central Chimney while I went up to the pinnacle at the side of Central Wall to see if Stephen George needed any help. He had badly burned his hand in trying to hold the hurtling rope and was, understandably, in a state of shock, trembling all over. Together we came down the crag by an easy route to the foot of Central Chimney, not knowing what we would find.

But, mercifully and unbelievably, Newton seemed all right. Remarkably, he had landed upside down, on what was probably the only patch of grass on the climb, the rope tightening at the very moment of his arrival. He must have fallen nearly a hundred feet. When we reached him he was displaying to the others what seemed to be his only injury: a neat hole in one of his knees. This was bound up, although there was not much, if any, blood and then he hobbled away. I don't remember him complaining. What I can clearly recall is that he made us all promise that we would never, under any circumstances, tell his mother about the accident. Then he and Stephen walked down the fellside to Torver or Coniston and rode home to Barrow on their bikes.

Writing of this fall on Eliminate B reminds me that my father, James Arthur Griffin, once had the courage to attempt this route when he was probably more than fifty years of age, and with comparatively little climbing experience. When I had started climbing in the late 1920s my parents had both been very worried about my safety in this, at that time, little-known sport, and my father, in particular, wanted to know what it was all about. So one day he told me he wanted me to take him climbing so that he could see for himself. We went to Dow Crag, of course, and I took him up some of the easier routes. He managed all right but, being strong in the arms (he had studied physical culture as a young man), he was inclined to rely too much on his strength and, to some extent, neglect his footwork. Eventually, he was able to cope with some of the severes, although he did no leading, and he also became interested in snow climbing in winter, becoming something of an all-round mountaineer. He was certainly fond of the Lake District hills, joined the Fell and Rock and became a reasonably competent climber, but he had started too late in life to achieve the higher grades.

How he came to get himself involved with a climb like Eliminate B I can't recall, except that I had nothing to do with it. Whether he had asked Jim Porter to take him up it, or Jim Porter had invited him to accompany him I can't say, but one day when I wasn't around they set off up the climb together. And Dad must have done most of the climb, as far as Central Wall, for that was where he was forced to abandon it. Jim told me afterwards that Dad, or Pop as we called him in those days, tried many times but just couldn't make those few, delicate steps across the wall. It was, I thought, a very gallant attempt by a man of his age, but perhaps, under all the circumstances, not a very prudent one. I bet he enjoyed himself despite being a little frightened.

It was about this time that as I was leaving the crag one day, walking down the screes on my own to the Cave, I noticed three climbers having some difficulty on Murray's Route, the splendid severe climb on B Buttress. They were climbing in nailed boots but it had started to rain, the rocks were slippery, and they couldn't work out how to manage either the delicate slab on the first pitch or the awkward corner that follows it. I agreed to help and went up, with stockings over my rubbers because of the wet rocks. With some difficulty, because of the lack of room for manoeuvre, I managed to get past them and into the lead. The four of us then continued up the climb to the top and, as the rain got worse and we gradually became more and more soaked, I expressed myself rather forcibly at times, urging the others not to waste time and becoming more and more impatient. I might even have sworn at them more than once.

However, the three of them seemed to be particularly patient and long-suffering men, and on our walk down to Coniston together I discovered the reason why. They were all parsons! About thirty years after this incident I happened to refer to it in one of my early books, writing of how ashamed I was to have used such bad language in the company of three men of the cloth. "Perhaps they are all bishops by now," I added. Then about ten years ago I wrote about Dow Crag in my Lake District "Country Diary" in *The Guardian*, and an elderly clergyman living in Sheffield, reading the piece in the paper, thought my name seemed familiar to him. He turned up one of the books of mine he happened to possess and read, for the first time, the story of the three clergymen and their adventure on the crag more than fifty years earlier. He had been one of the three clergymen!

This was the start of my friendship with the Revd Dr John McLachlan, a retired distinguished leader of the Unitarian Church, an old climber, in many parts of the world, and still, in a modest way, quite active. After all those years he had remembered my name and that I came from Barrow, realised we had been together in the little adventure, and wrote to me, telling me the names of his companions. I realised I had met one of them, the Revd Priestley Phillips, a former well-known climber, many years before in North Wales. The third, he told me, had been the Revd Arthur Chisman, a Congregationalist parson "and a fine gritstone climber". All three had been members of the Rucksack Club. John explained that because of the nature of their ministries none of them had been able to become a bishop!

John McLachlan and I have kept in touch since then, and on two or three occasions when he has been holidaymaking in the Lake District area he has looked me up for a chat. A few years ago he gave me a copy of his most interesting autobiography, *The Wine of Life*, a wonderful testament to an active career, both at home and abroad, working for the good of the people, and encouraging friendship, "the wine of life". He has also presented me with a copy of a second rewarding book of his: *The Wilderness Experience*. One of the many, many good men, in different ways, that I have been fortunate enough to meet through climbing.

Most of my climbing, especially in the early years, was done as leader. It seemed much more interesting and rewarding to lead rather than to follow, although, in later years, with experienced companions of roughly the same ability, we usually led through, that is, leading alternate pitches. This was a much quicker and neater arrangement since it avoided changing belays. Sometimes when I was leading I got myself into trouble, either through being scared or by making such a mess of things that I just couldn't get up.

With the Tigers most of my climbing was with Jack Diamond, Dave Birch or my brother Leslie. One day Dave and I were on Great Gable, climbing on the Napes Ridges. By that time I had done nearly all the climbs on the Napes, but for some reason had never done Abbey Buttress. Nor had Dave. So we went along to the foot of the climb and set off up the steep, pleasant slabs with me leading. It seemed an excellent route, with smaller holds and more exposure than its modest grading of "very difficult" might have implied, and we had almost completed the climb when I found myself on a narrow ledge with an overhang above me. There seemed as if there might be a hold just below the overhang, but I couldn't quite reach it, and I felt that if I lunged up to grasp the hold, and it wasn't there, I would overbalance on the narrow ledge.

So there I stuck for what seemed like hours but might have been as long as twenty or thirty minutes. Every minute or two I would shuffle about on the ledge, reach up to the possible hold, fail to reach it, and settle down on the ledge again. I must have tried a score of times, adopting slightly different tactics each time, but I just couldn't make it. The ledge was very narrow and restricting to the toes and it looked a long way down the steep wall, with perhaps fifty feet of rope strung out beneath me. And, of course, no runners in those days.

Dave was, of course, the perfect second. Quietly, he told me to take my time. There was no hurry; I would get up all right. But I was stuck and feeling more lonely every minute, the drop seemed to be steepening below me, and the narrow ledge getting narrower all the time. Then, suddenly, a voice from the screes far below us, "Are you all right? Would you like a rope?" Of course, with my courage ebbing by the second, I replied, "Yes, please." In a remarkably short time there was a noise above the overhang and a loop on the end of a rope came snaking down to me. Somehow I managed, while balanced on the ledge, to slip myself into the loop and then, reaching up, to find the hold and step up easily to the top. There had really been no difficulty whatever, except in my imagination. I felt an awful fraud. Fancy, having to be rescued from a v. diff! I would never live it down.

My rescuer was C.J. Astley Cooper, of whom I had known by reputation for some time, but had never met. He had been involved in several important first ascents on Great Gable, Scafell and elsewhere and had just returned, brown as an Indian, from a climbing holiday in Skye with the Wood-Johnson brothers. I was very fortunate he had spotted me. If he hadn't, and I don't recall seeing any other climbers about, I suppose I might have eventually found the courage to reach up for the hold, and risk the consequences – and everything would have been all right.

Several years later I was similarly stuck while leading a climb, but this time it was not quite so shameful for the route was Eliminate C, the splendid very severe on Dow Crag. Neither my second nor I had climbed the route before but we were managing very well until I was nearing the top of the first pitch above Intermediate Gully. There were only three or four feet to go, up a

Great Gable

steep corner, but I just couldn't work it out. My second read out the description from Bower's guide, which said that the corner had to be climbed direct, with the right leg remaining "in the gully". But what did this mean? I made repeated attempts to climb the corner, spending probably the best part of half an hour on the problem, but without success, and we were wondering what on earth we were going to do.

Then, much the same as on Abbey Buttress years earlier, we were hailed by another climber, this time on D Buttress, who told me exactly what to do. I had to make a couple of moves to the right and then go straight up. Stupidly, I had been trying the corner from the wrong place. As soon as I had made the move to the right the pitch proved quite straightforward and we continued on to the end of the climb, with its splendid, airy finish, well pleased with another v. s. in the bag. But I was ashamed I had made such a mess of the finish of the first pitch. This time not so much because of lack of moral fibre, but because of a shortage of common sense. Or my stupidity!

One year, in the early 1930s, my brother Leslie decided to walk to Scotland from Barrow-in-Furness with two or three friends. They had an old tent or tents and a few bits and pieces, and Les, no doubt remembering our walk to Wasdale some years earlier, looked forward to a carefree holiday. I had left home and was working in Preston at the time so knew nothing of their plans, but from what I gathered later, there were no plans at all. They had no transport, but they had a map or two. There was not nearly so much traffic on the roads as there is today, so they just started walking.

I never found out very much about their adventure, but although they might have got a lift here and there, they did an awful lot of walking. They crossed the Border, went through the Scottish Lowlands and eventually found their way to Glen Croe in Argyll, somewhere near the "Rest and Be Thankful" pass. Then they walked home again. They were away for two or three weeks, and heaven knows what they got up to. Eventually, they got back to the Lake District and Leslie arranged to meet our father, Pop, on top of Styhead for a trip up Scafell Pike. Mother and Dad were on holiday at a farm in Eskdale at the time, and it must have been thought that this would make a fine finish to the adventure; father and son coming down together to Eskdale from the roof of England. But it didn't turn out quite as they had hoped.

They met on Styhead all right, went up Scafell Pike and were coming down from Mickledore by way of either Rake's Progress or another path below Scafell Crag, when a loose foothold gave way and Les slipped off the track, plunging down over rocks on to the screes. How far he fell I don't know, but he was, obviously, pretty badly injured and probably unconscious for a time. Dad had never been on Scafell or Scafell Pike before, had never been to Wasdale Head, and there was nobody about, but he knew he had to get some help. He made Les as comfortable as possible with all their spare clothing and set off down the rough fellside, as fast as he could go, for the valley. Down he went, underneath crags he had never seen before, into Hollow Stones, down the long length of Brown Tongue, across Lingmell Beck to Wasdale Head, and into the porch of the hotel, where he told his story. His son had had a bad fall on Scafell. Could they help?

This was years before the introduction of mountain rescue teams but very quickly local farmers and climbers who were staying in the hotel were collected and they set off, with a stretcher and other necessities, for Scafell. Dad, unused to mountain walking, and after a hard day and a lot of stress, went with them to show them where he had left his son on the fellside.

I don't know how long the rescue took or if they had to come down in the dark, but I learned that Leslie was eventually stitched up as he lay on the floor of the entrance hall of the hotel, among all the boots and ice axes. He had rather nasty head wounds, among other injuries. He was treated by a Dr Abraham, a relative of the Abraham brothers of Keswick, perhaps a nephew, who, I believe, had a practice in Cockermouth at that time. Whether the doctor had been staying in the hotel, or whether he had been summoned to deal with the casualty I can't say. When Les had been stitched up and judged fit to travel, he and Dad were very kindly taken by car all the long way round the coast to the Eskdale farmhouse where Mother had been anxiously awaiting their arrival for many hours. Dad and Les were always very grateful indeed for all that had been done for them and were afterwards a little embarrassed that they had not been able to make a more tangible expression of gratitude to everybody concerned, although Dad made an effort to do something through the hotel. Nowadays, a donation to the appropriate mountain rescue team can ease this sort of worry. Leslie eventually made a full recovery, but Dad remembered his first visit to Scafell and Wasdale Head with a mixture of feelings, until his passing in his eightieth year.

Round about this time the Coniston Tigers began a series of annual visits to Scotland, the trips usually taking place at Easter. Clearly, judging by the photographs, they went for the snow and they always seemed to have a good time – often, it looks from the snaps, in blizzards or wild conditions. In the Lake District we had always enjoyed the winters, walking the snow-bound fells or climbing the gullies. We all had our own ice axes, mostly ex-army issue from the First World War, but it was to be many years later before we acquired our first crampons. In those early days modern ice climbing – front-pointing, using two short axes – had not been invented. We cut steps the old-fashioned way and felt secure enough in our nailed boots. In this way we tackled gullies on Dow Crag, Helvellyn and other places, once or twice getting on to Great End, but we could hardly have been described as technical winter climbers in the modern sense. Even so, we managed to get up some of the easier buttress climbs on Dow in winter conditions and I can remember desperate struggles on Woodhouse's when it was plastered in snow.

Tommy Tyson must have been the originator of the Scottish trips. For years he'd been going to Scotland to fish and, now and again, do a bit of shooting, and he knew several of the mountain areas. I believe he also had relatives or friends north of the Border. Regrettably, I never took part in any of the Tigers' Scottish expeditions. I was then working on an evening newspaper in Lancashire and couldn't get away so easily, but very soon I was having my own Scottish adventures which have continued throughout my life. Perhaps, more of this later. But the photographs of these early Scottish trips by the Tigers at least give some idea of the conditions they enjoyed. The earliest dated photograph, entitled simply 'Scotland 1933', shows Tommy Tyson, George Anderson, Jim Porter and Archie Stammers, our occasional London visitor, standing in the snow on what seems to be a summit.

At first I had some difficulty in working out where the photograph might have been taken. All are wearing nailed boots but Jim and Archie are roped together with a hemp rope, tied in a bowline around their waists. The summit looks something like Cairngorm but why are two of them roped together on top of an ordinary snow plod? Jim Porter, thankfully still around and in his late eighties in 1997, was able to help, for he clearly remembered that day, sixty-four years earlier. The photograph, he said, had been taken on a shoulder of Ben Nevis, he couldn't be more specific, and Archie, lacking winter experience, had had difficulty with a steep snow slope. Tommy complained he was wasting time so Archie was put on a rope, with Jim leading, and eventually they made it to the shoulder. Whether or not they went on to the top of the Ben that day Jim couldn't remember.

In the photograph Tommy, without a hat, is smoking his pipe, wearing what looks like a motoring jacket, and looking annoyed. The others are wearing balaclavas, George is in a sweater, and Jim and Archie in ordinary old tweed jackets. The ice axes are very long. Two of them are wearing scarves round their necks, and none have gaiters – just a second pair of socks. George is holding what looks like a drink in his hand, Jim (always correctly dressed) has a handkerchief in his jacket pocket and Archie has something on a cord from his lapel that could be a whistle or a watch.

Other photographs, taken at Easter 1935, show Tommy, George, Jim, and, this time, also Jack Diamond and Jack Atkinson, sitting by the roadside in the Sma' Glen on their way to the snows, and the same group, with their axes, on what looks like a snowbound summit. The next group of photographs, taken at Easter 1936, are all of Tommy, George, Jack Atkinson, Archie Stammers and, this time, Len Brown, in a very snow-bound Cairngorms. They are pictured in the Larig Ghru, by the Pools of Dee and, lower down, scrambling about on rock slabs. The weather looks pretty rough in the snow, with swirling mists and poor visibility, but they have ice axes and ropes and seem prepared for anything. On top of their old tweed jackets and knee breeches they are all wearing what look like old raincoats and George and Tommy have peaked motor-cycle helmets or Norwegian ski-caps on their heads. The others have balaclavas, pulled right down. I wish I knew more about these adventures in the Scottish snows more than sixty years ago.

But, by this time I had begun my own exploration of the Highlands and its mountains with a fortnight's visit to the Misty Isle of Skye – a place I had been longing to visit since my very first rock-climbs. I had heard that gabbro, the rock on Skye, was the best climbing rock in the world, and that the mountains there were rock mountains and quite different from any other British hills.

Tourism Gimmicks

Much-publicised demands for aerial cable cars strung across Windermere, observation towers with slowly revolving restaurants, "skydomes" – whatever they are – with shops and discotheques, and Florida-type marinas, all in the heart of the Lake District, are so outrageous and impossible that we can afford to ignore and forget them. Quite obviously, none of the proposals put forward by a Lancashire businessman for cashing in on "the pot of tourist gold" that we are told is waiting to be picked up would ever get off the ground. Any serious development applications – as distinct from propaganda – would lead to a national outcry. But this latest brouhaha does serve to show the ignorance of some people who do not seem to realise the difference between the Lake District national park and a seaside resort. They do not understand that while crowds, facilities and entertainments are the lifeblood of the average resort, these would ruin an area of unspoiled natural beauty and its opportunities for peace and quietude. To try to turn the Lake District into a different sort of place, just because it has become more accessible, would be criminal folly, and the area should not be ashamed of the charge that it is not "moving with the times", but should be heartily proud of its stance. The primary aims of the national park are the protection of unspoiled natural scenery and the encouragement of open-air recreation, with priority given to the first objective. They are certainly not to turn a sanctuary into an amusement park, get as many people inside it as possible and make the maximum amount of money out of them. Far too many people want to exploit the Lake District for their own ends and their efforts must be closely watched and nipped in the bud. The future of this area of unsurpassed beauty depends on the constant vigilance of us all.

April 1974

Chapter Seven

Over the Sea to Skye

This was going to be the most exciting holiday I had ever had, perhaps even more exciting than that first trip to Wasdale Head several years earlier. At last, for I had been dreaming of it for years, I was going to travel "over the sea to Skye" and climb some of the rock mountains, ridges and crags I had been reading about since my school days. And this would be something different, for the mountains on Skye, so I had read, were not like the Lakeland fells, but were rock all the way up. It was not my first visit to Scotland – I had been to Edinburgh in a school party – but this was to be the first time I had seen the Highlands. I didn't know then that eventually Scotland would be a country I would come to know, geographically at least, far better than England, the land of my birth.

Almost every detail of that first journey to Skye and our adventures on the island, more than sixty years ago, come back to me clearly as I write. It was the sunny June of 1935 and my companion was Mollie, the lovely, cheerful girl who, two years later, became my wife. We travelled together in the little, open Morris Minor I had bought some time earlier for £42, and apart from springing a leak somewhere between Broadford and Sligachan, that I mended with electrician's tape, it gave us no trouble in a thousand miles of motoring.

We crossed the Clyde by the old Erskine Ferry for this was more than thirty years before the bridge was built. In many later visits to Skye or the Highlands we always used to leave home in Kendal in the early morning hours to catch the first ferry at 8am but it was rather later in the morning when we crossed this first time. I can clearly remember the sunlit drive along the side of Loch Lomond, the shapes of the Crianlarich hills, the excitement of Glencoe, a glimpse of red deer from the old road to Glen Shiel, the Five Sisters of Kintail and lovely Loch Duich. And then, at last, our first sight of the Cuillin hills from the narrow, winding road to the Kyle of Lochalsh.

Especially thrilling was the drive through Glencoe – not only for the rocky heights and exciting crags on either side, but also for the road itself that had just been built. For miles it ran across the Black Mount and steeply down the glen, black, smooth and almost shiny tarmac. There were no other cars about, we saw hardly any traffic on the whole journey, and the temptation to see how fast the car could go was irresistible. I pressed my foot hard down on the accelerator and the little car bounced merrily along through the scenery. It was the first time I had ever driven at 60 miles an hour!

Much of the old Road to the Isles has now disappeared, replaced by fast, modern highways or drowned by hydro-electric schemes, and some of the old magic of the journey has, sadly, gone. Most of the roads – especially beyond Fort William, which was little more than a street with a few shops on either side – were narrow, winding and rough. Indeed, the way through the Glen Garry woods, along the loch shore to Tomdoun, and over the hill to Glen Loyne and, eventually, Glen Cluanie, was just a skimpy cart track, with little passing places scratched out of the heather, along which, over tree roots, we bumped and swerved. But it was all an absolute delight. We didn't mind the bumpy roads for this was the Road to the Isles.

I remember buying a new pipe for a shilling in a little store at Shiel Bridge, and taking a photograph of Mollie standing beside an old thatched bothy that disappeared sixty years ago. And, in a lonely part of Glen Shiel, in a tiny croft that was pulled down, or fell down soon afterwards – for we could never find it again – we had a meal of baps and bannocks with an elderly crofter and his wife. A distant relative in Preston, on hearing we were going to Skye, had given us their address and asked us to call on them. The old couple, who had little English and spoke Gaelic to each other, could not have been kinder if we had been their children.

There seemed to be only two rooms in the little croft, one of them the bedroom. Within a few minutes they had piled the table with food, including delicious oatcakes and a huge earthenware pot of tea. Then they quietly retired to their own room, leaving us alone. When we had finished, we knocked on their door and they came out, but they refused to take anything for their hospitality. It was the first time we had come into contact with the real highlanders of the northern glens, people we found to be always quiet and gentle of speech, kindly and considerate. But, over the years, I have met many more of their kind: real gentlefolk, proud and dignified and completely untainted by the march of so-called "civilisation".

The ferries – Ballachulish, Dornie and Kyle of Lochalsh – were primitive and adventurous. You drove on to all of them along two planks thrown roughly against the side of the craft. They were all very rickety and it needed a little driving skill to get your wheels exactly on to the planks when the boat was pitching up and down in rough seas. This was many long years (about sixty years in the case of Kyle of Lochalsh) before bridges replaced the ferries. I remember having to make quite an effort, this first time at Dornie ferry, to avoid driving straight down the hill into the boat or into the water. In those days the road took what is now known as the "scenic" route, high above the loch, and the descent to the ferry was not only steep, but also liberally surfaced with rough gravel. I came down the hill at a fair speed, saw the ferry below me, braked hard, and found myself skidding, helplessly, straight down to the edge of the water, just pulling up in time.

The ferry across the Kyle was just as rough and ready as the others in those days, and I remember that on this first visit they charged us six shillings to transport the car and ourselves across, which we thought highly extortionate. But once across the narrow stretch of water, with the gulls swooping and squawking overhead and the smell of the tangle in our nostrils, we felt we were in a new country. As, indeed, we were, for here was a Gaelic-speaking island. We saw for ourselves the rough roads creeping round a sharply indented coastline, a few, scattered, peat-burning crofts, the smoothly rounded Red Hills that guard the sanctuary in the foreground, and, behind, in the south-west corner, the most dramatic mountains in Britain, the Black Cuillin.

There were no bed and breakfast signs on Skye in the 1930s and some of the cottages or crofts were still the ancient "black houses", poor, blackened, grimy places with smoke coming out of roofs covered in thatch or roughly-dug turf. An old woman was scratching the ground outside one of these blackened cottages, little more than a hut, but when we asked her whether we were on the right road for Glen Brittle she didn't understand what we were saying. The roads round the island were unsurfaced and full of potholes, necessitating very slow progress. However, these were almost racetracks compared with the bumpy crawl over the hillside from Carbost and down to Glen Brittle, with two wheels in a rut in the track and the other two bouncing up and down, in the heather. And the main approach road to the Cuillin hills, round the coast, was not only unpleasantly rough but also incredibly circuitous, necessitating drives of ten miles or so round each of the sea lochs that seemed to bite deeply into the island every time you turned a corner. In other words, to go a mile or two towards a sighted objective you had to drive a dozen, or so it seemed.

At first we were a little disappointed with the rounded, heather-covered Red Hills, apparently devoid of crags, but somewhere near the Sligachan Inn, we had our first sight of Sgurr nan Gillean and the northern end of the Cuillin ridge and knew we had come to the right place. Probing the sky, only a mile or two away, was a jagged array of spires and pinnacles quite unlike our familiar Lakeland hills and looking different even from the big mountains we had glimpsed around Ben Nevis and Glencoe. These were, easily, the most dramatic mountains we had ever seen. And then, a little later, we topped the last rise of the rough track from Carbost to begin the bumpy descent to Glen Brittle and, all at once, saw the long line of the ridge from Bruach na Frithe to Sgurr Dearg and beyond. There they were, the mountains of my dreams, lighted by the setting sun, with blue-shadowed corries and foaming burns leaping down the rocky hillsides. These were the mountains we had come so far to see and we were well satisfied. And later that night, after supper, we stepped outside Glenbrittle Lodge, where we were staying, to sniff the air. In the darkness, with the ridge showing black against a purple sky, we sensed a stillness and peace as the hills went to sleep that I have rarely experienced since.

Glen Brittle had not been "developed" in those days. There was no youth hostel, climbing hut or camp site; just the end of the road with the Lodge, the post office and, just above the beach, Mary Campbell's, a simple croft, where all the great men who had "discovered" the mountains of Skye only two generations earlier had stayed. Indeed, it was less than forty years before my first visit when the last of Britain's unclimbed mountains, reputedly Sgurr Coire an Lochain, a modest peak near the main ridge, had first been ascended. We stayed with the MacRaes at Glenbrittle Lodge, as we did during the next forty years or so. Our later visits were with our children, and we watched a succession of MacRaes running the farm.

The next day, bright and sunny with a fresh breeze coming off the bay, we went up Sgurr Dearg, the rocky peak due east of the Lodge that overlooks the southern end of the glen. From the summit we looked out to the Outer Hebrides, the nearer islands of Rhum and Canna, the tremendous cliffs of Sgurr Alasdair, highest of all the Cuillin peaks, and its satellites, across the great gulf of Coire Lagan, and half the mountains of northern Scotland. We had never seen such a dramatic mountain scene before. This was the first time we had scrambled on mountains that were rock nearly all the way up. It seemed to add a new dimension to mountain walking - using your hands most of the time. On this first visit we didn't climb the Inaccessible Pinnacle, the vertical blade of rock that is the true summit of the mountain, the Munro. Mollie had done very little climbing at that time and I hadn't taken the rope that day. But in many later visits to Skye I came to know the Inaccessible very well, making several ascents of the different routes. So Sgurr Dearg can't have been my first Munro in 1935. That was probably Sgurr Alasdair or Bruach na Frithe.

Near the foot of Sgurr Dearg, as we were completing its descent, we met the only person we had seen all day – a man who asked us where we had been. It was only then that I discovered that "Dearg(red)" is pronounced something like "Jerrack". This was my first lesson in the Gaelic but I had many more later from old Mr MacRae at the Lodge. Years afterwards, I used to go into his cottage in the evenings for further lessons and the latest news of the glen. Gaelic is a most difficult language for an Englishman to understand, and after a lifetime I have never achieved more than a few simple words. It is, however, fairly easy to learn how to pronounce the mountain names more or less correctly and this is a useful accomplishment when you are collecting the Munros. There are half a dozen basic rules you can pick up in guidebooks, and you will quickly find that many of the formidable assortment of consonants in Gaelic are just not pronounced. Once you have got the hang of this, and found out how to pronounce the beginnings and endings of words, you can begin to understand, for instance, why "Mhadaidh" is pronounced "Vatee" and "Ghreadaidh", "Greeta".

Our second day on Skye was to be a little more ambitious. We planned to go round the coast by boat to Loch Scavaig, walk along the shore of Loch Coruisk into the heart of the Cuillin, and then climb back over the ridge and down to Glen Brittle. The one-inch map of the Cuillin, the only one we had been able to buy, was very poor more than sixty years ago. It showed so much rock and so many contours that it was almost impossible to pick out the lie of mountains that were obscured, anyway, by their names. About ten years before our visit a map of the Cuillin, at the convenient scale of three inches to the mile, had been specially produced for the Scottish Mountaineering Club, from a photographic triangulation, by Howard Priestman, but I knew nothing about this. Looking now at this map I see it doesn't show any of the passes across the ridge. Nevertheless, it is clear from the contours that the route to the "bealach" or "pass" we had selected would start about one mile after reaching the head of the loch and just before the entry of the fourth main tributary into the main Coruisk burn. If I had had this map I think I could have found the way.

All we had, apart from our virtually useless one-inch map, was a glimpse of a very small and quite crude relief map of the southern Cuillin which we had seen on a wall in the hall at the Lodge. I knew from my reading that there was a pass over the ridge – the Bealach Coire na Banachdich, between Sgurr Dearg and Sgurr na Banachdich. This rough relief map seemed to suggest that the second tributary of the burn that flowed into Loch Coruisk led upwards towards this pass. All we had to do, therefore, I thought naively, would be to follow this stream to its source and then continue in the same direction, and we would find the pass, no matter what the weather. What I had not realised was that scores of streams flow into the Coruisk burn in wet weather and that the relief map was a very rough representation indeed. Furthermore, the Cuillin, in mist, are far trickier mountains than the Lakeland hills and, indeed, perhaps the most formidable in Britain to negotiate under these conditions.

It was drizzling when we set off, with the clouds down to about 1000 feet, a really nasty morning that, nowadays, would keep me firmly indoors. But in the 1930s, fit and young, I didn't think the weather should deter us. After all, I had been climbing for years, knew my way about mountains, and we were only going to cross a mountain ridge by a known pass. Maybe it should be explained that a pass in the Cuillin hills bears little resemblance to a Lakeland pass, at least it didn't sixty-odd years ago. There were only two or three feasible routes across the ridge and none of them was a track as we know the term. The passes are on rock and I don't remember nail scratches on any of them. When I was last over the Banachdich pass some years ago, however, the way was marked, here and there, by an occasional cairn consisting, in the Highland fashion, of just two or three small stones perched on boulders or outcrops. To find these cairns in mist, forty years ago was not always easy, and in the 1930s I don't remember seeing any of them. But all this may well be changed by now with the bridge at Kyle of

Lochalsh, the new roads, the tourist exploitation of Skye, and the hills, no doubt, now being kicked to death by walkers and climbers, as has, so sadly, happened in the Lakeland fells. But in 1935 I knew nothing about Skye "passes", had only been up one mountain on the island, and could not imagine any difficulty.

We walked down to Loch Brittle in the rain and met on the shore, by arrangement, a man in oilskins with a tiny boat fitted with an outboard engine. We were dressed in our old clothes, we had no anoraks or other wet-weather equipment in those days, and were pretty well drenched by the time we had rounded the coast in a very choppy sea and pulled round the headland into the comparative shelter of Loch Scavaig. Here we were deposited on the beach at the foot of great, streaming slabs of rock that reached up, in the mist, towards the unseen summit of Garsbheinn, and left, unceremoniously, to our fate. For years we had been reading of the grandeur of Loch Coruisk, just beyond the sea loch, but there was no beauty in the loch or the corrie that morning. Our view was of wild waves on a half-seen stretch of water, a wet, cloud-filled glen, burns in lively spate everywhere and black screes and crags rearing up into the clouds.

Undeterred, for we were young, healthy and optimistic, we trudged for more than a mile along the shore of the loch, through boulders and across the burns. We then began to look out for the second tributary running into the main feeder for the loch, which I was confident would lead us to the pass over the ridge, nearly 3000 feet above. But it was only after we had passed the head of the loch that we realised that the expedition was not going to be the simple affair I had imagined: instead of three or four burns flowing down the hillside, as shown on the relief map at the Lodge, the whole of the corrie seemed to be alive with the sound of falling waters. There were white torrents racing down through the mist on all sides. Which one of these wild streams in spate was our ladder to the ridge? I got out my Ordnance Survey one-inch map to see if it would help but it was quite useless. We would just have pick out the most likely looking burn and follow it. If it proved to be the wrong one we would have to try the next.

Having made our choice we trudged, hopefully, up the screes towards the grey blanket of mist and I told Mollie, to encourage her, that we'd be on the ridge in an hour or so. But two hours later we were still in the corrie, visibility had been reduced to a yard or two, and we had no idea where we were. After following this first chosen tributary up steep, sliding screes and rock outcrops to a height approaching 2000 feet, we had suddenly and inexplicably come to a tremendous rock crevasse barring our way. In sixty-odd years of mountaineering since this epic I've never encountered a similar rock feature on any hillside in Britain, and I've never been able to identify the place since, largely because I've not often climbed on the Coruisk side of the ridge. But my memory of the crevasse, two or three generations on, is that it was pretty deep, maybe fifty feet or so, with almost-vertical walls, not easily climbable, on each side, and perhaps seven feet wide.

With an adventurous male companion I think we would have risked a jump, or tried to climb down into the crevasse and out again, but Mollie took one look at the place and announced she was going no further – not in that direction, anyway. She was wet through, miserable, and not really very interested in mountain exploration in one of the remoter areas of Scotland. Obviously, she said, we were on the wrong route, and I had to admit it certainly didn't look like a much-traversed pass over the ridge. So down we went, the way we had climbed with so much effort. Back at the foot of the corrie, we re-examined the maze of streaming burns and tried to decide which ones had been formed by the recent rain and, from the remainder, which one might be the key to the pass. Having made our decision, we set off once again, from somewhere near sea level, to try to reach the ridge and make our way down the other side to the comfort of baths, a hot meal, and a cheery fire.

Once again, it was the same steep, slippery trudge through the boulders and scree, the mist and driving rain, and soon we were in thick cloud and unable to see more than a yard or two ahead. We pressed on for an hour or two, beginning to feel a little tired now, and certainly exasperated, seeing no track, cairns or signs of previous passage. And then, all at once, we hit the ridge. I remember how completely unexpected it was – one moment, trudging blindly upwards through the scree, the next, finding ourselves in a narrow gap with a steep drop on either side. It was exactly how imaginative artists might have pictured a wild mountain pass in, say, the Hindu Kush: a rocky gap, perhaps six feet wide or less, almost as narrow as a tightrope, with steep crags soaring up into the mist at either end. We could only see a few feet up the cloud-wreathed crags and a similar distance down the pass on either side, and it seemed a very wild and lonely place indeed. However, we had reached the ridge at last and all that remained to be done was to scramble down the other side into Coire na Banachdich, which should lead us straight to the Lodge.

But it was the wrong pass, and probably not a pass at all. We didn't realise this until much later when we were climbing down near-vertical chimneys in approaching darkness, and had come to the conclusion that even mountain passes in Skye couldn't be like this. We had set off down from the gap in high spirits, hoping to be out of the cloud in an hour or so, but very soon found ourselves on steep, downward-sloping slabs, cleft at intervals by chimneys and gullies. There seemed no way to circumvent the first of the chimneys we encountered so we climbed down it. Or rather, I climbed down it, after lowering my battered but resolute companion on the rope. I'm sure Mollie often wondered during the trying hours we spent together on and around the ridge that day, what on earth she was doing with this madman on this wild, inhospitable terrain in thick mist or near-darkness. She can't really have enjoyed it.

Looking back on the whole sorry escapade, I'm convinced the only sensible thing I did that day was to take a rope. No doubt I'd done so because these were rock mountains and Mollie, although she'd done a bit of scrambling, was not a rock-climber. Indeed, this was the only time in a long mountaineering lifetime that I have ever taken a rope on a mountain walk in summer without rock-climbing in mind. But I don't know what we would have done without it.

In the mist and rain the slabs and chimneys looked quite nasty, and although I had been confident enough of the outcome all day, I was beginning to have some doubts. By now, of course, we had realised we were certainly not on the route we had planned, had really no idea where we were, and it would be dark fairly soon. Speed, it seemed, was essential, for if we could only get below the cloud before nightfall we should be able to make a reasonable guess about our position, and eventually retrieve our lost fortunes. So as soon as Mollie began to make heavy weather of the chimneys, losing valuable time, I kept her on the rope, lowering her as quickly as possible down each of the difficulties and then scrambling down after her. I don't know how many rope lengths we needed – it seemed about twenty but it could have been fewer – but I know that long before we had got down the slabs my arms and shoulders were aching with the strain, and I was feeling very tired. By now it was almost dark, but at least we were on easier ground and had got below the clouds.

The tale of the remainder of that uncomfortable day, during which we broke most of the rules of mountaineering, is soon told. We scrambled, slipped and squelched in the darkness down the hillside, fell into burns, tore our already tattered clothes, grazed hands and knees and, more than once, tripped headlong in the heather. At long last we hit a track that seemed to be going in the right direction. Following this, we eventually reached the road through the glen, which we followed for what seemed like two or three miles to the Lodge. Here, a welcome light in the darkness, Mrs MacRae, a kindly old soul, greeted our extremely late arrival with fervent expressions of relief for she had just been about to alert some sort of rescue team.

In those days this would probably have meant ringing up the police at Portree, many rough miles away, and hoping for the best. Where any rescuers that might have been assembled would have searched with the whole of the Cuillin to go at, I have no idea, for, in line with our long catalogue of mistakes, we had, of course, neglected to give the Lodge details of our intended journey. And, of course, there were no mountain rescue teams in those days. No doubt the boatman, when he had been traced, would have recalled he had last seen us, wet through and miserable, standing on the windswept beach of Loch Scavaig, and they would have had to work it out from there. It would have been a hopeless task.

Exactly where we had crossed the ridge I have never, in many subsequent visits, been able to discover. I think it most likely that we crossed between two of the several peaks of Sgurr a'Mhadaidh and dropped down the crags into Tairneilear and thence into Coire na Creiche. I've not been able to identify our likely route or work out how we reached the ridge from Coire an Uaigneis on the Coruisk side. Many mountaineering lessons I should have learned years earlier were hammered home that day, and I hope I have treated the Cuillin with proper respect since. Certainly, we seemed to have been looked after by some kindly, unseen power.

Having been brought down to earth by this rather shattering experience we spent the remainder of the holiday soberly exploring the island and tackling some of the more accessible peaks. We went up Bruach na Frithe, probably the easiest of the Skye Munros, and Sgurr Alasdair, the highest peak in the Cuillin. Certainly I remember the Alasdair Stone Shoot from this earliest visit, when it was much easier to climb or descend, by a clearly discernible track, than it later became. Indeed, it could be, in those days, a very fast and pleasant scree-run.

In many later visits to Skye, with family or friends, we collected all the peaks and climbed on the principal crags. Two of us, my son Robin and I, traversed the main Cuillin ridge. It was a day in a thousand, perhaps the best mountain day of our lives. Some of these adventures, most of them after the war, I shall describe later.

Skye, and also the Isle of Arran, were to become regular holiday places for our children: Robin, indeed, had his honeymoon on Skye. I have little desire now to go back to the Misty Isle with all its tourist trappings and the new bridge. Instead, I'm content to remember Skye when it was rough but unspoiled, a remote, exciting island where you almost felt you had come to a foreign land.

Looking back to this first visit, I remember that, apart from the man we met on the lower slopes of Sgurr Dearg on our first day on the island, we never saw one other person on the hills during the rest of our visit. There were the people at the farm, the MacRaes, but nobody else. It's not like that today, they tell me. But now I must get back to the Coniston Tigers and try to remember what we were getting up to in the years before the outbreak of the Second World War.

Lovely Buttermere

Not a cloud in the sky, the sunny slopes of Mellbreak perfectly
mirrored, upside down, in the glass-calm surface of Crummock
Water and a few Herdwicks wandering along the unfenced
lake-shore road. This was a recent still morning in lovely
Buttermere, in many respects my favourite Lakeland valley,
where once again we had been staying for a short break. One
day, on our way up Robinson by way of Buttermere Moss, I
recalled a previous, rather more challenging visit more than sixty
years earlier when, from our car on Honister Pass, two of us had
already traversed Fleetwith Pike, Haystacks, High Crag, High
Stile and Red Pike. We had also consumed, in the Fish Hotel,
several pints of foaming beer served, I remember sadly, in those
most suitable and delectable receptacles, now no longer available
– glazed earthenware tankards. As a result of this midday
carousal, our traverse of Robinson, Hindscarth and Dale Head
that immediately followed, was rather trying but quickly forgotten
during the consumption of a vast, mutton pie, covered with a
thick golden crust, in Janey Edmondson's kitchen at Seathwaite.
The mutton, as always, had been slowly cooked all day in her
huge fireplace oven and, as they say, "just fell away". Even now,
I smack my lips in memory. But the other day, we were merely
pottering up Robinson, and on the way enjoying the fantastic
view from the comparatively lowly summit of High Snockrigg
(1725ft). Buttermere and Crummock Water, with the smoke from
the farms and cottages drifting across the meadows, seemed
directly below our boots, and the steep, wooded fells across the
dale, split by the hanging necklace of Sour Milk Gill, looked a
vertical mountain wall. The best views are by no means always
from the highest places. We came down from Robinson to the
pass by the wild ravine of Moss Force and, thence, to Buttermere
by the lovely track above Sale Beck, which if walked in the
opposite direction and down Rigg Beck would have taken us,
easily and delightfully, to Keswick.

March 1998

Chapter Eight

A Terrible Accident

Working in Preston, far from the hills, and, from 1937, on a national newspaper in Manchester, even further away, regular weekend visits to the hut and Dow Crag were not always practicable. As often as possible, however, I drove north to the Lakes to uplift my spirits and persuade myself that, although now marooned in cities, not all was lost. The climbs we did in those pre-war years, the adventures we had, are now all consolidated into a pictured memory of measured progress up steepish rock, mostly in the sunshine, enviable physical fitness and a great deal of youthful high spirits. What wonderful, exciting times we had, leading through, with old friends, on climbs we had come to know so well! Until we had finished off all the routes in George Bower's red-backed guide to Dow Crag, the Langdale crags and, at holiday time, the Wasdale and Buttermere climbs, there seemed no need to seek out first ascents. Just ticking off the lists was enough. Perhaps we lacked ambition, but the pull of the crags and fells was enormous. I clearly remember, at the end of each visit, the sad trot down the fellside, with the evening shadows lengthening across the turf, the sweep of Dow dark against the sunset, and the realisation that all this beauty and adventure must now be set aside for at least a week or two.

The favourite climbs on Dow at that time were repeated most weekends. They were probably Murray's Route, Hopkinson's Crack, Hawk Route with the Direct Finish, Abraham's "B" and Trident. Most of us, certainly myself, preferred balance climbing on slabs to hauling ourselves up gullies and overhangs. Intermediate Gully and other struggles were climbed, of course – probably several times, but these inelegant postures were not really for us. Delicate climbing on walls was more our cup of tea and something like South-West on Pillar Rock our idea of a real climb, when we were on form.

Little pictures of those happy weekends, so long ago, come winging back across the years. For example, how, for years on our way up to the crag, we used to stop at the old gunpowder hut, on the shoulder of the Old Man, just before Goats Water, for a chat and a smoke. I remember on many occasions sitting smoking my pipe on a keg labelled "Gunpowder". We all did it, and nobody thought anything about it. Whether, in fact, the keg contained gunpowder we never knew. Many years later the Barrow Mountaineering Club took over the gunpowder hut as a climbing hut. I recall, too, the number of times when we were caught in heavy rain and took shelter under the arch of Cove Bridge, probably eating soggy sandwiches and arguing about whether we should abandon our climbing plans and just go for a walk over the tops. And there is another memory, this time of youthful vandalism, for which, after sixty years, I may perhaps be forgiven. Some authority had thought fit to erect a prominent white, wooden signpost beside the track leading up to the crag. Whither its arm or arms pointed, I can't remember, perhaps to Walna Scar, but we decided it was completely unnecessary and, indeed, unsightly: a blot on the landscape. So we uprooted it, threw it into a convenient gully and covered it with bracken. It was never re-erected.

I remember we practised bouldering (often in Boulder Valley, beyond Low Water Beck, on the other side of Coniston Old Man) quite seriously and, always, in nailed boots. We reckoned we could practise moves on boulders we wouldn't care to tackle when leading on proper climbs, since we couldn't do ourselves much damage if we came off. Nowadays, with nuts and runners, climbers can do this sort of practice with impunity on the climbs themselves, but we had none of these things. Nevertheless, it was in a fall from one of the steeper routes on the Pudding Stone, the biggest boulder in the valley, that I sustained one of the few climbing injuries that put me out of action for some time.

Nailed-boots practice was, we thought, very important. The exact angle of the boot on the hold had to be maintained when you stepped up; otherwise the boot would slip off. George Basterfield, I remember, also taught me how to practise balance in nails on rock. He would find a steepish rock slab and after his own neat demonstration, get me to come down it, in nails, facing outwards, without using the hands. Then he would have me climbing easy-angled slabs, again, without touching with the hands. I'm sure all these exercises greatly improved my balance until dithering old age set in.

We made a practice in the Tigers of always running, or trotting, down the screes below Dow Crag, and then the last mile or two down to the cars or to Coniston railway station. This trotting down the screes in our nailed boots, leaping across the huge boulders, certainly improved our balance, but the headlong dash down the contours at the end of the day did immeasurable damage to our feet. It certainly did to mine, for surgeons have told me that the troubles I have suffered with my toes and feet for many years were caused by a combination of this practice and the over-tight climbing rubbers and later PAs we used to wear.

Among the very few routes on Dow Crag I never climbed there's only one, Eliminate "A", that I have always regretted missing out. I never had any ambition to tackle Black Wall, believing it to be beyond my capabilities, and, despite several attempts, I could never work out how to lead the wall above the Bandstand on Great Central Route without assistance. Eliminate "A", though, looked a superb route that I might perhaps be able to manage. I had led Eliminate "C", but I kept putting it off and, perhaps lacking a companion, never got round to it. Many years later, Jim Cameron, the Coniston guide whom I had known for years and had climbed with as a friend on several occasions, suggested, knowing my interest, that we should climb it together some time. It was a favourite route of his. We would, of course, climb together as old friends, as we had always done, not as guide and client. But, although we tried on many occasions to fit in a day to do the climb, something always upset the plan, and we never got round to it.

And then Jim died, at a very good age, and, until near the end, remarkably active and fit. He was a kindly and knowledgeable companion in the hills and, in his day, a splendid climber. His enthusiasm, not just for rock-climbing but for hills in general, in all weathers, was always a tonic. His house near Coniston, above Haws Bank and not far from our hut, had originally been known as the Dow Crag Climbers' Hut, a guest house run by two redoubtable ladies, Mrs Bryan and Miss Pirie, both mountaineers and early skiers. Good days on Dow often ended at this welcome meeting place, either for a meal, a drink or just a chat with friends.

One little adventure that happened about this time had nothing to do with the Tigers or, indeed, with climbing. I had driven up from Manchester for a few days in the Lakes, staying with the Edmondsons at Seathwaite in Borrowdale. With me was a Cumbrian, Eldred Reeve, who was the news editor of the national newspaper for which I then worked. The holiday was memorable, as all Seathwaite holidays were, for the delicious Herdwick mutton pie, served with a thick, brown pastry crust, that Janey Edmondson would have been slowly cooking all day long in the huge kitchen oven. Leaving the car on Honister Pass one morning (no youth hostel or car park there in those days) we walked over Fleetwith Pike, Haystacks, High Crag, High Stile and Red Pike and then descended to the Fish Hotel at Buttermere, where we downed several pints of beer. I particularly remember the wonderful beer that day for it was served in the best of all receptacles for the job: glazed earthenware tankards, rarely seen nowadays.

Despite all the beer, I thought we might just be able to stagger the three or four miles to the car on Honister Pass, but Eldred had other ideas. We should go over Robinson, Hindscarth and Dale Head, he said. This would clear our heads. Under the circumstances, the ascent of High Snockrigg to Buttermere Moss seemed especially steep and, at the far side of the Moss, Eldred collapsed and lay down on the ground. It was not the beer, he said, but his legs; they were killing him. After a while, he insisted I should go on. He would recover, he said, when he had rested, and would catch me up. So on I went, looking back to see if he was coming, all the way up Robinson, on to Hindscarth, and along the Edge to Dale Head, where I sat by the cairn and fell asleep.

When I awoke, unaware of how long I'd slept, I was a little concerned about the non-appearance of Eldred, so decided to go back along the way I had come, shouting down the gullies on Hindscarth Edge in case he might have fallen down one of them. There was still no sight or sound of him and I was getting really worried so I went back all the way, over Hindscarth and on to Robinson again. I descended to the point where I could see where I had left him. He was not there! Nor, so far as I could see, anywhere else on this group of fells. What could possibly have happened?

There seemed only one thing to do – go back, once again, over the tops and down to Honister Pass to alert some sort of rescue team. This I did, traversing these now over-familiar fells for the third time, and running down the last easy slopes to the Pass. As I reached the foot of Dale Head, there was Eldred setting off up the mountain to look for me. Strong language passed between us for some time. When we had cooled down a little I learned that Eldred had, eventually, recovered enough to continue, and had made his way down the fellside to the Honister road, without traversing the tops – a ploy that perhaps I should have used.

But the day was not yet over. When we got back to the car I was still furious about all the worry and exertion to which I had been subjected. Consequently, I savagely manoeuvred the car off the grass at the side of the road and managed to drop the wheels of the vehicle into some sort of drainage ditch. It was impossible for us to shift the car so I went into the quarry sheds to try to get some assistance. Half a dozen quarry workers came out, lifted the car out of the ditch and then stood round in a circle in hopeful anticipation. But I had no money on me and Eldred only a few coppers: we'd spent all our resources on the beer. It was an awkward moment. Half an hour or so later, however, all our frustration and anger was forgotten as we tucked into Mrs Edmondson's delicious Herdwick pie, real food for mountain men.

Down at our Coniston hut I originated a climbing logbook in which the climbs done each weekend, unusual incidents or interesting people encountered were written down. The logbook was maintained for a few years but, probably during the war years, fell out of use and was then mislaid. It would have been invaluable in the preparation of this book. Among the "interesting people" encountered around this time could well have been the great W.P. Haskett Smith, widely recognised as the "Father of Lake District climbing". I saw him once or twice at Fell and Rock meets or social functions just before the war but, regrettably, never met him. My memory is of a quite large, old man with a big, drooping moustache, dressed in old-fashioned clothes. He didn't look much like a climber but, a little earlier, in his seventy-seventh year, he had taken part in the Jubilee ascent of Napes Needle, which he had first climbed, solo, in 1886. This was the occasion when Haskett Smith, having surmounted the top block, was asked by somebody in the watching crowd for "a story". To which the old man immediately replied, with enviable wit: "There is no other story. This is the top storey". I wish I'd been on the Napes that day to see and hear him.

The Tigers, like many others, were always climbing the Needle. Three of us, from the mantelshelf ledge, pulling and pushing together, would often try to rock the top block – a strange but popular pastime at the time. There was once even a wild plan, which, fortunately, came to nothing, to get some sort of token tent on top, and for two of us to spend a night, or some hours, in it. So far as serious climbing was concerned, Jim Porter, of course, wanted to do something different. His idea was to girdle the top block of the Needle without placing his hands on the top. There are two girdle traverses of the Needle: a higher severe route and a lower one, which is very severe. Jim didn't know anything about these, and, in fact, they don't involve climbing round the top block itself. Anyway, he set off and got three-quarters of the way round when he was told, by the rest, to come down as they were in a hurry to get away. Recalling the attempt for me as I was preparing this book, Jim remembers the traverse was "very thin".

But now I must recall the very serious accident on Gimmer Crag that, regrettably, put an end to Jim's most promising climbing career and very nearly killed him. Indeed, many of us are convinced that Jim only survived because of his superb fitness, expert surgical treatment and devoted nursing. It happened on August 26, 1937 when Jim was 28 years of age. I was working in Manchester at the time and only heard about the accident a day or two later. He had as his second, Isabel George, the sister of Stephen whom I mentioned earlier and the young lady with whom I had shared lessons at Barrow College of Art. Like her brother, she was a very able climber.

Jim recalls that he had got up at four o'clock that day and had felt very fit and anxious to do a good climb. On reaching Langdale, he and Isabel walked up to Gimmer Crag where they first climbed the strenuous very severe, Joas, on the north-west face of the crag. Jim has always believed this was the second ascent of this climb, but as its first ascent, by Macphee and Reynolds, had taken place in 1928, nine years earlier, I think this unlikely. As he completed the hard pitch Jim heard a man at the foot of the crag shout up, "You climbed that pitch beautifully." Several weeks later he was told that "an Everest climber" had been watching their ascent. Who this man was and whether he was the one who had shouted up to him, Jim never found out.

Anyway, having reached the top of Joas Jim decided to traverse across the face of the crag and finish up "E" Route, the delicate and rather exposed climb that, in those days, was graded very severe. Many years later, after the war, when I had managed to achieve some sort of climbing form, George Spenceley and I, leading through, used to climb down "E" Route and on to Ash Tree Ledge as a quick way off the crag. Listening to Jim's account of the accident sixty years later, I realise we must have climbed down past the place where he fell. At that time we had climbed up and down "E" several times and knew the small holds very well, but Jim had never done the route before. So he shouted across to Jack Diamond, who happened to be climbing another route on the crag, "How do I get across to 'E'?" Jack shouted back, "Traverse to the right."

For some reason Jim was wearing a pair of tennis shoes, women's tennis shoes, in fact, and in order to get "as close to the rock as possible", he'd no socks on. The climbing, in an exposed situation, was "quite thin" but Jim, as always, was confident enough. Indeed, as he has often confessed since, "over confident". He was on a steep wall, on small holds, and was reaching across with his right foot for the next move when the toe of the tennis shoe on his left foot curled over and slipped off the hold, and Jim plunged down the crag. Of course, they had no modern safety equipment in those days and the fall continued unchecked. Then the rope broke – at the belay, it is thought – and poor Jim continued down the cliff, finishing his headlong descent jammed between two corners of rock. It was estimated he had fallen between 180 and 200 feet, and Jim says he has been told that if the rocks had not halted the fall he might have fallen another 200 feet.

Clearly, he was very seriously injured. It was thought, at first, he had been killed. But Jim has no memory of the terrible fall, although he clearly recalls everything that happened up to the moment his left rubber slipped off. A team of local farmers and others carried him down the fellside, and he was taken to Ulverston Cottage Hospital where he remained unconscious for a fortnight.

When we recently discussed the fall Jim couldn't explain the breaking of the rope, which would have been paid out by Isabel across the waist and over one shoulder, as was the practice in those days. All he knew was that the shock of the fall had swung Isabel round on her stance, smashing her face into the wall. And I couldn't question Isabel for she died some years ago, as did her husband, Douglas Robinson M.C., an old Preston friend of mine to whom I had first introduced her in the 1930s.

For his convalescence Jim went for six months to Granton House at Moffat, a place where the Tigers had sometimes stayed on their Scottish trips. Tommy Tyson, who was friendly with the proprietors, had no doubt recommended the place. Here, he was given every possible attention. The main injury had been to his head and Jim has since told me that in the operations six square inches had to be removed from his skull. There were other injuries, too, mostly to a knee that has left him with a more or less permanent limp. But he doesn't complain, regards the accident as his own fault, and has nothing but praise for all the people who looked after him, including a bone-setter in Dumfries, an engine driver by trade, who, apparently, did wonders for his knee.

But, especially, Jim speaks of Betty, the nurse who cared for him, so devotedly, in Ulverston Cottage Hospital. For years they corresponded by letter and then, in 1947, ten years after the accident, they were married. Together they had a happy life. Jim was eventually able to return to his job in insurance and they brought up a family of two sons and one daughter. But, of course, Jim could never climb again or, even, seriously walk the fells. Later they moved to Kendal and we often met for a chat but, sadly, Betty died in 1991 after 44 years of contented marriage. I sometimes bump into Jim, quietly shopping in Kendal, and now and again we have a meal together to talk about the old days with the Tigers. A year or two ago Jack Atkinson, one of the four surviving Tigers, travelled from Barrow for an evening with us at Jim's home. The other survivor is Len Brown. Jim is a quiet, uncomplaining soul. He never moans about his lot, the blow that Fate gave him, or ponders what might have been, but is just quietly grateful to be alive. He is now having increasing difficulties with his vision but, again, doesn't complain. He is a gentle man whom I always feel honoured to have had as a friend for so many years.

Two months after Jim's terrible accident, on October 23rd 1937, Mollie and I were married. The ceremony had had to be delayed some months because of my move to Manchester and the uncertainty, in those days, of survival on national newspapers. We decided, on the recommendation of Tommy Tyson, to have our honeymoon in Aviemore at the foot of the Cairngorms. This was not because Tommy had some wonderful honeymoon hotel in mind, but simply because he considered it was high time I had a look at the Cairngorms. In fact, we didn't book into any hotel, not thinking this would be necessary, but as it turned out, we were fortunate to get any accommodation at all.

When we reached Aviemore, which in those days consisted of a railway station, two hotels and very little else, we discovered, first of all, that one of these hotels had just been burned down and that the other, the Cairngorm, was packed full with desperately keen-looking fishermen. The blackened ruins of what had been

A unique photograph. Siegfried Herford on top of the Great Flake on the first ascent, in April 1914, of Central Buttress, Scafell. For many years, this was the most difficult climb in England. (Picture from the collection of the late G.S. Sansom who, with C.F. Holland, was with Herford on the first ascent)

Sambo – a wonderful mountain companion

Outside the hut, above, left to right: George Anderson, myself, Len Brown, Jack Diamond, Jim Porter, Jack Atkinson

Left: most of the Tigers (myself, with scarf).

Dave Birch (left) and Jim Porter

Mountain rescue practice in 1948 on Kern Knotts, Great Gable. The climber taking down the stretcher is my old friend Lt Colonel "Rusty" Westmorland.
(Ivor Nicholas)

Lower Kern Knotts, Great Gable. My first climbing companions: left to right: Tommy Tyson, Dick Mackereth, myself, Bryan Tyson.

The Tigers in Scotland in the snow. Mostly in poor weather.

the Aviemore Hotel, its turrets and lawns suggesting the opulence and comfort we craved, was our first disappointment, and the "Full" notices at the Cairngorm, further down the road, the second. However, we looked around the small cluster of houses and eventually found a bungalow with a pleasant garden in front, where they were prepared to put us up for a week or two. There was only one other guest, a bishop, so I suppose our honeymoon could be said to have been blessed, or, at least, to have got off to a satisfactory start.

The next morning was sunny and crisp, with plenty of snow on the hills we had seen on our drive up the valley. We set off for Cairngorm. I can't remember the car I was driving except that it wasn't the little open Morris Minor that had served us so well on our trip to Skye, but it would have been a small car. A large car couldn't have squeezed through the trees that we found so constricting. None of my old maps of the Cairngorms show the route we took; they aren't old enough. I know the road, as such, ended at Coylumbridge or, more likely, Inverdruie, and, from there, in the car, we just followed an unmade track through closely packed woods. This was generations before new roads, mountain highways, ski paraphernalia, shops, hotels and all the fun of the fair had transformed a quiet railway halt and its surrounding unspoiled countryside into a modern winter and summer resort. All I can remember about our drive from Coylumbridge or Inverdruie to the Cairngorms is that most of it was over tangled tree roots, that we had to keep stopping the car to work out how to manoeuvre it around particular trees, and that it took a long time.

Eventually, we came out of the trees, through which there had never been even a suspicion of a road, on to sandy shingle, and found ourselves on the shore of a large loch – Loch Morlich, as it turned out. In those days there was no campsite, youth hostel, Forestry Commission Information Centre, reindeer house, boathouses or anything else on the loch side. We saw only the sandy beach, the reflection of the Scots pines in the water and, right at the back and pretty high, the snow-covered mass of Cairngorm and all her attendant peaks. We parked the car on the sandy beach and set off walking. There was nobody about and, indeed, we saw nobody all day.

We followed the main burn up the valley south towards the summit, probably partly along the line of the present ski road. We didn't take the hairpin line of the modern road and nor did we go up by the present White Lady run or into Coire Cas. Instead, we made for the big boulder, Clach Bharraig, and then followed the long ridge to the summit. It was the last week in October and the snow was down to about 1000 feet. Stupidly, we hadn't taken ice axes, not expecting much snow, but, then, not many people take ice axes on their honeymoon. We just kicked steps in our clinker-nailed boots and found no difficulty. Whether or not there was a track under the snow we had no idea, but there were certainly no footprints anywhere.

Photographs we took of each other by the snow-plastered summit cairn show Mollie in thick sweater and corduroy knee-breeches, and myself in breeches, a white polo-neck sweater and a splendid tweed sports jacket, with a handkerchief in the breast pocket. Both of us are wearing clinker-nailed boots. I don't look much like a present-day mountaineer: far too dapper. The view from the summit was superb – mile after mile of sunlit, untracked snow stretching as far as we could see, with white summits dotted around the horizon. From the map we identified Ben Macdui, the second highest summit in Britain, three or four miles away to the south across the snowfields. It didn't look all that impressive from that angle, but in later visits we discovered its steeper sides.

The most remarkable feature of the view, when compared with the scene any late October afternoon nowadays, was that in all those miles of sunny, unbroken snow there was not one person to be seen. Today, there would be scores, if not hundreds, of skiers scurrying about the snow like ants, with many cries of exhilaration or despair, and all the rattle of ski lifts. But 1937 was years before the skiing revolution hit Scotland. True, there were some Scottish skiers around, and a handful in Lakeland and elsewhere, but nothing had been done to ease their access to the snow and their enjoyment of it; no roads, no ski tows, no huts, nothing. Cairngorm and the other ski mountains of Scotland were still completely "undeveloped", and no doubt looked exactly the same as they had looked a hundred years earlier.

Mollie and I walked back down the mountain to Loch Morlich, admiring the wonderful effect of the late afternoon sunshine on the snow slopes of the Cairngorms, and drove back through the forest, over the tree roots, to our honeymoon base in Aviemore. In later days we explored the area around Loch an Eilein, along Gleann Einich, into Strath Nethy, and, one day, as I described earlier, drove to Perth ice rink for me to take a lesson in doing back loops. We were not then to know that we would be returning to the

Cairngorms many, many times, that we would watch, and become involved in, the later transformation of Aviemore and Cairngorm, and that skiing would become an important part of my life for forty years or more.

Strangely, I had nearly started skiing two years earlier. It happened this way. One day in the early 1930s, I had been travelling in a bus in Preston, reading a climbing guidebook for Dow Crag or Langdale, when a young man sitting on a seat behind me leaned forward and asked me whether I was a climber. When I replied in the affirmative he asked me whether I would take him climbing, and that was the start of a close friendship. The young man was Walter Ingham, an astonishingly handsome youth with an attractive Austrian accent. He was trying to sell typewriters in Preston, had been born in Vienna, where his father was the European director or manager of Remington typewriters, and was passionately devoted to Austria and skiing.

We went climbing on Dow Crag and, several times, from Wasdale, and, as young men do, we spent a lot of time discussing our futures and how to make a lot of money. Walter, the driving force, was bored with selling typewriters and kept producing schemes for transforming our lives. We examined all these very seriously, but for a variety of reasons ultimately rejected them all. One of them, which nearly got off the ground and might well have ruined us both, was to start a chain of cheap libraries. Eventually, Walter started up his winter sports travel business and, as I knew he would, worthily became a very rich man.

But one day, when he was still trying to sell typewriters, he announced that he and I were going for a fortnight's skiing holiday in Austria. I had taught him to climb, he said, and he, in return, was going to teach me skiing. Incidentally, he had been schools' skiing champion of Austria some years earlier. We were going to stay at Hochsolden in the Tyrol with a friend of his, Serafin Fender, mountain guide and chief ski instructor. The holiday would cost me nothing, except the price of the journey there and back. The food and accommodation, the ski instruction, the ski lifts, all the gear, would be thrown in, free. Regrettably, I was busy planning my first trip to Skye, with Mollie, and I couldn't take the time off for two holidays that year. It would have to be one or the other, my first skiing holiday or a first trip to the magic Isle of Skye. In the end, after much discussion, I decided on Skye. Skiing would have to wait for a while.

As it turned out, I didn't start skiing until I came back from the war. A year or two later I happened to be in Hochsolden, on a first visit, and who should I bump into on the slopes but my old friend, Walter Ingham? Having brought much prosperity to the area by his successful skiing holidays, he had become something like the uncrowned king of that part of Austria, and I was entertained royally by him and his wife on several occasions. We also did some skiing together. Regrettably, we lost touch in later years, but I kept hearing stories of his continued success. Years later, when I was booking a skiing holiday through Inghams and happened to mention that I knew Walter, I was treated with increased respect, nay, almost deference.

"You mean you actually know Major Ingham, personally?" queried one lovely, tanned ski courier, as if this was scarcely credible. I will always be grateful to Walter Ingham for initiating my love for Austria (he used to teach me the lilting mountain songs, in German) and, probably, for getting me into skiing, although this came years later.

Three months before the outbreak of war, in June 1939, Mollie and I had our first visit to Arran; another Scottish island that, with Skye, was to became a favourite family holiday centre for years. My son, Robin, was born four weeks after the outbreak of war and Sandra, five years later, and the first holidays of both our children were in these two delectable islands. On this first visit we rented a bungalow in Lamlash and did all the usual things: climbing Goatfell and some of the ridges, exploring the Rosa and Sannox glens, and cycling all round the island on hired machines. But the holiday was cut short by a telegram from my newspaper requesting my immediate return to help in the coverage of the submarine Thetis disaster off Anglesey, so some of the Arran hills had to be left for another holiday.

But it was to be many, long years before I saw the hills again, British hills, that is, and the thrills of rock-climbing had to be set aside for other less joyful thrills. I joined the army, as a volunteer, not as a conscript, in the first months of the war. After some years of service in this country, during which, as part of my intelligence job, I had become reasonably well informed about the dispositions of the German army in occupied Europe, I was suddenly dispatched to the war in Burma – about which I knew nothing. At the beginning of the war I had been stationed in Orkney for about a year and remember seeing the Old Man of Hoy, which had not then been climbed, but don't recall being particularly anxious to attempt it.

Anyway, I went through Burma with the "forgotten" 14th Army, up to Mandalay and down to Rangoon, where, at last, I was able to organise some leave. The travel warrant must have been quite complicated for I went by plane from Rangoon to Calcutta; by train, a terribly long journey, from Calcutta to Rawalpindi; by bus, a very rickety affair, to Srinagar in Kashmir and, then, by pony, to the hill-station of Gulmarg. From here, some huge mountains were glimpsed and some small ones climbed, but before my leave had expired, I was ordered back to India where a 12th Army, for the invasion of Malaya, was being assembled, and then to Ceylon, where the operation was to be planned. But we were all forestalled by the dropping of the atomic bombs on Hiroshima and Nagasaki and, thankfully, the end of the war. By keeping my nose clean and looking industrious, while avoiding any actual fighting, I contrived to finish the war as a lieutenant colonel, but it was the spring of 1946 before I could get myself demobilised, collect my extremely ill-fitting suit, and look forward to climbing the crags again. But, before then, while I was in Kashmir, I had been involved in an adventure – the snow-climbing fall mentioned earlier that had very nearly killed me.

High Street and Haweswater

A Rewarding Hill

The summit of Lingmell, that lonely and little-visited outlier of the Scafell range, is really one of the most rewarding mountain tops in the Lake District. It boasts, when not decapitated by vandals, the most splendidly sited and beautifully built summit cairn in the district, but there's no other evidence of the hand of man up there – no piles of old tins and orange peel and not even a track across the top. Few people bother to go on to Lingmell because it is so close to the highest mountains in England and just off the main highway, but it is one of the most superb grandstands in the country. With the Scafells just across the col, no other Lake District mountain is so closely ringed with soaring fellsides, rock and scree. And the view of Great Gable across the great trough of Wasdale and Lingmell Beck must be the most detailed sight of one mountain's architecture in the national park. From just north of the cairn on Lingmell, you appear to be looking across the valley at the district's most shapely mountain as though through a telephoto lens or zoom camera. Every feature of Gable, from top to toe, leaps into sharp focus – you can easily pick out the Needle on a good day – and you have the impression of tremendous depths dropping below your feet. As if this tremendous panorama of peaks was not enough, Lingmell also happens to display, sliced into its eastern flank, the biggest ravine in the fell country: the dog-legged Piers Gill, large enough to hide an army and, especially in wet weather, a formidable challenge to the climber. The longest rock-climb on any of our crags, the 2000 feet Pilgrim's Progress, leads out of the Gill to the top of the mountain. All this on a mountain the crowds don't bother to explore or, often, even notice – a mountain for the connoisseur.

June 1972

Chapter Nine

Kashmir to Kendal

Possibly inspired by Amy Woodford-Finden's "Indian Love Lyrics", which I used to play on the piano, but, more likely, because of what I had read of high mountain adventure on the great peaks beyond the Pir Panjal, I had for years dreamed of going to Kashmir. This was the beautiful state at the western end of the Himalaya, overlooked by Nanga Parbat, the tenth highest mountain in the world, and then still unclimbed. Burma was an unpleasant experience, hot, sticky and full of flies – quite apart from the tragedies of the conflict and the widespread destruction of what had, no doubt, been a pleasant countryside. Often in the oppressive heat I thought of the cool delights of snow, especially high mountain snow that crunched underfoot. Consequently, when I had this chance of leave, Kashmir, although so far away, seemed the obvious place to go.

The first disappointment, after the long journey that took several days, was the discovery that the hotel where I had booked to stay in Gulmarg, Nedou's Hotel, had been burned down. I had assumed this penchant for incineration to be confined to Scotland – our would-be honeymoon hotel in Aviemore, for instance, and many other similar establishments in the Highlands had met the same fate – but had not thought the practice would have spread to Kashmir. They say the reason these Scottish hotel fires are rarely extinguished is because the fire stations are so many miles away, possibly fifty or more, and if the nearest fire station to Gulmarg was in Srinagar, a few thousand feet below, it's not surprising they couldn't put this one out. Anyway, I was installed, on my own, in a splendid bell tent, fitted not only with duckboards, but also a proper bed. After sleeping for so long inside a mosquito net, on my own army camp bed – when I was lucky – this was luxury indeed. I was also provided with a bearer who brought in the food and looked after me.

But the real delight, when I opened the tent flap the next morning, bright and sunny, was the incredible view. For there, miles and miles away, across the lake and the Vale of Kashmir, and unbelievably high in the sky, was the peak of my dreams: Nanga Parbat. Its snows seemed to float like a cloud at the far end of the valley. On other days I could sometimes pick out the soaring ridges, and try to imagine what it must have been like for Mummery and the later German expeditions in their early attempts on the summit. It was to be another eight years after my first view of the mountain before Hermann Buhl finally reached the top, alone, after an astounding feat of endurance. This, then, was the view I had every morning throughout my stay; the biggest and most beautiful mountain I had ever seen.

Much closer to hand were much smaller mountains, perhaps only half the height of Nanga Parbat, and one of these, an easy peak called Apharwat (about 13,000ft), I decided to climb. By this time I had met two other officers, their names escape me now, and the three of us trudged up the snow slopes and the rocky bits until we reached what looked like the top, and then came down again. A day or two later I decided to go up Apharwat again because I wasn't completely satisfied we had reached the actual summit. The other two weren't interested, so I went on my own.

I was wearing ordinary army boots, without nails, and had no ice axe, but on my way up through the forest I picked up a stout stick which I thought might be useful. This time I found a different way up: a pleasant snow and rock ridge that led easily to the summit plateau and, eventually, to the obvious summit. On the descent I kept to the same route, following my footsteps in the snow, and then began descending the snow and rock ridge, climbing very carefully, and using the stick as I would have used an axe. But when I had climbed some distance down the ridge I noticed a parallel ridge some distance away to the left that looked altogether more interesting. The two ridges were separated by a steep snow couloir but I thought I could easily kick steps across this and thus get on to the better-looking descent line. About fifty kicked steps would take me across, I thought.

So I set off, facing into the slope, plunging the stick in the snow as if it had been an ice axe and kicking good, solid steps. But after I had kicked fifty steps and was beginning to tire a little, I realised I wasn't halfway across, and the snow was getting much harder. I had to kick several times to make a step and soon it became difficult to make even a nick in the hard snow. Suddenly, the hard snow changed to ice, and I knew I was in trouble. Without an axe there was no way I could tackle the ice. Already both feet were most precariously placed on tiny nicks, I was not yet halfway across the couloir, and it was impossible to guess when I might get back on to good snow. I decided to go back. To do this I had to put the stick in my other hand, turn round slightly to face left, and change the positions of my feet, tip-toeing carefully across the ice. Without an axe it seemed a most complicated manoeuvre. I was halfway through it when one of my toes suddenly slipped on the ice and away I went down the slope.

The feeling I most remember about that awful slip is one of utter helplessness. With an ice axe I might have been able to arrest the fall – we had often practised this – but the useless stick had been snatched away and there was nothing I could do. I had started falling on my back but managed to turn over to face into the ice. Then my head must have swung down and I continued down the slope, looking straight down into the abyss, with my fingers and toes desperately clawing into the ice. It was a very steep gully indeed: virtually bottomless, falling away into crags. If nothing happened in the next second or so I was going to be killed.

Then, as I hurtled swiftly downwards, I noticed a snow-covered rock, perhaps three feet square, further down the steep gully. If I could hit this rock, I thought, I might be able to stop going down and over the edge. But it seemed to be slightly left of the line I was taking and I might miss it. "Please, God, help me," I'm sure I must have prayed. By digging in my toes and fingers, I did manage to change course very slightly, and then, miraculously, I crashed into the rock.

Then came the most desperate part of the whole descent. I simply had to hang on to that rock in any way I could and stop the impetus of the headlong swoop from carrying me over and past it, and down to my death. Even now I can recall that struggle, although it probably lasted only a second or two. I put every atom of strength I had into it and almost literally hung on by my fingernails. Eventually, I managed to struggle to my feet.

I could now see what lay immediately below. The gully, hard ice in its centre, seemed to tilt down towards the vertical, and then just drop into space. Crouched on the rock, however, I could see I could kick steps on reasonable snow leading to the ridge towards which I had been making when I started to cross the couloir. Almost in a dream, I carefully crossed the snow to the ridge, sat down on a ledge, and then began to shake and shiver in every part of my body, as if I was in some sort of fit. It took me perhaps ten minutes or so to get over this violent reaction to a very narrow escape from disaster, but then I was able to walk down the mountain without any other sign of the desperate struggle I had just been through. The next morning, after a good night's sleep, I discovered that most parts of my body were very badly bruised in a startling variety of colours, and this bruising remained for several days to remind me of a very nasty experience.

One other rather more pleasant incident of that day may be worth recording. When I got down below the snows and on to a little grassy alp above the forest, I saw, with some surprise, for this was a fairly remote area, a rather ornate tent. Out of this tent stepped a man, a Kashmiri, who asked me whether I would like some strawberries and cream! He must have taken a photograph for me for among my snaps of that trip is one of me sitting at a table, just below the snow, apparently enjoying a meal. The caption reads, "Strawberries and cream at 10,000 feet". There is a white cloth on the table, and two or three nice chairs. The strawberries must have had a restorative effect for, despite my rather nasty experience an hour earlier, I look fairly normal.

I have often wondered how far I went in that fall. When I had recovered from my shaking and trembling I looked back up the slope and thought I had swooped about two hundred feet. Since then I have sometimes looked at similar places in the Alps and tried to come to some more reasoned estimate, but I think my original guess was about right. The fall felt longer than that, but it can't have been. Certainly, it was the most frightening mountaineering experience I've ever had.

By the following spring, 1946, I had been demobilised. Soon after that I found myself living and working in Kendal, where I have remained ever since, and where I will remain until I am translated into the upper air. In moving to Kendal I had come back to the hills for good – my homeland hills. We had always stopped at Kendal when driving north from Manchester to Borrowdale, I knew the Kendal climbing gang, and I liked the pubs. Now, at last, after years of incarceration in industrial Lancashire and six years of war, much of it abroad, I could get back to climbing every weekend and every holiday. I could see the hills from the windows of my new home. Later, when I had moved a little nearer the fells, I could see hills in the four counties of Cumberland, Westmorland, Lancashire and Yorkshire every day, simply by looking out of my windows. Life was good again.

During the last twenty years or so I have kept a rough diary of my mountain days, but apart from my fortnightly contributions to *The Guardian's* "Country Diary" (nearly fifty years of them) I have almost nothing else to remind me of hundreds of days on crags and hills. The single exception is the start of a diary, scribbled in ink on lined paper, and entitled "Mountaineering in 1948". I have recently discovered this diary among some old papers. These bits of paper, starting twenty years after I had begun climbing, finish at the end of May of that year, after just five months of entries. Perhaps I had got bored with them or possibly there was nothing worth putting down. Here is a selection of some of the entries, showing the not-very-exciting things we were doing at that time.

Jan 18. 1948. Went to Farleton Knott with E. Arnison and T. Philipson. Cold and windy, but pleasant for scrambling. Dinner afterwards at the Plough.

Feb. 22. (Coniston Tigers meet). Staying at the hut Saturday night: J. Diamond, Pop, R. Shaw, D. Birch and myself. These, with J. Blackshaw, C. Smith and Syd Brown met at Goats Water. Extremely cold and wintry. A little snow and ice on the crags. Led Blackshaw up Giant's Crawl – others fell-walked. Dinner at Black Bull.

(Pop was my father. Jack Blackshaw was elderly and completely stone deaf. When climbing with him communication had to be carried out by agreed tugs on the rope. I remember on this climb, trying to fix a belay while balancing on icy footholds at the top of the long, rather exposed slab, and discovering Jack climbing up just below me, with yards of rope hanging down the pitch. He had not felt any tugs and had decided to come up. Jack, a determined little man despite his disability, took up skiing and ice skating in his seventies.)

March 7. Practice on Kern Knotts with H. Westmorland and Borrowdale mountain rescue party. Very heavy rain and very cold. Waded knee-deep through R. Derwent on return. Tea at Mrs Edmondson's.

(This was the start of what became the Keswick mountain rescue team, founded by Lt. Col. H. (Rusty) Westmorland, who later became a close climbing and skiing friend.)

March 14. To Dow with P. Wilson – lovely, warm sunshine. Did Woodhouse's in boots and down Blizzard Chimney and then Branch Chimney in rubbers. Dinner at the Black Bull.

(Paul Wilson, a generous Kendal friend, became Lord Lieutenant of Westmorland and, later, Lord Wilson of High Wray.)

March 26 (Good Friday). From Barrow went to Dow with Pop and J. Diamond – very hot walking up. Led Pop up Arête, Chimney and Crack and then up Lazarus. Lyna Kellett, Dick Cook etc also on crag. Rock in good condition. Rubbers.

March 28. Glorious sunshine but a little wind. To Gimmer with R. Crompton. Led him up Herdwick Buttress, Ash Tree Slabs and Main Wall. Found. H. B. distinctly hard but others easy.

(Dick Crompton was the Planning Officer for Westmorland. I introduced him to climbing and he introduced me to dinghy sailing. He and his wife were later killed in a car crash.)

April 11. Glorious weather. To Honister with E. Arnison. Met Miss Joy. Walked over Moses Trod to Beckhead and climbed on Boat Howe for first time. Did Hatchway and Rigging, Starboard Arête by Clinker and Breakwater Slabs and Lighthouse (leading alternate pitches). Down to Gatesgarth via Scarth Gap. Tea at Miss Nelson's. Home via Newlands, Keswick and Penrith.

April 18. To Dow with M. Ferguson. Rain in the morning. Crags wet but otherwise a fairly good day. In boots went up D Ordinary, down Blizzard, up Giant's Crawl and down again to Easy Terrace.

(Myers Ferguson is a Kendal lad who became the captain of the famous Kendal rugby fifteen. We often climbed together. He is still keen on the fells and pretty fit but, like me, no longer climbing.)

May 16. Dow with Les and Pop (who came up from Torver on his own). Les and I tried Murray's Crack but, when leading, I found final pitch too steep and turned it down. Then took Pop and Les up Southern Slabs and Central Chimney.

May 20. Dow again with Les. First did Raven, finding it easy, and then embarked on Hopkinson's Crack. Leading, I found it hard but I finally won out. Just about my limit at this time.

May 22. (morning). To Longsleddale and Buckbarrow. In boots did Dandle Buttress, leading alternate pitches. Les on better form than me.

May 23. Dow again. We (presumably Les and I) decided to climb in boots and, leading alternate pitches, did Giant's Crawl and Giant's Corner.

May 30. Met E. Arnison and V. Veevers in Keswick. Intended climbing on Scafell but, owing to shortage of time, went to Napes. Intended doing Tophet Ridge but found it too windy. Went on to Gable Crag and did Smuggler's Chimney and down Central Gully, finding the chimney very strenuous because of its extreme narrowness (or width of paunch).

And there the diary suddenly finishes. I have left out several of the entries, but the picture is of careful climbing up v. diffs. and severes – still without any security, and paying out the rope in the old-fashioned way. Eric Arnison and Vince Veevers, mentioned in the last entry, have both been dead for a few years now. I recall that a few weeks before Vince died he and I, with Jim Birkett, then in his last days, had a splendid evening together in Little Langdale, talking about the old times we had enjoyed together. This was the last time I saw either of them. I had first met Vince, a splendid climber, about fifty years earlier. He was thinning tree seedlings in a little plantation below Castle Rock of Triermain, which set us off talking about climbing and soon a long mountain friendship began. We often climbed together on Dow or in Borrowdale.

I first met Jim Birkett in Langdale just after the war. We were both floundering about on skis at the time. Langdale is hardly ideal skiing terrain and both of us were beginners, bumping into trees and falling down in snowdrifts. That was the first and last time I ever saw him on skis. Of course, I had known of him by reputation for years. He was then starting his new climbs in White Ghyll, Langdale, but five months before the outbreak of war he had made his important bold leads of Overhanging Bastion and Zigzag on Castle Rock of Triermain, the first great climbs in an outstanding career.

An early memory of Jim is when he showed me Lanty Slee's cave in Moss Rigg quarry, Little Langdale, where he (Jim) worked as a quarryman, and later became the manager. Lanty Slee, born in 1802, was the famous illicit whisky distiller and smuggler who had several stills hidden around the Langdale area. Many years later I had a long talk with Lanty's son, Adam. Adam lived until the 1960s when he reached more than 100 years of age, so that I just fail, by two years, to have a direct link with the 18th century.

Jim and I roped down into the entrance to Lanty's cave, which is now walled up. With a torch, we discovered the spring where he obtained his water, a sort of covered tank in the floor, pieces of the pipe that carried the exhaust steam back into the water, the place where he had his still and "worm" and, at the back of the cave, his concealed whisky store. There were also the ashes from many of his fires, several pieces of rusted barrel hoops and a broken clay pipe. You can easily imagine the scene, with Lanty keeping his ears cocked for the sound of the excisemen and wondering whether they might spot the smoke escaping through the entrance.

Jim Birkett was not just a brilliant rock-climber, probably the leading figure of his day and certainly the best nailed-boots climber in the country, but also a gifted ornithologist, botanist and countryman. He had first got into climbing by seeking out birds' eggs in dangerous places, but later the poacher became game-keeper and Jim was transformed into a staunch environmentalist. A walk with him could be a revelation. Besides his intimate knowledge of birds he had an instant recognition of every type of tree, even in winter, seemed to know the different species of grasses by their names, and was an expert on most forms of plant-life, especially wild flowers.

He was immensely strong in the arms and shoulders but won-derfully neat in his footwork. I have written earlier of him climb-ing on Dow in quarrymen's clogs, rimmed with steel "caulkers", and putting me to shame. On another occasion, probably walking to a climb, we were crossing the foot of Hart Crag, high up in Link Cove above Deepdale, and I had to follow him as he tripped and danced across a mixture of steepish rock, grass and wet earth at speed. "The trick," he told me, "is to go so quickly that as soon as you slip off one hold you're on to the next." I learned a lot in that wild traverse, but I couldn't keep up with him or match his casual confidence.

Another memorable early expedition with Jim Birkett was a

descent of Tilberthwaite Gill in spate. We'd been climbing some-where and, seeing all the water rushing down the gill, Jim sug-gested its descent would round off the day nicely. The idea was to climb down the streaming walls of the gill, keeping as close to the water as possible. Several times we fell in; at least, I know I did. It was a wild, hair-raising descent with many exciting moments and we finished up among the boulders at the bottom of the gill like a couple of drowned rats. Years later, possibly inspired by this peril-ous descent, I started "collecting" the gills of Lakeland by climbing as many of them as possible. This was long before the "new" sport of gill scrambling became popular.

Jim took me up one of his new climbs in White Ghyll, Hollin Groove, and I happened to be around, a year or two later, when he led the first ascent, with Len Muscroft, of the very severe Haste Not on the same crag. There was an exciting moment on the sensa-tional overhanging pitch when an expected "jug-handle" turned out to be either rounded, flat or non-existent. For some reason Jim, despite his extremely perilous situation, thought this very amus-ing; we, just looking on, were quite alarmed.

Round about 1948, when Jim Birkett led the first ascent of Haste Not, another great climber, Arthur Dolphin, was preparing for his first lead of the remarkable Kipling Groove on Gimmer Crag. A day or two before this bold lead I watched Dolphin climbing down the top part of the climb, unroped, to check on the sequence of holds, and then climb back up again. I couldn't work out what the climb might be, but it looked incredibly steep and frightening. Some years later I was again at the foot of Kipling Groove when a Russian climber, on a visit to the Lake District with a number of his compa-triots, was attempting to lead the climb. For a long time the Rus-sian was stationary, high up on the climb, at the sensational crux. One or two of the others in the watching group knew exactly what he should do, but as none of them could speak Russian there was nothing they could do to help. Eventually, however, after an agonising wait, the Russian made the move and we breathed again.

One day Jim Birkett and I went to explore a "new" cliff, Raven Crag above Pasture Beck, Low Hartsop. It had never been climbed, was very steep, and had a sensational traverse line across it. There was a large raven's nest at the right-hand end of the line. Jim wanted us to climb up to the nest, do the traverse and climb down at the other end. The ensuing couple of hours are indelibly stamped on my memory. Jim would climb, with some difficulty, towards the traverse, get me up to him with considerably more dif-

ficulty, make several abortive attempts at progress and then abseil
off, leaving me to do the same. We would then repeat the attempt
from different points below the traverse line, all without success,
abseiling off each time. I had never before abseiled in such desperate, awkward situations, and was greatly relieved when Jim called
off the attempts. Somehow, there was the feeling that my inepti-
tude had been the main cause of our failure, but then I always
seemed to climb badly with Jim – a natural sort of inferiority com-
plex.

However, we went on to do two quite challenging first ascents
round the corner up the south end of the crag, which, after the ter-
rors of the traverse, I thought rather enjoyable, but Jim didn't think
them worth while entering up in the book. A. Wright eventually
led a traverse of Raven Crag, named Echo, in 1964, but, reading the
description, I doubt whether this was the exact line Jim had in
mind.

We had several other days together on the crags and adventures
on the fells, but having no diary, it is difficult to recall many of
them. He took me, I remember, on an early ascent, possibly its
second, of Curving Gully on Hutaple Gully, when we spent much
of the time hurling down loose rock. Another day, not long after
the war, I was walking along the High Spy-Maiden Moor ridge to
Dale Head when I was struck by the line of crags overlooking the
Newlands valley. There looked as if there should be some good
climbs on them, but I didn't know of any, so I suggested to Jim that
we should have a look at them. Jim said he knew all about these
crags, had already had a look at them and had decided they weren't
worth exploring. "Not enough good rock," he said, "too much loose
stuff, and grass. No good lines." In the next few years, however,
Rushworth, Dirkin, Dennison, Peascod and others put up several
interesting new routes on these crags, notably on Miners' Crag, so,
perhaps, for once, Jim had got it wrong.

But I did happen to be in at the "birth" of another Lakeland crag,
Eagle Crag in Grisedale, in 1954. Later, I'm glad to say, Jim, too,
was involved. About this time George Spenceley and I were spending a lot of time on the eastern crags, on the lookout, rather casu-
ally, for likely-looking first ascents – provided they weren't too
desperate. We lacked the drive of the really hard men. Walking up
Grisedale one day, perhaps to have a look at the Dollywaggon gullies, we noticed, across the beck and at the foot of Nethermost Pike,
the sunlit, clean rock of the South Crag of Eagle Crag. No climbs
had been done on this crag so far as we knew and the rock looked

Tigers in Lakeland snow. Jack Diamond is in the foreground.

The entrance hall of the Wastwater Hotel (now the Wasdale Head Inn) in about 1930.

A post-war reunion of the Tigers outside the Old Dungeon Ghyll Hotel.
Left to right: Sid Cross, myself, Dave Birch, Len Brown, Jack Diamond,
unknown, Ronnie Shaw, Jack Blackshaw.

Another post-war Tigers reunion. Jack Blackshaw, with bald head, in front
row. Myself (with pipe – and hair) on the back row with Sid Cross to my left.

Kashmir: strawberries and cream at 10,000 ft

Jim Birkett *(Tony Greenbank)*

The Tigers on Ben Nevis in 1933.
Left to right: George Anderson, Tommy Tyson, Archie Stammers, Jim Porter.

Mollie and I on the summit of Cairngorm on our honeymoon in October 1937.

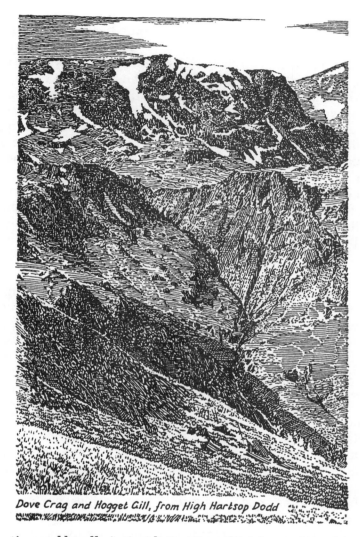

Dove Crag and Hogget Gill, from High Hartsop Dodd

attractive and hardly intimidating. Just the job, we thought. As if to confirm our opinion, a sheep that had been idling around the cliff easily climbed the top pitch of our intended first route. Impressed, we hurried across, roped up, and during the next couple of hours worked out three pleasantly airy routes.

By a strange coincidence, however, it happened that the crag had first been visited just four weeks earlier by members of the Sheffield University Mountaineering Club, who had taken over Ruthwaite Lodge, 500 yards away from the crag, as a climbing hut. They had climbed one of our three routes, now named Original

Route, and in later months did several much harder routes on the crag. Before we left the crag George and I noticed what seemed a very good line, starting up steep slabs. Either because we'd no time or, even, because it looked too hard, we left it alone. But I'd already named the unclimbed route, Kestrel Wall, for there was a kestrel hovering overhead at the time. A fortnight later I showed it to Jim Birkett, and he and I did it together. It was an enjoyable route, quite steep with small holds, and I understand it is now regarded as a minor classic in its grade. More importantly, this severe happened to be the very last new route, out of dozens, to be led by Jim Birkett, master climber and gifted countryman. I will always remember his elegant footwork on the steepest rock, his eye for the best line in impossible places, his expert knowledge of birds, trees and flowers, his patience and his tolerance. And always treasure his friendship.

The war over, I had soon got back with the Coniston Tigers again, picking up the threads as if they'd never been broken, but, in addition, I was meeting up with other old friends and finding new ones. There were also new experiences to enjoy, including skiing and potholing: the first of these to remain almost a way of life, in wintertime, for another forty years or more; the second, a pastime in which I dabbled for just a few years. Eric Arnison, the Penrith climber mentioned earlier, was probably largely responsible for attracting me to skiing. George Spenceley, also from Penrith in the immediate post-war years, my companion on the Eagle Crag climbs and on many others, certainly steered me into potholing. In wintertime, Eric was always abandoning climbing trips and disappearing towards unseen, distant snow patches with his skis, which he always seemed to have with him, besides, occasionally, a fishing rod. He was always so enthusiastic about skiing that I thought there must be something in it, and soon I was involved.

Eric was a senior member of a family firm of solicitors in Penrith and about ten years older than me. He was an active, all-round mountaineer, a member of the Alpine Club and, some years later, the President of the Fell and Rock. His other activities included fly-fishing, a bit of rough shooting now and again and, when it seemed desirable, (dare I write this of a clerk to the magistrates?) an enthusiastic poacher. George Spenceley, about ten years younger than me, had been in the RAF, flying in bombers, but unfortunately had finished the war in a POW camp. He was a member of the Yorkshire Ramblers Club, the senior potholing club, a keen rock-climber and a teacher in Penrith. Round about the first time we met he went to the Alps for his first season, with Eric Arnison. During much of the next half-century I was to spend very many happy and, sometimes, slightly desperate days with either Eric or George or, sometimes, both of them.

But I must get back to the Tigers where, for the first time in the club, we were struck by tragedy and the unexpected loss of an especially well-loved member.

Pavey Ark and Stickle Tarn

A Wooded Height

The now-afforested upland of Claife Heights, high above Windermere, where Beatrix Potter loved to wander, seems to be undergoing yet another change. At first, it was a delightfully unspoiled, naturally wooded fellside with splendid, unrestricted views of the surrounding fells and, far below, the long length of Windermere. Then the foresters moved in, planting tens of thousands of conifers so densely packed that for years this became the best place in Lakeland for getting yourself lost. Of course, the views disappeared as well. The next stage, no doubt following complaints from tourists about going round in gloomy circles for hours, or finishing up in the wrong valley, was that a narrow corridor was cut through the forest and the way clearly indicated by white-topped posts hammered into the ground. You could now work your way through the forest with ease, but, except in one or two places, the views were still either restricted or non-existent, although now and again you might get a peep at the sky. But now another change is upon us for during the past year thousands of the conifers have been felled, and the top of the Heights is now as bald as a battlefield and, in places, nearly as ugly. No doubt, there will be even more changes, if only to clear up the mess. At least the distant views are back, for the time being, but at a price. But despite all the noise of the felling, roe deer still roam the woods, and sometimes peep out at you, and buzzards soar overhead. And the five miles round from Far Sawrey, past the lovely pools of Moss Eccles Tarn and Wise Een Tarn, with their dramatic mountain backdrops, and then into the waymarked forest, is still a splendid way to spend a summer afternoon. Not far from the ancient ferry is an old ruin, one of the principal "stations" of Thomas West, the scholarly Jesuit who wrote the first real guide to the Lakes. From here the first tourists looked down at the view through windows of coloured glass, but the views from the Heights just now are far better than anything these early visitors might have seen.

June 1998

Chapter Ten

Sadness and New Friends

Right from the earliest days of the Coniston Tigers Jack Diamond had been our secretary and organ-iser-in-chief. He looked after the blankets and the beds, paid the rates, repaired the stoves, ordered the coal and arranged the annual dinner that had kept us together, despite a war and many changes of address, all those years. And such was his affection for the hut and the surrounding fells and crags that after his army ser-vice, he threw up his job, learned another, school teaching, and went to live and work in his beloved Coniston. Then, on a cold February day in 1956, in a city hospital a hundred miles away from the hills, he died from a rare disease. Tragically, he was only 45 years of age. A few days later, the Tigers came back to Coniston, and we buried our old friend in the churchyard, not far from where the old hut stood, in the very shadow of the Coniston hills.

I will always remember my old school friend for his deceptively long stride across the fells, his stolidity and common sense on a rock-climb, and his ready smile when things were going wrong. He would be cheerful in a wet, draughty shack, with the fire out and the matches lost, and stuck on a climb together, with the issue very much in doubt, he would always be optimistic and philosophical. He must have introduced scores of people to the fells and the rocks, and his devotion to mountain huts, and everything to do with them, was quite remarkable.

In a way, Jack, with his tall, gangling figure, looked almost out of place in a house, but he seemed to fit into a hut all right. When we eventually gave up the Coniston hut Jack bought out all our shares, took over the beds, blankets, stoves and everything else and started looking round for another base. Eventually he found one, a derelict miner's cottage above Church Beck, and here he would spend his weekends and holidays, fitting up beds, shelves, stoves and tables so that he and his friends could sleep as high up the fells as possible. Many a time I've known him leave his comfortable home on a dark, wet night to trudge up the fellside with a load of food, wood or tools on his back for a solitary night in his two-roomed bothy in the fells.

But his real aim was to acquire a base really high up in the fells, as near the tops as possible. In time, he found what he wanted: the ruined shell of a stone hut, without a roof, above the old gunpowder hut in Cove Quarry, high up on Coniston Old Man. This he decided to make into a climbing hut for his friends and, in particular, for young people learning to love the fells. Its eventual completion, after his death, was, in a way, a memorial to a wonderful man and sincere lover of the fells.

He had some of us crawling about on the beams trying to fix up the roof, hauling wood and coal up the fellside, or struggling to shelve up collapsing walls. More than once, when gales had torn down the roof yet again, or the rains had flooded his little chest of valuables, we tried to persuade him to give up the idea, but he refused to be beaten by the elements or anything else. When other people were huddled over fires or sitting at the "pictures", Jack would be trudging up the Old Man to see whether the tarpaulin was still in position over the hole in the roof, or dragging sacks of coal up the fellside so that his friends might brew themselves a cup of tea during the coming weekend. And when he was not labouring at the hut, as likely as not he would be working out the number of new slates or laths he needed for the roof, or drawing pictures of what he hoped it would look like when it was finished.

It seems a long time since Jack and I compared notes about the Alps, longer still since I took him on his first rock-climb, and almost a long lifetime since we endured our first French lessons together, but it will never be easy to forget him. That crude building of Coniston slate, set among old spoil heaps and facing the great buttresses of the Dow Crag we both knew so well, should last out my lifetime. It will be a constant reminder of an old friend who loved the simple things of life, and taught scores of others to do the same.

And there are other reminders for me of my old friend – his many cairned paths about the fells. Jack was a great one for new tracks: discovering long-lost ways across the fells or working out new ones. One of his inventions was an ingenious track from just above Goats Hause to Levers Hause, thereby avoiding the trudge up the Old Man, and his cairns are there to this day. But his best new route on the fells (he was also involved in several new rock-climbs on Dow Crag and Gimmer) was his delightfully cairned, zigzag route up the Old Man from Boo Tarn, past Bursting Stone quarry, to the south ridge just below the summit. In his guidebook to the Southern Fells Alfred Wainwright described this route, enthusing about its "succession of fascinating and unexpected zigzags, making use of grassy terraces scented with thyme and tiny alpines". He then adds, "The man who worked out this delightful, well-graded and ingenious route clearly hated the sight of the big quarries. He deserved a medal."

Alf Wainwright, whom I knew well, never met Jack, did not know who had pioneered this route and I never told him. Now I am revealing the name of the originator of this splendid route for the first time. Jack took a long time working it out. In those days Bursting Stone quarry had not been reopened and was only a small hole. He and his wife, Peggy, then spent many weekends building the cairns, carefully placing them exactly where they were needed, and nowhere else. When they had finished the job he told me all about it, and then gave me a privately conducted tour up the route. I believe I was the first person to be told about this new way up the mountain, and the second, after the originator and his wife, to use the route. Since then, more than forty years ago, I have probably used the route on dozens of occasions, always preferring this quiet, usually-deserted way up the mountain to the ugly, stony tourist route through the old quarries. For me, this lovely way past Bursting Stone quarry, or "Brussen Staen" as they say in those parts, is always Jack Diamond's way up the Old Man, and the best way. I will always think of it as his special memorial in the Coniston fells he loved so well.

Two years later the Tigers were sadly mourning another of our little band who had been stricken down – again, far, far too early. The brilliant, immensely likeable Dave Birch, by far our best entertainer, died immediately from a heart attack in the street just after returning from a short holiday in Borrowdale. He was just fifty years of age, in his prime, you could have said, and he left Irene, his wife for 12 years, and his lovely nine-year-old daughter, Susan, to face their lives without him. David had given up rock-climbing when he married Irene, he didn't think the risk was fair to her, but they had both continued to enjoy the fells together, and he was always a regular attender at the annual dinners. His other big interest was in drama – naturally so, with his superb gifts for impressions and mimicry. He was highly regarded, at county level, as a drama producer and coach, and his funeral was attended by a large number of friends and admirers. In grammar school days together, although he was three forms ahead of me, we had both been very interested in classical music and good literature, and often met socially at each other's houses. As with Jack Diamond, I felt the sudden passing of my old friend David, so young and with so much, we thought, ahead of him, very deeply indeed.

Inevitably, with the loss of some of the original Tigers, the abandonment of the hut, and a declining interest in rock-climbing among some members, my own activities on the crags were now being shared with other mountain friends who lived closer to my Kendal home than the Barrow and Ulverston crowd. But the annual dinners of the Tigers, now usually held at the Old Dungeon Ghyll Hotel in Langdale, with our distinguished honorary member, Sid Cross, as host, continued for many years, and these kept us together.

Many of my post-war memories are of long, often exciting, days with Eric Arnison and George Spenceley – both, always, wonderful companions, in their different ways, on crag or fell and, often, in Eric's case, on skis. George and I were regular climbing partners for many years, especially after he moved from Penrith to Kendal. When we started seeking out first ascents he persuaded me to join the Yorkshire Ramblers Club, of which he was a prominent member, and in return I got him into the Fell and Rock. The idea, I seem to remember, was not so much that we were great club men, neither of us were, but that we could get our first ascents written up in two club journals instead of just one. Neither of us used the club huts very much, if at all, for we were within easy reach of the crags from our homes, but we both met many more interesting climbing people through our club membership.

Through George I got into potholing in a modest way. This was in the early days of carbide lamps and very heavy rope ladders, but down below I missed the fresh air and the sunshine. Certainly, potholing had its interests and excitements, but it was extremely hard work in those days, pushing and crawling with heavy equipment, and the climbing involved never seemed as neat or satisfying as on the crags. George and others took me down a few potholes, and then he announced one day that we were going to attempt the second descent of the Bar Pot entrance to Gaping Gill. It had first been descended a fortnight earlier and he was sure nobody else had been down.

It was all very exciting but very strenuous. Crawling in complete darkness, pushing or dragging heavy rope ladders, through passages only a foot or two in height, was hardly my idea of enjoyment. Eventually, we got down all right and explored many of the wonders of this enormous underground system. The trouble for me was getting up again, for I was not as skilful at climbing the rope ladders as the others. It is an acquired art to climb them with minimum effort when they are hanging clear for over 100 feet, as they do on the big pitch on this route, and I began to tire quickly. Near the top, when I reached a sort of ledge, I managed to get the safety rope tangled with my anorak, and then my acetylene lamp came apart and I was in complete darkness. Of course, I eventually got up all right, things are rarely as bad as they seem at the time, but I was certainly quite relieved when I saw the sky and the sunshine again. We did a few more holes over succeeding months and years, and I was glad I had sampled the sport, but I don't think my heart was really in it.

The Yorkshire Ramblers were a wonderful crowd of men, many of them also excellent climbers and mountaineers, and I used to enjoy the annual dinners. We had to attend in dinner jackets and famous mountain men usually provided the speeches. However, I realised I wasn't a two-club man and that potholing, however exciting, was not really my scene, so after a few years I resigned from the YRC and, eventually, George came out of the Fell and Rock. But many years later, when I was in my seventies, I went down a pothole again, in quite distinguished company: with Lord Hunt, formerly of Everest. We both happened to be guests at a National Park function at Whernside Manor, near Dent, then used as a potholing training centre. After the speeches and demonstrations, we were all given the choice of a walk over Whernside or a trip down a pothole. Being well familiar with the delights of Whernside I opted for the pothole and found myself with John Hunt, a couple of others, and an instructor who was to take us down the Long Churn entrance of Alum Pot.

Both Lord Hunt and I knew Alum Pot – we had each descended the main pot more than once, many years before – so that the Long Churn trip, a bit of a scramble down a waterfall, didn't present any problems. We had met several times in the past and had a most interesting chat, as we slid down the water, about many of the things that mountain folk discuss. I recall discovering, when we were discussing the longevity of some climbers, that Lord Hunt was just two or three months older than myself, but still remarkably fit and well preserved.

But George Spenceley and I, as a partnership, were much more into rock-climbing than potholing, and I must deal with those happy years in some detail. George has always complained that despite everything we did together, the only reference I had made about him in my many books had been an account of how the heavy skylight of the toilet at Glenbrittle Lodge in Skye had once, inexplicably, fallen on him while he was performing his morning operations. As a result, he had suddenly appeared at breakfast, moments after the enormous crash, with blood streaming down his head and face, and had to be cleaned up and bandaged later by the kindly and efficient Mrs MacRae. I'm afraid I thought this funnier than did poor George.

Many interesting climbs were done on that holiday with George in Skye but I mostly recall an ascent of the splendidly exposed White Slab route in Coir' a'Ghrunnda, largely because we did much of the route in company with a golden eagle. We were getting well up the climb when we heard a swishing sound and, looking down, saw a huge golden eagle almost brushing the face immediately below us. The bird looked absolutely enormous, we reckoned up to seven feet from wing-tip to wing-tip. We could study the dark, golden ridge along the leading edge of the great wings, see the long pinions, the folded claws and the head, with its powerful beak, sunk into its shoulders. Clearly, the eagle wasn't going to soar away quickly. He (or she) wanted to know exactly what we were doing on its crag. So it flew backwards and forwards, just a few feet below us, and, when we thought it would surely fly away, back it would come for another look, virtually accompanying us up the upper part of the route.

Neither of us had seen an eagle so closely before, nor for so long, but many years later I was coming down Coire na Creiche alone when I saw a golden eagle perched on a large boulder, just ahead of me. By standing perfectly still I was able to watch him for several minutes before he slowly took off, with a languid, disdainful sinking of his wings, into the higher part of the corrie.

In the Lake District, George and I climbed regularly, at the weekends, on most of the crags, but at one time concentrated on the eastern crags, mostly in and around Deepdale. We were inspired, perhaps, by the first ascents of Duckworth and Batty, and, earlier, by those of the Everest climber, Alf Gregory. An old mountaineer, William Allsup, a founder member of the Himalayan Club, who happened to live at the entrance to the dale, also encouraged us. He was always most interested in our adventures, insisting on hearing all about them over afternoon tea in his drawing room when we came down, and often studying our progress through binoculars.

George and I did some not very demanding new routes in the area, always leading through. The one we thought by far the best of the batch was Cofa Wall, a hard severe on the steep pillar of Black Crag in Deepdale. Unfortunately, the guide-writer, Harold Drasdo, could not identify it from our description. We were sorry that succeeding generations of climbers (we did the route on May 30, 1954) were thus denied the excitements of this climb for it had given us many anxious moments, including, I seem to remember, some fiddling, when in extremis, with pitons.

Some time before Cofa Wall, George had been given the job of writing up the new Fell and Rock Climbing Club's Eastern Crags climbing guide and, mainly because I had transport, I was enrolled as his assistant. For months we happily traipsed up and down old routes, measuring pitches with pieces of white tape tied on the rope at five-feet intervals, and then suddenly realised, with alarm, that young tigers were putting up new routes of startling severity all over the place. Just one of many shocks was when Donald Hopkin, stopping beside my garden gate on his way to the crags, cheerily informed me there were already nine new V.S.s on Raven Crag, Thirlmere. I then realised, with dismay, that this was part of our area.

Not regarding ourselves as anything approaching the leading climbers of the day, but rather as fairly knowledgeable potterers, we realised the only way we could tackle the guide would be by employing trained leaders to do the hard routes. But then an even more serious obstacle appeared on the scene. George was selected to go to South Georgia on one of Duncan Carse's expeditions, along with another old friend, Tom Price, and, among others, the great Scottish iceman, John Cunningham, whom I had met several times in the Cairngorms. When George eventually disappeared southwards towards the Antarctic a lot of new thinking had to be done, and, in the end, with considerable relief, I was able to hand over the climbing aspect of the guide to a far better man, the gifted Harold Drasdo.

Nevertheless, before that happened George and I had had our moments, sometimes in company with Eric Arnison, who always seemed to be around when odd things were happening. For example, we were always having excitements with loose rock. Once, on a very wet day in Dollywaggon Gully with, I seem to remember, Jack Carswell in attendance, large portions of its retaining walls peeled off during our ascent. We managed to escape relatively unscathed but wondered whether this scrappy ascent had been among the first since Lt. Colonel "Rusty" Westmorland had first discovered the route many generations earlier.

On another occasion, not concerned with the Eastern Crags guide, Eric Arnison had, inconsiderately, dropped a large rock on me in Newlands Gully on Miners' Crag. We were leading through at the time, and I didn't see it coming down, but it felt just like being crushed by a heavy sideboard. "Tie yourself on in case you faint," Eric shouted down helpfully, "and sit down for a bit." I was trying to follow his instructions when he dropped another lump of rock on me. I saw this one coming but, being a sitting bird, there was not much I could do about it, and he winged me, painfully, on the arm. Of course, such are the rigours of the game that I had to lead out the rest of the climb to steady my nerves.

Eric was also involved with me in some rock-juggling on Migraine, on Hutaple Crag in Deepdale. George was with us and it was my turn to lead. I was pedalling about in a little crack, not making much progress, so Eric climbed up and took a poorish belay just below me. Now feeling a little safer, I made my effort, reached up for the top of a jammed flake and the whole mass below it suddenly lurched outwards. Several things then happened very quickly. Eric reached up and pressed me on to the rock, just holding me in balance. I managed to hold the huge rock in place for a second or two with my knee, and George, who was still on the screes, was told to get himself and Eric's dog out of the way as quickly as possible. All this took about three seconds but it seemed like many minutes. At the end of it, when I was able to let the huge mass fall, a few tons of rock crashed to the screes. We discovered after explorations from above and below that I had so wrecked the pitch that it was now impossible. The route now goes to the left.

One of the "discoveries" that George and I made during our explorations of the eastern crags was the Dove Crag cave, high above Jim Haggas's appropriately named Hangover. Clearly, shepherds and, no doubt, some others knew of the place, but climbers and walkers were generally not aware of the cave at that time, and it had never been used as a bivouac, as it is nowadays. George and I often used to climb up there when we were in the area, to shelter from the rain or for a smoke. The outward view is sensational and George got into the habit of spending a night in the cave every now and again. He kept a little stove, some fuel and emergency food supplies up there in a tin box and, no doubt, had some interesting nights out, although he was never able to persuade me to share his experiences. Nowadays, there's a logbook in there to record your adventures, and somebody's built a low wall to deter somnambulists. If you walked only two or three yards in your sleep you would fall down the overhangs of Hangover on to the screes – and, of course, never wake up again.

While we were still supposed to be busy with the guide, George felt it necessary one day, for some strange reason, to check the already-excellent description of Hangover, and secured the services of a young tiger to do the leading. I felt no urge to attempt this overhanging cliff and my presence didn't seem necessary with George involved so I opted out, although agreeing to walk up to the foot of the climb with them. Having thus washed my hands of the whole affair, I then spent the previous day in helping an attempt by a very fit young mountaineer on the Bob Graham 42 peaks fell record, mainly by motoring pacers all over the Lake District. The attempt failed through bad weather, but that seemed no reason for cancelling the planned celebration, and we carried on, I'm ashamed to say, until the early morning hours.

The next morning, suffering as I was from my personal hangover, the screes below Dove Crag's Hangover seemed nearly vertical. I was not, however, allowed to wait at the foot of the climb as planned. Instead, despite all their promises, I was bullied into tying on. One little matter, right at the start, shattered my creaking confidence: the discovery of the largest and rustiest piton I have ever seen, something like a piece of railing. But the leader had more up-to-date ironmongery of his own and eventually they dragged me up the climb to the top. As I scrabbled about on the overhangs, I thought longingly of the comfortable grass ledge far below where I had planned to sleep and smoke. My hangover perhaps made the climb seem harder than it really is, but I certainly could not have led it that day. Nor have I led it since. The crux, I remember, seemed to demand neatness (in an off-balance situation) and strength in roughly equal proportions.

George Spenceley returned from his adventures in South Georgia and later went to the Himalayas with a Yorkshire Ramblers Club expedition during which the leader, Crosby Fox, had the misfortune to be killed. He was a friendly and determined mountaineer with whom we had both often climbed in the Lakes. Thereafter, George continued to seek out an active, indeed adventurous, life, travelling frequently to out-of-the-way places like Lapland and Ethiopia (this one with Eric Arnison), as well as canoeing down the Danube and, with Tom Price, on a remote lake in northern Canada. To accommodate his widening interests George embarked on a new career as a lecturer, and when we were last in touch, quite recently, he still seemed to be in popular demand for his varied, illustrated talks. He had always been an exceptionally good mountain photographer. Unfortunately, we now live too far apart for regular joint outings, but now and again we do meet up to chat about our very happy years together on the Lakeland crags or go for a walk in the fells.

It was with George that I first went to the Alps. I'm uncertain of the year, but it was a year or two after the war. All those dozens of years when I foolishly neglected to keep a mountain diary are now coming back to haunt me. I can't now remember, for instance, whether we went to the Alps before all our caperings on the eastern crags of Lakeland, or after them, but perhaps it doesn't matter. Another old climbing friend of mine, Ivan Waller, who has now, sadly, passed on, kept a mountain diary from his very first climbs in the 1920s until his very last outings with me, and could always produce exact dates for adventures long, long ago. I always admired his providence and engineer's attention to detail.

Anyway, George and I went to the Alps. We went across the Channel and then by train and bus into the heart of Switzerland, and for me it was all a tremendous adventure. George had been to the Alps before, with Eric Arnison, and knew the ropes – or some of them. Between us, we coped all right, although we didn't carry out anything like the programme we had in mind.

My first sight of the Alps, at dawn, with my head stuck out of the railway carriage window, excited me almost as much as the first sight of the Cuillin: vast, white shapes, just tipped with the gold of the sunrise, and unbelievably high. I couldn't wait to get up there. We planned to get the Matterhorn out of the way first, and then progress to better things, including the Weisshorn, Dent Blanche and perhaps one of the Mont Blanc routes. In the event, we did none of these things. First, we were told the Matterhorn was out of condition, with far too much snow, and had not yet been climbed that season. So we changed our plans, went to Zinal, which looked a convenient base, and set up our tent in a wood just above the village. From here we moved up to two or three huts in turn, crossed a couple of passes and, in rather changeable weather, did some modest peaks including the Trifthorn, Petit Dents de Veisivi, and Pointe Zinal. The next on our revised list was the Zinal Rothorn. We were, of course, climbing without guides.

By that time I was well accustomed to the exposure of vertical rock, and also of Scottish snow and ice climbs, but the exposure on the long snow arête of the Rothorn took my breath away. Smooth, steep, snow slopes seemed to fall away on either side for what looked like thousands of feet. It took some time to become accustomed to the scale, to steel myself to look down and not be afraid. Perhaps memories of my fall in Kashmir came back to haunt me. I remember George and I carefully rehearsed what we should each do in case of a slip from the near-knife-edge. If one of us slipped down one side of the arête, the other should immediately throw himself down the opposite side, and thus, with the rope taut between us, save us both. Fortunately, we had no need to try out these heroics and soon I began to enjoy the exposure.

Other little memories, tiny pictures really, of that first trip to the Alps nearly fifty years ago come flooding back as I sit over my word processor trying to remember what we did. Buying my first crampons, with long leather thongs, for instance, in some Alpine village and getting them fitted to my boots by, I seem to remember, a blacksmith. Then there was my first bergschrund; our first glacier together, and the crevasse rescue rehearsals; the rock-hard bread and the delightful snacks of jam mixed with snow. Particularly vivid are the memories of the early morning starts from the huts, with lanterns illuminating the frozen snows; and the vast, sunlit views from the summits of wave after wave of snow mountains reaching, all round, to the horizon.

In the huts we mostly lived on pemmican – we had both read all the Antarctic books – which, mixed in with the soup, wasn't too bad. This was before the days of special convenience foods for mountaineers. George had insisted we must cut down on weight so we had one small piece of soap to last the two of us for the whole fortnight. One morning, having a quick wash at our camp in the woods above Zinal, I foolishly placed the soap on a rock and a goat that had been hovering around us ate it in one gulp. So that was the end of our washing.

On this first, very modest, Alpine trip I found the rock-climbing easy; the moving together, roped, on mixed ground, a fascinating challenge; and glacier travel, exciting, but more skills needed to be learned on later visits. I also found the exposure of steep snow more difficult to accept, on this first visit, than the exposure of steep rock. My most evocative memory of this first trip to the Alps is of one evening at the Mountet Hut, where some German climbers were singing their mountain songs, in harmony, on the terrace outside. The lovely melodies were echoing across the frozen valley to the surrounding snow peaks and away up to the stars. The camaraderie of the heights came across very strongly that night. We were all climbers together, no matter what our nationality.

I returned to the Alps on many occasions: for climbing, for walking from hut to hut with Mollie, collecting modest summits as we went, and, often, for skiing. But that first trip with George, learning the scale of big mountains and the feel of steep snow and ice, was an important stage in my mountain career. It was the first time, for instance, that I had climbed with crampons. Earlier, in the Lakes and Scotland, we had relied on our nailed boots for climbing on ice or hard snow, cutting steps as required.

Coming down to earth and back to the Lake District, my old friend Eric Arnison lived only 25 miles away from me, near Penrith, so we continued to meet regularly. This pleasant arrangement carried on even when I had become elderly and he, being ten years older than me, could almost be described as "old". He certainly didn't look it, however, and in his eighties he still walked miles to his office every day. Two or three stories might help to flesh out the picture of my old friend. He once rang me up to say the retired town clerk of Penrith, Mr Bert Rayworth, thought he would like to go round the Mosedale Horseshoe, and Eric thought I should lead the expedition. It was important, said Eric, that we should have an early start so we stayed the previous night at Brackenclose, the Fell and Rock hut in Wasdale. Neither of us had thought of getting the key and we only gained entry, late at night, by getting an irate member out of bed – an indignity for which he has never forgiven us.

Despite our ages – both the retired town clerk and I were approaching seventy so Eric must have been nearly eighty – we got round the Horseshoe all right and finally reached the last summit, Yewbarrow, after the little scramble up Stirrup Crag. From here it was decided to make a beeline for the Wastwater Hotel down the steep, rough and untracked east face of the fell since our need for liquid refreshment, on a very hot day, was becoming urgent. I had been up and down this unattractive fellside on two or three previous occasions but the others had not been there before, and were stumbling on the rocks, skilfully concealed among the bracken and heather, for the first time. As we struggled down Eric realised we were wasting valuable time, with closing time approaching, and told me to run on ahead and get the beer lined up in readiness.

This I was able to do, after a quick pint or two before their arrival, and an excellent day ended enjoyably.

The point of the story is that the closing time about which Eric was so worried was after the lunchtime session, not the evening one. For Eric's day was not yet halfway through. He had suddenly remembered, he announced to our disgust, that he had promised to conduct several of his grandchildren along a very distant section of the Pennine Way, so he'd no time to hang about. And off he went for a long drive, and probably an even longer walk – his second of the day – along Yorkshire heights or the rolling Northern Pennines. Everything about Eric was unconventional or unexpected, that was his charm. Our geriatric round of the Mosedale Horseshoe, which might have taxed much younger pedestrians, was not enough for this old fellsman. As always, he wanted to make the most of his day.

Another odd adventure with Eric occurred on a trip to Ben Lomond. Although I had collected nearly 200 Munros by that time I had never been up Ben Lomond, the nearest Munro to my home, so my friend Ted Stacey, who will be introduced later, and I decided we would make the trip. At the last moment Eric said he would like to join in and would take us up there in his camper-van. We arrived at Rowardennan, at the foot of the mountain, all right, but then Eric, typically offbeat, announced he couldn't be bothered going up the Ben and would go fishing instead. Ted and I decided we would come down the untracked east face of the mountain and meet up with Eric, after his fishing, somewhere near Loch Ard. We fixed a time in the early evening, got out our maps, found a place called Teapot, a mile or two from the loch, and arranged to meet there. (Teapot, we discovered later, was a cottage formerly used by illicit whisky distillers. The first step, apparently, in negotiating a purchase of the stuff was to ask whether they could provide a cup of tea.)

Ted and I managed the ascent of the Ben by the tourist route easily enough, despite the great heat, and got down the steep, rough, untracked east face of the mountain all right. We were then completely nonplussed by the many square miles of the Queen Elizabeth Forest Park, not shown on either of our antiquated maps, into which we stumbled. But, by working east through the forest and after a few mistakes, we eventually reached civilisation, in the shape of Teapot and the main road. No sign of Eric and his van! This was fairly serious as the van contained our change of clothes and all our money, and it was now growing dark. We hung around for half an hour or so and then, since it seemed the only thing we could do, set off along the loch-side road to Aberfoyle, perhaps eight miles or so away. Somewhere along the road Eric's van loomed out of the darkness, coming from the opposite direction to the one expected, and several harsh words were said, each one blaming the other. We spent the night in the van with Eric's large dog, and awoke the next morning to another scorching day.

The suggestion from Ted Stacey over breakfast – bacon and eggs cooked by Eric in the van – that we should ascend some pointed peak in The Trossachs before driving home was greeted with scorn by me. Eric, who was equally against any form of exertion in the great heat, supported me. Instead, I suggested a cruise on Loch Lomond. I had seen notices at Balloch about a jubilee trip on one of the steamers and Eric thought this would be a splendid idea. "We can spend the whole voyage in the saloon, getting nicely pickled," he said with enthusiasm, although Ted thought it would be a sad waste of a good day. Anyway, we made the trip, accompanied by pipe bands, girl pipers, dancers and all the fun of the fair. We soon realised that with what seemed like civic receptions at every port of call up and down the lake, it was going to be a very long voyage. Long before we came ashore at Balloch, at last, we had had more than enough of Loch Lomond and eightsome reels, and even the long journey home in the darkness presented unexpected problems.

We all thought we knew Scotland pretty well, but with our antiquated maps, none of them showing motorways, we made a ridiculous job of driving south from Balloch. Eric, whose map was even older than my 1940s issue, would drive one way, I would tell him he was on the wrong road, and Ted would argue that neither of us was right. In the end, we made it, but the balls-up was a fitting conclusion to an unusual weekend.

I remember, too, an unusual evening with Eric. He had heard that a local, well-to-do farmer had his own aeroplane, and although he did not know the farmer, Eric had the nerve to ring him up and ask whether he would take him and a friend (me) for a flight over the Lake District. His excuse was that his friend (me) wanted to view the Lakeland "three-thousanders" round from the air. It was a wonderful flight, with me acting as navigator. This was an easy job with the familiar lakes, fells and crags laid out below us, exactly like the relief map of the Lake District on the wall of my study. We first flew over Skiddaw, then the Scafells and finally over the Helvellyn range, surprisingly seeing not one person on any of the summits around which we slowly circled at what seemed about fifty feet above the cairns. I recall two principal impressions of that most interesting flight. Firstly, the deeply scored tracks across most of the fells. The second revelation was the way the big crags, including Scafell Crag, Pillar Rock and Gimmer Crag, seemed, from the plane, to lean back from the vertical and to be nowhere near as steep as they feel when climbing them.

We flew down the whole length of Ullswater at the end of the flight, just above a lone water-skier making his last run of the evening, with the white wake reaching behind him. It was also the very last time that any water-skier has skied on Ullswater, the final day for power-boats on this lake, so those interested can check the date of our flight over the Lakes. The kindly farmer, who had gone to considerable trouble and expense to accommodate two people he had never met before, was Mr Brian Berry of Great Strickland near Penrith. He refused any payment for providing us with a really memorable evening.

But I must leave the Lakes for a while and return to Scotland. This has been my second home, in a way, for more than sixty years, ever since that first visit to Skye in 1935 and, two years later, my honeymoon with Mollie in Aviemore and the Cairngorms.

Ullswater from the
north-east ridge of
St Sunday Crag

Helvellyn in the Snow

The polished black ice of Red Tarn, glinting in the morning sunshine, mirrored the gullies and snow slopes sweeping up to the Helvellyn summit ridge. Overhead, an unseen jet aircraft silently traced a vapour trail across cloudless skies and the reflection lay like a golden pathway across the ice. A rare day for winter mountaineering in Lakeland with hard, frozen snows, the whole corrie, except for the shadowed snow wall below the ridge, flooded in sunlight, and not enough wind to blow out a match. Out of the sun, on the snow wall, rearing to the vertical below the cornice, the snow was polished and rock-hard, perfect for our axes and crampons, making the climb a measured delight. At our backs, far below, Patterdale drowsed in the sunshine, beyond, the mountain wall of High Street, was bare of even a handkerchief of snow. And eastwards, to the Pennines, there was not one sign of winter. Yet here, in front of our noses, snow several feet thick, and when we reached the summit ridge we could see east-facing snow slopes on the Scafells. Tiny specks of people crept along the rocky roof-trees of Striding and Swirrel Edges that enclose the corrie and now and again we could hear their voices. Several hundred feet below us we watched little figures cautiously walk out on to the ice on the tarn, hesitate, and walk back. A pair of ravens tumbled, in daring acrobatics, above the black crags and a group of youngsters on a mountain course, in brightly coloured anoraks, picked their way down the first icy steps from the summit. The snow cornice, just below the survey pillar, was split by a huge crevasse: when the thaw came all these tons of snow would avalanche down the face. But today, with the frozen snow ideal for our crampons, we climbed easily up the wall and over the cornice, stepping out of the dark shadows into blinding sunlight and views across half of Lakeland.

January 1969

Chapter Eleven

Scottish Stravaiging

The Highlands of Scotland, especially the north-west corner, are the finest part of Britain for grandeur, unspoiled beauty and the promise of adventure. This is the opinion of most mountaineers, although for me the whole country, excluding the industrial belt, has always had an almost magical appeal. Although I live only an hour's drive from the Border, and have crossed it scores of times in the last sixty years, this first step into Scotland is always an exciting moment. And it's not only the mountain scene – the snow-bound hills, the lonely crags, ancient forests and rushing torrents – that unfailingly attracts: it is also the sad, wild history of the land, the battles, the heroes, the legends and the songs that are so fascinating. Here, indeed, among the biggest and most rugged mountains in Britain, is a land for adventurers and poets.

Often the beauty has been breathtaking: half of Scotland seen in a glance from some rocky pinnacle high above a deserted glen; sunlit snows reaching down to shadowed crags; the northern hills rising like ancient obelisks from watery plains; or the magic of dawn from hills on the edge of the sea, the horizon crowded with islands. Or it might be sunset by a quiet loch, the water a pool of flaming gold, the Scots firs above the farther shore black against the sky, and the snows, very high and far beyond the glen, rimmed with fire. There are places beyond the Grey Corries, the Fannichs or the Rough Bounds, remote corners in the purple hills around Loch Carron perhaps or above the lochs reaching out to the Atlantic, with nothing moving and nobody about, where the beauty, the loneliness and the quietude can be so overpowering as to bring a man to search his soul.

Much of my early exploration of the Scottish hills, following the pre-war visits to Skye, Arran and the Cairngorms, was done on family holidays, especially with our son, Robin, who'd already had plenty of early training in the Lake District. Sandra, our daughter, had walked up Catbells at two and a half, refusing to be carried, but Robin had led his grandfather, who had never been up the mountain before, on an ascent of Coniston Old Man at five and a half years of age. The young guide already knew the way quite well. Two years later I took Robin on his first rock-climb, Middlefell Buttress in Langdale, but he complained afterwards that the holds were "too far apart". Mollie rightly argued that I was pushing the boy too much, so I told Robin I wouldn't take him climbing again until he asked me to do so. This he did when he was twelve years old and, thereafter, we climbed regularly together.

In Scotland, as a family, we sometimes camped, occasionally used hotels, and often stayed in guesthouses, caravans, huts, farms, or bed and breakfast places. But mostly in the early days we used youth hostels, which, so far as comfort and amenities were concerned, could hardly have been more diverse. On our first visit to the one in Glen Nevis – although I'm sure things have changed since then – we were disconcerted to find a man sitting on the front step eating fish out of a bucket. Yet at Garth youth hostel near Fortingall there was a beautifully furnished quiet room where the facilities included a Steinway grand piano on which I was able to enjoy myself, undisturbed, in the evenings.

I remember, with particular affection, one of the first of the youth hostels we used, a small, rough building on the beach at Inver Alligin in Torridon. It closed down, fell down or was pulled down many years ago. We arrived there in some disarray, pots and pans dangling from Robin's rucksack, to see wet socks hanging over soup simmering on a blackened stove, and a rough-ish-looking bearded man sitting on the floor, in semi-darkness, cooking sausages on a Primus. There was no fuel, but we managed to scratch some earthy bits of coal out of the ground where the heap had been. The entrance to the women's dormitory was by way of a rickety ladder. Mollie took one look at the place and announced she wouldn't be seen dead in such a howff, but there seemed nowhere else to go. In the event, we had a very happy holiday there, once we had grown accustomed to the conditions, for the company was the friendliest imaginable.

One day I foolishly agreed with the bearded man to drive his motorcycle to the eastern end of Liathach so that he could do the west to east traverse of the mountain. Meanwhile, Robin and I, leaving our car at the western end, would do the traverse in the opposite direction. As usual, it was pouring with rain. Many of our early Scottish visits, taken, perforce, in the often-wet school holiday weeks, were beset by awful weather. The road from Torridon to Kinlochewe in those days was little better than the bottom of a riverbed, I hadn't ridden a motorcycle for many years and I had to drive with Robin on the pillion. It was, therefore, with some relief when we were finally able to take to the steep slopes of the mountain, although the cloud was down to about 500 feet and remained so all day. And I had lost my compass.

In those days there were no mountain shops in Fort William, or anywhere else that I knew of, where I could have bought one. Robin produced a tiny Boy Scout's compass I had once found at the top of Walker's Gully on Pillar Rock and given to him, and we had to make do with that. We managed to find a steepish scree gully leading in the right direction and eventually, despite the thick cloud and driving rain, reached the first summit. Thereafter, we traversed west along the whole ridge, including the Fasarinen Pinnacles, which we carefully climbed, up and down each one. Nowadays, I believe a track avoids the actual pinnacles, but we didn't see any tracks anywhere on the mountain that day. Nor did we see the bearded man on his traverse in the opposite direction, although with visibility reduced to a yard or two, this was understandable.

Problems began when we reached the west end of the ridge, where it broadens into a shoulder. Here the compass, which up to that point had served us well enough, began playing tricks, the needle pointing to any direction when we turned it round. As a result, the next two or three hours turned into something of an epic. However, we eventually managed, in the appalling conditions, to feel our way down to Coire Mhic Nobuil, remembering the lie of the land from our now-sodden map, and stagger, like drowned rats, down the then-trackless corrie. We were drenched to the skin, our boots full of water through wading, knee-deep, the burns that seemed to be everywhere, and the river itself was in furious spate – an exciting sight had we been in the mood to enjoy it. Down on the road at last I sent Robin on to the hostel, and then squelched the mile or two back to the car. On the way, miserably wet through and dripping with water, I met the Torridon postman. "Nice drop of rain," he said, but I hadn't the strength to argue.

And there were many, many other wet days during these early Scottish holidays, one of the worst of them being reserved for a traverse of that splendid mountain, An Teallach. That morning I had taken the precaution of ringing up the baronet who owned the hill to enquire whether he would be deer stalking that day. Consequently, I was wet through before we started from the 50-yard walk to the telephone kiosk from what was then the Dundonnell Youth Hostel. He told me that stalking was out of the question in those conditions, that fell walking would be extremely foolhardy and that many people had come to grief on the mountain, even in good weather. He urged that we should abandon our plan and come back the next year, in May. In turn, I argued that we were very experienced mountaineers, a long way from the truth. After a while, sensing our determination, he finally gave his permission and his blessing, after asking us to do as little shouting and banging on tins as possible, so as not to disturb the deer.

We traversed the hill in the drenching rain but, as with so many of our ascents in those dimly-remembered summer days, saw almost nothing of the mountain, not even the famed Loch Toll an Lochain, although we later stood on its shore. On the lower slopes, when we eventually emerged from the cloud, the water slurping over our boot tops at nearly every step, we saw about fifty of Sir Michael's deer but, as requested, passed them without making a sound, apart from the squeaks and squeals from our squelching boots.

A year or two later Robin and I, from a tent by the shore of Little Loch Broom, traversed the mountain again, in brilliant weather, and this time collected all ten of its summits, including the outliers. At the end of the traverse, having viewed much of the Northern Highlands from the tops, we slithered down a scree gully to the scenic mountain lochan we were seeing for the first time. We then trotted across a thyme-scented hillside to enjoy a fried Angus steak outside the tent on the loch shore.

One year, during a wet family holiday in a cottage at Lochinver, we wanted to collect Suilven. We had not yet even seen it because of the thick cloud, but, as we discovered later, it was the most prominent feature of the countryside for miles around. Using map and compass – we must have acquired a new one by then – we were able to set off, in the usual rain, in the right direction, but encountered considerable difficulty in negotiating a way through what seemed like dozens of small lochans. We never found any track but had to take compass bearings on identifiable features on the far side of each lochan in order to keep the right direction. In the end we bumped, almost literally, into the cliffs of Caisteal Liath (The Grey Castle), so our compass work must have been competent enough. We then scrambled up steep heather and scree to the summit ridge. The top is supposed to be one of the best viewpoints in Scotland but all I could see from it was my son, standing about three feet away, with the rain streaming down his face and bubbling out of his boots.

Our first visit to the bristling porcupine of An Stac was also on a day completely without views; just cloud, depressing rain and streaming rock. This was years before the car park had been established at its foot and the eroded tracks to the summit ridge kicked out. We had to take a compass bearing for the top from what looked like the foot of the mountain (usually the spiky ridge is very obvious from below) and just walk up. On the ridge, we now and again bumped into an interesting rock pinnacle, but that was all. It wasn't until later visits that we discovered the superb views from the top and the splendid rock architecture, with so much scope for the climber.

Occasionally, of course, during these weeks of miserable weather and interminable bog-trotting, there was the consolation of a clear, sunny day. I particularly recall one perfect afternoon. We had set off, in the usual heavy downpour and thick mist, to explore the Ben More Coigach group and had reached, with the aid of the compass, the top of Beinn nan Caorach, when, almost miraculously, the rain stopped and the clouds began to lift. Pressing on quickly, in case the clouds came down again, we reached the top of the remarkable summit of Sgurr an Fhidleir, with its 700-feet precipice. From it we saw An Stac and, beyond it, Suilven, peaks we had climbed but never seen. And beyond these summits we saw some of the most northerly mountains in Scotland, scores of lochans, now glistening in the new sunshine, and a wild, lovely countryside.

With growing excitement, our wet clothes now steaming in the sunshine, we hurried on to Ben More Coigach and then along the rocky ridge to the last peak overlooking the bay. And there was the view that made the whole holiday worthwhile. Far below, sparkling in the evening sun and seemingly so close we felt we could have dropped a stone into the depths, was the deep, blue sea. The waves were breaking white on a dozen yellow, sandy beaches fringed with grey-brown rocks, and the sea birds were wheeling and screaming over the tide. Just off the coast, like ships at anchor, lay the magical Summer Isles, while across the sea we could pick out the Outer Hebrides and, far to the south, the dark turrets of An Teallach.

Year after year we returned to places all over the Highlands for these and kindred delights, sometimes in disappointing weather, but often enjoying wonderful, sunny days. Apart from some modest routes on Ben Nevis and in Glencoe, several of the better-known rock-climbs in Skye, and a certain amount of adventurous scrambling, we didn't do a great deal of climbing but tried to seek out the best and biggest hills. Sometimes, especially in later years, Mollie and I were on our own, often using the same large, comfortable caravan at Glencoe, or renting cottages at Tyndrum, Killin or, much further north, at Ullapool. I remember the two of us once traversing the Ben Cruachan ridge when the temperature was well into the eighties – the hottest day in Glasgow for a century, said the newspapers. Yet we were able to kick steps in old, hard snow up to the summits and glissade down steep drifts several hundred yards long. That was the day when, returning to our parked, open car on the Pass of Brander, we found it was only possible to use the seats, blistering hot from the sun, by sitting on our rucksacks. And, in this way, we drove down to the pub at Taynuilt. It was a Sunday and they had only a six-day licence then so we had to persuade them that having been over the Cruachan peaks we were, indeed, bona fide travellers and, therefore, entitled to a drink.

An early ascent of Ben Lawers when the children were youngsters had its special difficulties. Sandra was very young then, only a few years old, and firmly against the idea of climbing any mountain, let alone one nearly 4000 feet high. But we discovered that the promise of a slide on an old cape down the patches of snow that liberally covered the mountain could encourage her to scramble higher and higher. She would slide down a snow patch, refuse to go any further, and insist on spending the rest of the day there, sliding down the same patch. But then I would point out an even better snow slope higher up and she would be persuaded to make for that. Another slide down, another refusal to go higher, and the process would be repeated, with several slides down each succeeding snow patch. In this way we eventually got her to the summit, in the process probably climbing the mountain twice over.

Apart from the problems during the children's school holidays of frequent wet weather or the mountains taken over by the deer-stalkers, there was also, often, the midge menace. At that time I was a pipe smoker, more or less enshrouded in smoke when on the hill, so that, mostly, the midges avoided me, but others found them an abomination. We were once camping at Kinlochewe when the midges were the worst we could remember, millions of them regularly emerging in clouds out of the bracken and heather to make life pretty well unbearable. One man camping near us seemed to be having a particularly bad time. We would often see him running around, jumping up and down, shouting, swearing and waving his arms about, while swathed in towels and sweaters, and showing all the signs of advanced madness.

To try to escape the midge hordes the four of us went up Slioch one very warm day. At the end of the walk, back again at the foot of the hill, we had to go through a particularly vicious belt of bracken, as tall as ourselves, in which the midges were lying in wait in their millions. As a result, freely perspiring as we were, we got back to the camp covered in the things, and wondered how on earth we were going to make a meal. On this visit I was sleeping in the car, Mollie and Sandra in a small tent and Robin in his own, even smaller and very dilapidated bit of canvas. When I scurried inside my vehicle to escape the pests I couldn't see out of the windows, they were so thickly covered by the creatures, and in blindly trying to manoeuvre the car, managed to drive over the cooking utensils, squashing them flat. This seemed the final straw, driving all thoughts of cooking out of our heads. Without a word, dishevelled as we were, we all trooped into the Kinlochewe Hotel for dinner. This area, we later decided, was the worst for midges in Scotland.

Gradually, but without making an issue of it, we were working through the Munros, but, lacking the required single-minded ambition, and also the energy, I never completed their collection. To date I've done about 200, with many Munro tops, but am now unlikely to complete my list, and not sufficiently interested to try to do so. I remember accompanying Ivan Waller, a bit older than me, on the collection of his penultimate Munro (Mullach Coire Mhic Fhearchair in the "Whitbread Wilderness") in 1980. We were staying in Cannich with our wives – the Wallers in his "caravette", we in a tin hut – so it was quite a long drive to Loch a'Bhraoin, near the Destitution Road, where I parked the car.

It was a very wet day with low cloud, so we saw very little and were wet through for most of the time. After the long trudge beyond the loch we tiptoed up the great, grey slabs of Sgurr Ban and then swarmed over the rock towers of the Mullach on to the summit. Here, in the mist, we had a disagreement about the right way down and parted company, although there was a sort of arrangement to try to meet at a rough bothy we had noted on the way up. This we managed to achieve, although we took widely different routes, and then squelched on together back to the car. Here, we had to make a complete change of clothing, for we were drenched to the skin. The trip ended convivially at the Altguish Inn.

Most outings with Ivan ended convivially. One day, some years after he had done all the Munros, he and a friend went up Stob Dearg on Buchaille Etive Mor in Glencoe. Back down at the Kingshouse Inn Ivan happened to say, since he was then getting on a bit, "Well, that's my last Munro." Overhearing the remark, and thinking that the old gentleman had just polished off his Munros that day, a man at the bar insisted on purchasing what turned out to be a succession of many glasses of malt whisky for him and his friend. Ivan, seeing no reason to explain, accepted the man's generosity with gratitude, and the evening proved such a success that his friend had to be carried back to the car in glorious delirium.

Many memories of hundreds of mountain days in Scotland have survived the years: the Glencoe peaks, shrouded in late spring snow, with Mollie, and merry evenings afterwards at the Clachaig Inn; happy days on Ben Nevis, with all the family – when Sandra wasn't grumbling or yelling; collecting the Glen Shiel Munros with Robin; and long walks over the tops in Glens Affric, Cannich and Strath Farrar. Often, especially in later years, I went on my own into the hills, although Mollie would sometimes go part of the way, return to the car or tent, and, at a prearranged time, have refreshment awaiting my return. On one poor day I went off on my own to collect the four Munros in Strath Farrar. After completing the traverse in heavy rain, when swollen burns had to be waded, I came down further up the glen, with five miles of road walking remaining. On the way back a man in a car, an unusual sight in that glen, offered me a lift, but I felt far too drenched to accept. I asked him, however, to let Mollie, waiting in our car a few miles further on, know that I was down off the hill and on my way. Getting back into dry clothes in the deluge was, I recall, quite a feat.

Every year, sometimes two or three times a year, we walked, scrambled and climbed all over the Highlands – from the Arrochar "Alps" to the lonely peaks in the far north, from the Rough Bounds of Knoydart to the Cairngorms, from Mam Soul to the Mamores. The only important areas we failed to explore were the Ben Alder country and some of the most northerly hills. One year, from the youth hostel in Glen Clova, Tom Price and I walked to Lochnagar and back. I thought it would be too demanding for Robin, who was quite young then, so we left him behind, but I think he would have coped all right. At that time, and no doubt still today, Tom was addicted to hard living in the hills, rough mountain howffs being his ideal type of accommodation. He was then living, in rather cramped conditions in a small car already crowded with gear, and I had the greatest difficulty in persuading him to share the luxuries of Glen Clova youth hostel with me.

Early next morning, Tom woke me up and suggested I took a look at the foot of my bed. To my astonishment, a large owl, looking rather ferocious at that time in the morning, was perched there. Neither of us felt much like going back to sleep in the circumstances, so we spent the next half-hour, often, we thought, in some danger, trying to get the bird out of the window. Exhausted by our efforts, Tom swore that that was the last time he would use youth hostels. In future, he said, he would stick to howffs or his car, where at least he could get a decent night's sleep.

Another time I bumped into an old friend, Neil Mather, who was camping with a Munro-bagging party at Shiel Bridge. Among them was Jimmy Dawson, a remarkably sprightly retired surgeon, who, after he had inspected my grievously deformed toes, immediately suggested he should amputate their ends – not then, but on a mutually acceptable date and without any cost to me. He was very persuasive but I was able to put him off, although I have since wondered whether I did the right thing in hanging on to my funny toes. The next day we all went up a succession of Munros to the north of Glen Cluanie, including Sgurr nan Conbhairean, racing up them as if we were competing in the Grasmere guides' race. After we had completed half a dozen summits Jimmy, stripped to the waist, had to be dissuaded from going on and adding several more. I clearly remember him pointing longingly to distant ranges, urging that they should be included.

Eventually, we all ran down from the last mountain – dawdling was not allowed – and, after a most energetic day, trooped into the Cluanie Inn for our well-deserved pints. When they got back to their tents, Neil, who was in training for the Lake District Mountain Trial, insisted on going for a run around the hills in his trainers. He needed the exercise, he said.

On another holiday in the Glen Shiel area, I remember having a wonderful day with Robin on the Forcan ridge of The Saddle, which was covered with just enough snow and ice to make it interesting, without being too awkward. Near the top we came upon a lone walker in some trouble and had to rope him down.

As the children grew older we seemed to experience much better weather for our Scottish visits; perhaps we were getting away from the usually wet school holiday weeks. I can remember long, sunny days in Glen Affric on the Mam Soul-Carn Eighe round, the Torridons, the Strath Carron hills, the Fannichs and the lonely heights of the Beinn Dearg range, reaching out to the remote outlier of Seana Braigh. Dimly remembered in old age, these mostly seemed dry, sunny days with contented strolls down long, shadowed glens in the evening. Indeed, my memories of the misty isle of Skye, more than sixty years of them, are rarely of cloud and rain, but mostly of dry, sun-warmed rocks, airy ridges with views across the sea to far horizons, and quiet corries, with nobody about, and the only sound, the splash and gurgle of mountain burns. Skye may not be like that today but that is my memory of these most delectable mountains.

Every year when the children were young we went to either Arran or Skye, and came to know both islands, and especially the hills, fairly intimately. In Arran we stayed in many different places around the coast, collected all the hills, and did a bit of climbing and plenty of scrambling. One day Robin hired a bicycle and rode all round the island while I took the others up Goatfell. Arran has always seemed to me a particularly friendly island, so easy to visit, with its delightful sea crossing, from our home in Cumbria. Its mountains are almost as enjoyable, although with different rock, as the spectacular peaks of Skye. I was last there in my eighties, revisiting the once-familiar granite ridges, treading the delightful glens of Rosa and Sannox again, and glorying in the wealth of spring flowers – just before the midge season!

But Skye, for several years, really became our home from home. We always stayed with the McRaes at the Lodge in Glenbrittle and came to know several generations of the family quite well. Through the MacRaes we met Dame Flora McLeod of Dunvegan Castle. Another acquaintance was Gavin Maxwell, long before he became famous through his *Ring of Bright Water* and other successful books. He was trying to establish a shark fishery on the island of Soay, just off Skye, at the time. He once took us far out in the bay in his boat, pointing out what he described as killer whales in the distance. But most of our sea trips were with Ron Macdonald, the Skye boatman, in his leaky old boat, overladen nearly down to the gunwales, with no life-saving equipment, and many maritime regulations breached or disregarded. You took your life in your hands when you went to sea with Ron, but he was always good company and we usually came back with plenty of fish. Once or twice he took us across the Sound to the Isle of Rhum, just giving us enough time to scramble up some of the rocky peaks – very like the Skye Cuillin – and then trot down to the boat on the loch shore.

One year my brother Leslie and I decided to have an April rock-climbing holiday in Skye. The Lakeland hills were clear of snow after a good winter of skiing and climbing so, stupidly, we never thought of taking our ice axes. But when we arrived in Glen Brittle we found the hills draped in snow and ice: perfect winter conditions. We couldn't get hold of axes in the glen and I think that holiday was the most frustrating I have ever had. All the crags were glazed in ice and several attempts to get on to the ridge proved hopeless; without axes or crampons the ice and hard snow defeated us every time. I remember one attempt on Sgurr Dearg that failed only a couple of hundred feet from the top. We even resorted, that day, to hacking out footholds with bits of sharp rock. One day we managed to get up Bruach na Frithe, almost like an alpine climb, but that was all. In desperation we crawled round the coast, explored some of the corries and pottered about the Quirang. One notable feature of that holiday was the fierce strength of the wind that battered us every day. There was never a hint of sunshine all week but we got home brown as berries – burned by the wind.

Robin and I came to know the Cuillin hills quite well. One memorable day was when we did the Clach Glas-Blaven traverse together. It was wonderful scrambling on perfect rock and from the summit there was a superb view of the whole, long line of the Cuillin Ridge. There were also great days on the round of Coire Lagan, "doing the Dubhs" or swarming up and down the Pinnacle Ridge of Sgurr nam Gillean. On one visit, when Robin was 18 or 19 years of age, we decided to attempt the traverse of the main ridge. My old Coniston Tigers friend, Jack Diamond, had died three years earlier, and I remembered he had once made a gallant solo attempt on the ridge on a very hot day. He had got as far as the Bhasteir Tooth, but had then become so dehydrated that he had had to abandon the walk and escape down Fionn Choire, practically on his hands and knees, with his tongue hanging out. Perhaps our attempt was in his memory.

It was a dry, sunny week in September and we were able to use the fine days before our attempt in checking up on those parts of the ridge with which we were not fully familiar. These were, I seem to remember, around Sgurr Dubh na Da Bheinn, and on the triple peaks of Bidean Druim nan Ramh which, if not taken in the right order, can cause delays. We also cached bottles of water along the ridge but only two of our planned three caches succeeded: the bottle intended for Bidean Druim nan Ramh, filled at the last spring in Coire na Creiche, burst in Robin's rucksack on the way up and ruined most of the contents. In hot, dry weather it is desirable to cache water for the traverse as the only supply is from the spring in Coire na Creiche, some hundreds of feet below the ridge. An alternative might be to take tubes or straws for sucking up water caught in crevices among the rocks.

On the day before our attempt I drove the car to Sligachan and left it there, against our return. In the evening, after dinner, we left for the walk along the coast to the foot of Gars-bheinn, intending to camp at its foot so as to cut down the night walking and be able to leave the first summit at dawn. But this, as it turned out, was a poor arrangement. It would have been far better to have had a decent sleep at Glen Brittle and then to have walked unencumbered round the coast and up the mountain. In addition to the tent we carried sleeping bags, cooking stove, food and a decrepit alarm clock that had no glass front, only one finger and a reputation for unreliability. As a result, after carrying it gingerly round the coast, neither of us dared to go to sleep after we'd pitched the tent and swallowed a bite of food. In fact, we only dozed off about five minutes before the alarm went off at 3.30am.

The ascent of the "perpendicular" screes of Gars-bheinn at night, and this was a particularly black night, "is a realistic foretaste", according to the late, great Scottish mountaineer, W.H. Murray, "of what awaits climbers in another world". And as we clawed at the sliding screes with our hands, while holding the torches in our mouths, I was reminded of the remark of another famous climber, H.W. Tilman, when similarly struggling on a Himalayan peak, "Thank God, at least we're holding our own." We each had two cheap, disposable torches, and these just about got us to the summit, but it was an experience I would not care to repeat and by far the worst part of the whole trip. Indeed, we both reached our first summit, with another nineteen to climb or thirty-one separate pinnacles and tops, completely exhausted. Fortunately, our condition rapidly improved as we went along, and the only other time I felt tired was during the toe-grinding descent of the screes of Coire a' Bhasteir at the end of the day, when we had finished the ridge.

Memories of that wonderful day forty years ago are easy to

recall. I remember that as we sat on top of Gars-bheinn, recovering from the ascent of those awful screes, and waiting for the new day, the surrounding peaks were still only shadowed, black precipices and the islands, far below, just vague shapes floating in a grey sea. It was not yet dawn but light enough to see without the now-useless torches so, after a rest and a bite of food, we set off, at the trot, for the long, exciting procession of rock peaks that lay ahead. Eventually, at just ten minutes to seven, when we had gone some way along the ridge, the sun that had been slowly creeping up behind the distant peak of Blaven suddenly flooded the grey, misty world with sparkling light and dancing shadows. We could now clearly see the whole line of the Outer Hebrides, far out on the horizon, like great ships at anchor; and the ridge ahead, the peaks and towers now glowing in the sunshine, looked friendly, almost smiling on our endeavour. And so it remained for the rest of the day – unbroken sunshine, cloudless blue skies and little or no wind. We could not have had a more perfect day.

As a result, everything went well and there were no difficulties, either with the route or with the climbing. The Thearlaich-Dubh gap was easily tackled with a quick abseil and then the scramble up the other side on dry holds for the first time in several crossings. We hadn't even bothered to rope up for this first problem, feeling very fit by then, and both knowing the route quite well. The slightly awkward slabs down to the foot of Sgurr Mhic Coinnich, however, needed care, unroped. I have to confess that to save time and to avoid roping up we avoided King's Chimney, which we knew, and went up by Collie's Ledge, new to both of us, which proved a pleasant, delightfully exposed scramble. The magnificent round of Coire Lagan finished with the toil up An Stac and the ascent of the Inaccessible Pinnacle by the longer, eastern ridge.

And there we had a pleasant, even exciting, surprise. I was fixing the rope round the big, perched boulder on the Inaccessible for the abseil down the short side when I saw a man sitting on top of Sgurr Dearg. This was, to say the least, unusual so early in the morning, but the surprise came when he addressed me by name. I then saw that he was John Jackson, director of the Plas y Brenin mountain centre in North Wales, who had been a member of the successful British expedition to Kangchenjunga four years earlier. I knew him slightly but had no idea he was in the country, let alone on the same ridge in Skye. He had been camping in the glen, had heard we were making an attempt on the ridge – how, I never found out, for we had tried to keep it quiet – and, forgoing his breakfast, had decided to come up to see if we needed any help or encouragement. When he saw we were well provisioned, not needing anything, he grabbed our rope and rucksack and led us, at great speed, over the several summits of Sgurr na Banachdich before trotting down to the glen to make his breakfast.

Our acceptance of this friendly assistance, together with the avoidance of King's Chimney, might well invalidate our round as a really genuine performance, but no matter. Furthermore, John took some of our useless kit and the news that we were at least one hour ahead of schedule down to Mollie at the Lodge, leaving there for us, against our return, two bottles of beer. It was, altogether, a kindly and most generous gesture. We enjoyed the unexpected meeting and the talk, but John was the only person we saw from leaving the Lodge the previous evening to our arrival, nearly a day later, at Sligachan. Indeed, the only other encounters with living creatures were with a friendly dotterel walking about on the top of Sgurr Mhic Coinnich and a mountain hare sitting in a little chimney on the western ridge of Sgurr nan Gillean. Both gave the impression they had never met human beings before, the mountain hare, in particular, studying me for about two minutes, when two feet away from my face, before disappearing into a hole at the back of the chimney.

Our schedule had been based on Murray's timings when he did the ridge with Blaven and Clach Glas, which I had extracted from one of his books and adjusted to take into account several stops and possible complications, such as losing the way or twisting an ankle. In fact, we were moving so quickly, trotting along in the easy places, that we were even further ahead of our schedule at the Bhasteir Tooth, but lost some time there by, inexplicably, getting off route for a while. Robin and I had done Naismith's Route only two days earlier when the holds had been coated in slime, and our time-wasting on this second ascent, when the rock was perfectly dry, can only be ascribed to tiredness, which neither of us felt, or, more likely, to the swig of whisky I had taken on Bruach na Frithe. The whisky flask, in case of emergencies, the map, the compass and the rope (120 feet of it, full-weight, since I hadn't a shorter length) was my only load. Robin carried the rucksack, with the food, the torches, the slings, the Kendal Mint Cake, the raisins and the spare sweaters. Looking back on it all we took far too much food. Most of it we left for the gulls on Bruach na Frithe after Robin had carried it for five-sixths of the way. Water, raisins, mint cake and glucose tablets seemed to be all we needed.

After a leisurely sprawl in the sunshine on top of our final summit, Sgurr nan Gillean, we descended by the way we had gone up, the Western Ridge, and then carried on down the Coire a' Bhasteir screes to Sligachan. I had thought this descent would save time, but it proved, after the ascent of the Gars-bheinn screes in the darkness, to be the most tiring part of the whole trip, and was probably the start of the gradual deterioration of my feet and toes. I thought later that a far better way down, after the descent of the Western Ridge, would have been to cross over the shoulder of Am Basteir into Fionn Choire. We could then have finished down easy slopes to join the road through the glen, thus avoiding the need to leave the car at Sligachan, and providing a much more satisfying round. It had been a mistake, too, to take such a long and heavy rope.

Nevertheless, it had been a really splendid day – probably the finest mountain day, everything considered, I have ever had in Britain. We had had the Cuillin Ridge completely to ourselves on a perfect day, with unequalled views far out to sea and, all around us, every step of the way, the most dramatic crags and precipices in the country. The climbing and scrambling on dry, sunny rock had been delightful, the scampering along the easier parts of the ridge, often exposed, with great drops on either side, provided interesting tests of balance and agility. Furthermore, the views from the summits were as clear and widespread as I have ever seen. Perhaps the long drag up Bruach na Frithe was the least interesting part, but by then the end was in sight. The best bits, apart from the rock-climbs, were the superb, slabby rock of the Dubhs and the airy dance up and down the little summits of Bidean Druim nan Ramh. To these I would add the splendid traverse of Ghreadaidh and Mhadaidh and the scramble along the fine Western Ridge of Sgurr nan Gillean, both ways, passing the famous "policeman" which toppled over many years later.

The ridge had taken us less than twelve hours, but had it not been for our route-finding problems on and around Am Basteir we would have put up quite a respectable time. Later, we heard we might have been the first father and son to do the ridge and Robin must have been one of the youngest to have completed the traverse up to that time. We finished, of course, in the Sligachan bar, where Ron Macdonald, the boatman, was completely unimpressed. "Wasting your time," he said, "stravaiging about the hills." But he did kindly volunteer to take us down the coast in his boat the next day to collect our tent at the foot of the dreaded Gars-bheinn screes and I seem to remember we caught some fish.

The Silence of the Snows

Absolute silence is a state rarely achieved – even in lonely hills. Almost always there is the noise of falling waters, however distant, the sighing of the wind, the whisper of the grass, tiny sounds of moving sheep, a tinkle of sliding scree, or the faint drone of unseen aircraft. Only on a totally windless day, when the becks are frozen into immobility and the fells blanketed in deep snow, can you sometimes stand and savour the complete absence of sound; an utter quietude that is almost uncanny. I experienced this the other day on the east face of Wetherlam: nobody about, nothing moving, bright sunlight on hard-frozen snows, and not enough wind, even on the summit, to flicker a burning match. The steep snow gully to the right of the crag of Hen Tor, in superb condition for crampons and axes, provided an exhilarating ladder to the heights, and a nearby gully proved a quick way down. For some time after my climbs I sat in retreating sunshine in the corrie, enjoying the exceptional stillness of the late afternoon. Far to the east the sunset glowed pink on the snows of Helvellyn and Fairfield but the gloom of dusk was already beginning to fill the valleys. Frequently I strained my ears for the slightest sound but it never came. Motorcars on the roads, quarrymen and foresters at work, and all the bustling life of the dales only a mile or two away but not the slightest sight or sound of it on my lonely snow slope. Not even a moving sheep or the trickle of a spring. At the summit I had slowly scanned the skyline ring of snowbound fells for sight of the moving speck, against the white, of some other pilgrim, but without success. So far as I could see I was quite alone in a white, white world, frozen into awesome immobility. Thus the often overcrowded fell country on a rare day of winter perfection.

February 1982

Chapter Twelve

The Magic of Snow

For almost as long as I can remember snow has had a magical appeal: the first snows of winter dusting the fells; carol singers in the snow, under the Christmas lights; the crisp crunch of crampons on a frozen snow slope; or long, slow turns on skis across a glistening white carpet reaching down to the valley. As my confidence on snow or ice gradually increased, winter became a favoured time of the year; a time when the fells looked twice as high and the crags vastly more dramatic and challenging. There seemed so many things you could do in the winter fells – hill walking, climbing the snow gullies, seeking out the ice on frozen waterfalls, ski mountaineering, piste skiing, skating on the tarns, or just pottering about with either crampons or skis. Indeed, in later years my car was usually laden, in winter, with skis and boots, climbing boots and crampons, ice axes and all the impedimenta. There was also a bag of sand, to hold down the back of the car, a strip of carpet for putting under the wheels when stuck in snow, and a large shovel or spade. More or less, ready for anything.

It had been the sight of two skiers descending High Raise towards Grasmere in long, elegant turns that had first inspired me to try the game. This was a couple of years before the war and skiers were very rarely seen on the Lakeland fells in those days, but the neat way these two came down the steep snow slopes greatly impressed me. A year or two earlier I had had to turn down an invitation from Walter Ingham to accompany him on what would have been, for me, an introductory skiing holiday in Austria because it clashed, most unfortunately, with my long-planned first visit to Skye. These two on High Raise were the first skiers I had ever seen, but it was not until immediately after the war that I was able to make a start.

In those early days piste skiing, using lifts and tows, had not reached this country, and skiing in Britain was, really, ski mountaineering – going up and down mountains on skis. Accordingly, most skiers were mountaineers who found skiing an enjoyable alternative to ice-axe work in the gullies, and skis, useful pieces of equipment for exploring the hills in winter. They fitted skis to their nailed boots, wore their ordinary mountain clothes, often carried axes for the steep, icy places and fastened on their skins (originally sealskins) as soon as they reached the first snow. In these explorations of the winter hills – as distinct from careering down selected bits of fellside – the ascent, using skins, working out the best line through steep or rocky terrain, was just as important, and sometimes as interesting, as the descent.

My own first skiing was in the same mould, using primitive skis, without steel edges, fastened on to nailed climbing boots, after first gouging out grooves in the heels to take the elementary bindings, for an ascent and descent of Harter Fell from Longsleddale. The ascent, using skins that had been acquired, naturally, at the same time as the skis, proved straightforward enough but the descent, since I had no idea how to turn, was quite disastrous – a succession of falls, all the way down. Fortunately, the experience didn't put me off skiing – the delightful sliding along the easy bit at the top and the dramatic views across winter Lakeland must have been factors – and I was able to carry on enjoying the sport for more than forty years (until I was eighty).

After gaining a little confidence on the Lakeland fells I drove up to the Cairngorms, last visited on my honeymoon in 1937, where I knew there would be plenty of snow. Aviemore was much the same as I remembered it from ten years or so earlier – a small Highland village with a railway station, a hotel, a few small shops made of wood at the side of the road and splendid views of snowbound hills. But skiing, except for a handful of devotees, had not yet "hit" the area; there were no facilities of any kind for the sport, and not even a road to the slopes. Carrying our skis, we simply walked up to the top of the mountain, Cairngorm, from Loch Morlich, and then skied down, perhaps pausing halfway down to practise on a suitable slope. And in one of these training sessions we came upon Bill Blackwood experimenting, somewhere above Coire Raibeirt, with a primitive, portable, rope ski-tow, based on a small farm tractor, and he kindly allowed us two or three runs. This was the first time we had ever used a tow – my companion was my brother Leslie who I had introduced to skiing a little earlier – and this tiny contraption must have been one of the very first tows to be used in the Cairngorms.

Years later they built the first ski road up the lower slopes of Cairngorm and I was an early subscriber, making a small contribution, following an appeal. The road was washed away the following winter and a new road had to be built, and gradually extended. We usually stayed in Aviemore with a Mrs Fraser who lived in what was then the last house in Aviemore, on the left, going north. Mrs Fraser, a kindly soul, had been the cook at the big hotel before it was burned down and Mr Fraser was the local coal merchant, so we always had good food and great roaring fires. When the mountain road was built Mr Fraser had the contract for supplying the sand for helping to keep the road open in winter, and often when we enquired after him Mrs Fraser would tell us, "Och, he's awa' with the sond."

Sometimes, when Mrs Fraser was full up with visitors or I had neglected to book in advance, she would allow me to sleep in my car, a "traveller" type of vehicle in those days, in the coal-yard at the back of the house. I had my meals and used the bathroom facilities inside. Another occasional port-of-call in Aviemore in the early days was an adjoining guest house, later converted into an hotel, where the proprietor, a Mr le Mesurier, must have been one of the first entrepreneurs in the village, hiring out some of the first skis, as well as bicycles. Gradually, over the years, the facilities on the slopes and in the growing village were developed, and soon big business was involved. Nowadays the area, with its hotels, shops, mountain roads, ski lifts and even a restaurant perched on the slopes, higher than the top of Scafell Pike, is unrecognisable from the place we knew half a century ago.

At one time, in the early days, there were three ski schools (Norwegian, Austrian and Scottish) teaching slightly different techniques on the Cairngorm slopes, but eventually the Scottish instructors assumed command. Probably the first of the continental ski experts was Carl Fuchs, who established a successful hotel and ski school at Carrbridge, north of Aviemore. Later he set up a brand new ski area high up near the Lecht road. I would often encounter him in the winter hills, usually wearing a curiously long cagoule that reached down to his ankles. Occasionally we would ski together, although his standards were far above mine. Another skiing acquaintance was "Plum" Worrall, a Lancashire-born ski instructor living in Aviemore, who, like me, enjoyed ski mountaineering in preference to "piste-bashing". When he was not involved with ski classes we would sometimes go together for a ski tour round the tops, and I remember, in particular, skiing several of the Cairngorm four-thousanders with him on the most perfect day for powder snow, weather and sunshine I can remember in this country.

There was not a cloud in the sky, although, strangely, there was just one greyish wisp of it down in the depths of the Lairig Ghru, and the views of waves of snow-clad peaks were startlingly clear. We sat perched on top of Cairn Lochan, on the very edge of the precipice, and, for the fun of it, "Plum" pulled out a lightweight survival tent from his enormous rucksack and we sat inside, with the flap open, marvelling at the view. Then, remarkably, he produced two bottles of beer, and contentment was complete. We saw nobody on the tops that day, which we finished off with the swoop down Lurcher's Gully and the fast traverse across the floor of the corries. As we reclined in the heather on the Fiacaill Ridge we looked down at the scurrying ants on the White Lady and in Coire Cas and listened to the distant rattle of machinery and the cries of colliding skiers. "What about a couple of quick runs?" I asked. "Plum", more wisely, replied, "Too much of an anti-climax. Mustn't spoil a marvellous day. Let's go down for a pint." Which we did, leaving the noisy, crowded snows to the mob.

Although skiing the tops using ski mountaineering boots with special release bindings and skins for the ascent became my preference, we had plenty of fun on the piste runs, although icy "moguls" usually defeated me. When he was old enough, I introduced my son Robin to the game, and I recall one of his early descents of the White Lady on Cairngorm – without stopping and grimly persisting with his snow-ploughs all the way down. We also often skied in Glencoe and Glen Shee before these places had uphill transport, and around the Lecht road before this was "discovered" as a skiing area. To reach the early rope tows high up on Meall a' Bhuiridh, near Glencoe, we had to cope with the steep slog to the shoulder of the mountain, now equipped with a chair lift, carrying our skis. Among the regular early skiers on the Glencoe slopes in those days were Frith Finlayson, who later established a successful ski school on Cairngorm, and Tom Weir, the writer.

The Glen Shee runs were easier to approach in the days before ski lifts, provided you could negotiate the often-icy, snowbound

Devil's Elbow with your car. We also skied in the Ben Lawers area, one of the earliest centres for Scottish skiing, and explored the likely-looking slopes above Dalwhinnie and the Drumochter Pass. Year after year we kept going up to Scotland for the skiing, sometimes twice a year, but the crowds grew bigger, the once-lonely snows were transformed into ski circuses, the queues for the lifts became a boring frustration, and Scottish piste skiing began to lose its appeal.

Most of my skiing, however, was in Lakeland or in the Northern Pennines, and, incredible though it now seems in these global warming days, we could often count on up to four months of skiing each winter. This was often no better than short drifts high in the fells, but at least, we were able to keep fit stamping up the slopes. Sometimes, though, the skiing was superb for weeks on end and I can remember many days when we climbed Raise from Glenridding on skins and, after hours of sport in the sunshine, skied all the way down to the mines in the evening. There was splendid skiing on Savage's Drift on Raise in May 1947 – regrettably, I wasn't there, but I've seen the photographs. In the middle of June 1979, a few days before Midsummer's Day, some token runs were made on the slopes of Cross Fell. Some years the skiing in Lakeland began in November and lasted until April, although, admittedly, weekend conditions could sometimes be poor, if not appalling. But every winter Saturday or Sunday, or both, we would trudge up the fell from Glenridding or Thirlspot carrying all our skiing paraphernalia, hoping for good snow but prepared, if necessary, to put up with windswept ice, driving rain or snow and thick mist.

Skiing in Lakeland began to move towards the modern era when the first rope tow, originally based on a two-wheeled garden tractor, appeared on the upper slopes of Raise soon after the war. This primitive tow and later improved models were the brainchild of Frank Kieser, an enterprising Penrith motor engineer and indefatigable skier. In 1946 he had, with friends from the same town, notably George Morton-Rigg, "discovered" the northern slopes of Raise and identified them as the most promising ski area in Lakeland. Frank also persuaded his fellow members of the Lake District Ski Club, founded in 1936, to place a ski hut on about the 2500 feet contour on Raise.

I have many happy memories of helping to build the hut and later, with many others, dragging it back after it had been blown down the fellside! I recall, with pleasure, helping to haul engines, ropes and other ungainly objects up the side of Keppel Cove, and countless skiing days on Raise and elsewhere. There were also exciting days on Great Dun Fell in the Northern Pennines. We put up guideposts across the fellside, dug out culverts to improve a rough mountain track for vehicles, persuaded a specially built snow-truck up the mountain road and fixed up rope tows and snow fencing – mostly inspired or bullied by Frank Kieser. Four of us: Eric Arnison, an early ski mentor; Teasdale Stephenson, from the Carlisle Ski Club; Frank and myself, became trustees to represent skiing interests in this area and negotiate a licence from the landowners, the Nature Conservancy. But, despite all this labouring and long hours of committee meetings there were also happy skiing days.

Often we went exploring, far from the tows, and I remember one gloriously sunny day, with a biting wind, when Eric Arnison and I skied across the tops to Cross Fell. Down in the Eden valley the sun was smiling on the fields nearly 3000 feet below and glinting, here and there, on little streams or the windows of distant farmhouses. But eastwards, all we could see was mist and cloud hanging over dreary, snow-streaked moors falling away, in miles of bare desolation, towards the industrial north-east. We skied to the summit along rippled snow, hard as ice, in dazzling sunshine and in the teeth of the wind, but on the return journey, with the wind at our backs, sailed for miles along the plateau, quite effortlessly, as if we had little engines on our skis. The only sound was the hiss of the thin planks sliding over the snow and the flapping of the hoods about our ears.

Another wonderful ski mountaineering day, plucked from dozens on sunlit or icy snows, was a traverse, just two of us, of the Kentmere Horseshoe on superb powder snow. The view from the summit of Ill Bell, looking back the way we had come, before the swoop down to Hartrigg, was particularly impressive; wave after wave of snowbound peaks, just like the Alps. I can recall, with a little effort, many of these ski mountain days along the Helvellyn ridges, the traverse of the Dodds, around the Coniston fells, the hills to the east of Kirkstone Pass and, once, on to Esk Hause and the Scafells. All of them were adventures in a way, stored away in one's hidden memory, ready to be taken out and savoured on the right occasion. But all the hundreds of days of downhill skiing, highly enjoyable at the time, are now merged into just a blurred memory of hard exercise and good fun.

I can't now even recall my last day of piste skiing, or whether it was on Raise, Great Dun Fell or, perhaps, Kirkstone, but I clearly remember finishing off a lone ski traverse of the Dodds a few years ago. It had been bitingly cold but there was plenty of untracked snow, feet deep of it, and the sun had shone all day. I felt tired after all the miles of skinning up and skiing down – and thirsty. When I was down from the snow-plastered tops at High Row at last, I found the lane down to Dockray still well covered so I skied down it in slow, easy turns, wondering how long the snow would last. And my luck was in! Remarkably, I was able to ski all the way down to the front door of the Royal, take off my skis, prop them up against the side of the door of the pub and go inside for my reward. Apart from this occasion, only in Austria, at Hochsolden, have I been able to ski right down to the door of the inn.

Quite early in my skiing days, not long after the end of the war, we began going to the Alps – Austria, Switzerland or Italy – for the skiing. Strangely, I never went to France. At first, we went across the Channel and then, in rather primitive "sleepers", to the resorts. Later we went by air and coach. Remarkably, these early holidays used to cost less than £40 each for the flight, the accommodation and all the trimmings for a fortnight. I remember an early holiday at Gargellen in the Voralberg where, although we were accommo-dated in the very superior Hotel Madrisa, the total cost of the pack-age was only £39. The hotel, I remember, had recently had to be rebuilt because an avalanche had taken out the middle of it. This was the place where the village priest annoyingly started tolling his bells about 6am. Later we would bump into him, morning mass over but still wearing his cassock, on the chair-lift with his skis on his way to the slopes.

At first we attended a few ski classes to try to improve our rough and ready techniques, but soon abandoned these in favour of ski tours to the tops with visits to the mountain huts. Some gnarled, elderly instructor, probably a retired mountain guide no longer up to fancy turns on the piste but a sound mountain skier, usually led these. Just what we wanted! My companion in much of this foreign skiing was my brother Leslie, and sometimes we were accompa-nied by our wives. But Mollie's skiing activities came to an end rather abruptly when she broke a leg while with the ski school at Galtur, when Leslie and I were doing a tour in the Silvretta.

There were a couple of climbing seasons in the Alps, and Mollie and I did several summer tours in Austria, walking across the mountains from hut to hut, carrying all our gear, with a short length of rope and one axe between us, in case of emergency. One year my son Robin, who was working in Holland at the time, joined me in Innsbruck and we climbed several modest peaks including Wilder Frieger, Zuckerhuttl and Wildspitze. Another year I had a week's ski mountaineering in the Otztal and Silvretta, but it is many, many years now since I was last in the Alps.

In my seventies, I was fortunate enough to steal many ski outings in Canada and the USA through the hospitality of my daughter Sandra and son-in-law Tony who were then living in Vancouver, and are now retired there. You can see the high snows and the ski slopes from downtown Vancouver and I became quite familiar with the runs on Grouse Mountain and Cypress Bowl. A little further away are the twin peaks of The Lions, prominent in the skyline view from the city streets and, on one summer visit I was able to climb them – four thousand feet of steep forest, then the snow and finally the summit rocks. "Rusty" Westmorland (Lt. Col. Horace Westmorland), the second president of the Lake District Ski Club, with whom I often climbed and skied in the Lake District, had made the first ascent of one of the routes up The Lions. In those distant days it took several days of hard travel and "bush whacking" just to get to the foot of the mountain. Later we compared notes about our ascents, made about half a century apart, and also about a lone attempt of mine on Mount Temple in the Rockies, which he had climbed many years earlier but from which I had had to retreat.

In later visits to Canada I was fortunate enough to ski on several occasions on the beautifully-laundered pistes of the fabled Mount Whistler in the Garibaldi National Park and on Mount Baker in Washington, USA. In these resorts you drive along superb mountain roads to the foot of the chair lifts, ski all day in the sunshine on compacted snow, without the need to walk more than ten yards, and then settle down to food and drink in your fabulously appointed ski chalet at the foot of the slopes. Here, where skins and even rucksacks seemed unknown, and where fancy downhill boots were used instead of heavy, ski mountaineering gear, it all seemed so flattering that I began to wonder whether, after all those years, I could perhaps ski a bit. Indeed, there was the temptation to settle for this sort of thing – or there might have been if it had been more readily available. But, back home, the sight from my windows of snow-covered High Street, Harter Fell, Red Screes or the Howgills was still as alluring as ever. So, ignoring the effort involved, I would go out on the tops again with my skis and quietly potter around in the old way, the dream skiing of Whistler and Cypress Bowl forgotten.

Even now, seven years after I put away my skis, I often sigh for the remembered joys of mountain skiing, and sometimes feel that skiing the fells would be far kinder to my funny feet than walking them along the stony, eroded ways that pass for paths nowadays. I wish I could have completed fifty years of skiing to rank along with my sixty years of rock-climbing, but although I started skiing long before there were any facilities in the Lake District or Scotland, I started too late for this.

Pillar Rock in August

*There's a couple of hours' hard walking from anywhere to get to
Pillar Rock, which makes it a different sort of climbing venue
from these "modern" crags, quarries or climbing walls within
handy reach of main roads and hotel bars. Climbers met on the
Rock, therefore, tend to be determined devotees quite prepared to
walk up mountains to find their climbs – rather than
single-minded gymnasts for whom an urban quarry face would
serve equally well. They are also likely to be much thinner on the
ground, and the other day, with the crags in superb condition,
there were only two people beside myself on the biggest lump of
rock in England. The walk to the Rock from Buttermere in August
can be long and hot, but the steep scramble up from the Liza and
the massed conifers of Ennerdale was made enjoyable by the
sight of the heather in bloom and the refreshing state of the
bilberries that grow hereabouts in great profusion. But the real
lodestone of this walk is always the sight, high up and straight
ahead, of the great bulk of the Rock – rather like two cathedrals
piled on top of each other, but bigger than any cathedrals in the
world. I reached the top of the Rock by a modest route befitting a
lone and slightly decrepit climber and joined the other two, who,
strangely, I happened to know, as they finished the last pitch on
one of the much steeper west face climbs. As we contemplated the
splendid scenery far below I remembered my first visits to the
Rock around 1930 when there were no trees in Ennerdale and the
valley was just a barren moor: today you look down on tens of
thousands of closely packed spruce trees. Strings of walkers,
looking like moving matchsticks from High Man, were crossing
the high ridge of Pillar mountain but there was no other
movement, except for the changing cloud shadows, over the
whole wild landscape. Westwards, towards the lake, the sea and
the sunset, stretched the dark forest, and northwards rose the
blue evening hills around Buttermere as we smoked in silence on
our steeple top, oblivious of the busy world so far away.*

August 1982

Chapter Thirteen

Mountain Companions

Hundreds of mountain days in the last thirty years or so have been spent alone which, when not rock-climbing, can be the ideal situation. You go as fast or as slow as you like, enjoy the scenery without the distraction of talk or anything else, and have plenty of time to think or, perhaps, work out an article or recall a symphony. Indeed, it may be that mountain beauty is best appreciated alone or, failing that, in the company of a tried and trusted friend with whom, since you know each other so well, there is no need for continuous chatter. During my mountain years I have been fortunate enough to climb, ski or walk with many valued friends. The ones with whom I have spent most time since the sixties have been my brother Leslie, staunch companion since boyhood days; Ivan Waller, especially after his retirement to Crosthwaite and Kendal; Ted Stacey of Levens; my partner and companion Josie, and my wonderful Border Collie, Sambo.

It was a very sad moment when Sambo, at a good age, died in my arms, for he had been my faithful companion in the hills for most of his life – always trusting, never complaining. In many ways he was the ideal mountain companion, keeping his thoughts strictly to himself. Indeed, I can't now remember him ever barking, although I suppose he must have done now and again. He had been up and down almost all the Lake District two-thousanders, climbed many of the Munros, been dragged, in a harness, up several moderate rock-climbs, been washed down waterfalls in the River Sprint, been lost for hours on a remote crag, and had once crawled along miles of frozen snow with bleeding paws after a slip down an ice slope. On one holiday in Skye six other Border Collies had savagely mauled him at Glen Brittle Farm. He was carried to the vet at Portree and, after treatment for a terrible wound, several inches long, in his stomach, climbed up and down Sgurr Dearg the following day, refusing to be left behind.

I often used to take him with me when I went climbing on Dow Crag, leave him at the foot of the climbs with instructions to wait, and always find him there, his tail thumping away, and his eyes brightly shining, on my return, probably an hour or two later. Throughout the years we were together I never once used a lead: there was no need. When required, he would always walk "to heel". In a whiteout, in thick mist or in darkness Sambo could usually find the path, even if it was hidden under snow, and would often take the lead under these conditions, when I was uncertain of the way. I'm convinced he had a wonderful mountain memory. Once, on a very hot day, he ran a hundred yards ahead to the tiny spring near Kern Knotts, previously visited two years earlier.

There was only one difficulty with Sambo, and that was when I went piste skiing on Raise. If ski mountaineering or ski touring there was not the slightest difficulty: Sambo just followed behind, the best he could. But on Savage's Drift on Raise or some other piste slope, with several other skiers around, Sambo would insist on darting at the ski points of the others, usually when they were in the middle of complicated turns on hard snow or ice. He never went for my skis, only for the skis of others. In the end I had to stop taking him to these crowded places, which was probably a good thing anyway. But I still miss Sambo in the hills.

My brother Leslie was always game for any adventure, no matter how madcap, was never put off by bad weather, was usually the first of us down black ski runs in the Alps, and generally managed to keep his summer tan throughout the winter. Bathing, in all seasons, was one of his passions. He could never pass a mountain pool without wanting to jump in. Four bathes during a day's outing in the fells were nothing to him. I remember one of our last bathes together. We had done a round of the Lake District central fells one very hot and sultry day and coming down from High Raise towards Easedale Tarn, Les suggested a bathe. Quickly undressing at the side of the tarn we waded in, after stuffing all our clothes into our rucksacks as the sky looked a little ominous, and swam out to the middle of the tarn.

Suddenly a cloudburst and thunderstorm of epic proportions assailed us. The rain deluged down, the thunder cracked and the lightning flashed but, out in the middle of the tarn, there seemed no reason to panic. We were in no danger and we couldn't get any wetter. It was still pouring down when, after swimming around in the deluge for some time, we got back to the shore, so we just

Leslie (on the right) and I in Skye.

Leslie and I at the foot of Pavey Ark in 1956

Napes Needle (photographed by Tommy Tyson by moonlight at 4.30am on March 11, 1933).

Eric Arnison (right) and myself in the 1950s

Above: Ted Stacey

Right: Ivan Waller – he was
passionately fond of motorbikes.

"The Last of the Summer Wine" in the 1990s.
Left to right: myself, Ted Stacey, Ivan Waller. *(Stephen Greenwood)*

Myself scrambling up Brim Fell slabs above Low Water, aged 80.
(Sir John Johnson)

pulled on our boots and, shouldering our rucksacks, set off down the track without a stitch of clothes on our bodies. Fortunately, there was nobody about. And we continued down the track, completely naked, until we reached the woods by the side of the road into Grasmere where we changed into our dry clothes in the shelter of the trees and, the cloudburst now over, strolled down to the village respectably dressed.

Apart from all the skiing holidays in Austria and Switzerland, a lot of rock-climbing and regular mountain walking together – Leslie driving up to the Lakes at weekends from his home in Stourbridge or in Cheshire – we began exploring the Lake District gills. At that time these were rarely visited but we sought out as many as we could find and, when possible, climbed them. Among the earliest were the Oxendale (Langdale) ravines of Browney Gill, Crinkle Gill and Hell Gill, but soon we were going much further afield. One of our favourites was the splendid ravine that drops down, below Ern Nest Crag, from Link Cove into Deepdale. We always called this Ern Nest Gill and climbed it many times in all conditions, including winter ascents in snow and ice. Later I continued our explorations alone and considered writing a guide to Lakeland gill climbing and scrambling in general, but eventually abandoned the idea, believing this would tempt too many novices into dangerous situations. Instead, I wrote discursively about the subject in one of my books without providing any guidebook information, although guides were later written by others.

One day I suggested to Leslie that we should walk the length of the old Roman road of High Street, collecting all the summits en route. "We'll do it from north to south so that we're facing the sun the whole way," I said. In the event, we saw little more than our feet all day for the weather was quite appalling. Leaving the car just north of Windermere, near Troutbeck, we were taken in another car to Celleron, between Pooley Bridge and Eamont Bridge, and left to our own devices. Soon after the disappearance of our transport it started raining, and very soon the drizzle became a downpour and the cloud level dropped to below 500 feet. Once committed, however, we had to continue, although we were soon facing a very strong headwind that battered us all the way, while visibility was restricted to a few yards. Indeed, we had to navigate by compass the whole way and, even so, towards the end, got badly off route, missing the Scots Rake on Froswick and finding ourselves on very steep, rocky ground that seemed unfamiliar.

Thinking we might be coming down the craggy side of

Thornthwaite Crag, by mistake, we decided to retrace our steps, although by now we were very tired, and climbed several hundred feet back to a recognisable feature on the ridge. Eventually, after several attempts, we were able to find the Rake, and the way down. We decided afterwards we had been descending Blue Gill on Froswick which, had we realised this at the time, would have been a reasonable way down to the valley. The atrocious conditions, especially the strong headwind and complete lack of visibility, made this one of the most exhausting walks either of us had ever done. As a final slap in the face, when we got down to Troutbeck Park we found the fields about a foot deep in water. By then, though, we had been wet through to the skin for several hours, and nothing mattered. I remember it was quite a problem, the two of us changing into dry clothes in what was then the tiny toilet of the Troutbeck pub.

To celebrate his sixtieth year Les decided to do the round of the Lakeland three-thousanders – as I had done to mark my sixtieth year two years earlier. Instead of starting from Keswick, as I had done, he chose Seathwaite as his starting point, leaving the ten miles of road walking from Keswick back to the hamlet under Styhead to the end of the walk. Very soon, however, he ran into bad weather and his traverse of the Scafells, including the descent of Broad Stand, had to be done on his own, in heavy rain with the accompaniment of thunder and lightning. By arrangement, we met him, wet through and battered but fit and cheerful, near the toe of Thirlmere as he came down the flooded Wythburn valley, and he was soon being fed and watered at the Wythburn car park before his climb over Helvellyn.

I was suffering at the time, from a bad respiratory attack: otherwise, I would have accompanied him at least part of the way. We met, of course, in the pub at Thirlspot, after his traverse of the Helvellyn tops, and at Keswick we met my old friend, Eric Arnison, then in his seventies, who had kindly agreed to accompany Les over Skiddaw. The last ten road miles back to Seathwaite must have been very trying for Les, after such a battering day on the tops. I managed to walk part of the way with him and he finished quite strongly. Under the appalling conditions it was a very gallant performance.

Earlier, Leslie and I had made many climbing visits to North Wales, staying mostly at Glan Dena, the hut of the Midland Association of Mountaineers, of which he was then a member. We climbed on several of the main crags and walked most of the ridges and summits. On the way back from one of these trips, driving through the rather depressing town of St Helens at midnight, I had the misfortune, through a catalogue of misunderstandings, to topple a nightwatchman into the hole he was guarding. My argument that he had walked into the side of my car was not accepted. For this offence, despite my profuse apologies and offer to recompense, I was, in due course, hauled before the local bench, fined and disqualified from driving for a short period. The case was reported in the local paper and my name was given, to which was added: "described as a journalist".

My brother and I had also spent some time familiarising ourselves with the Yorkshire hills, including a round of the Three Peaks: Whernside, Ingleborough and Pen y Ghent. I had earlier done the round on my own but had been disappointed with the time taken – about eight hours. This was in the days when the route had to be worked out, no eroded paths or, indeed, paths of any kind then. Leslie and I decided to see if we could improve on this and managed to get round together in seven hours. Years later, when doing the round as a sponsored walk, I was able to bring my time down to just over six hours by not stopping at all, and trotting along and down the level and downhill sections. Runners, of course, do the round very much more quickly, and arrive at the finish far less exhausted than I was. I remember stopping at a cottage on the drive home, after a shower at Giggleswick School arranged by the organisers, and buying tea in a huge, glazed earthenware pot that provided me with six large mugs of lovely liquid, rapidly consumed. I must have been completely dehydrated.

I recall one wonderful climbing day on the Napes with Les, probably our last rock-climbing day together. We had arranged to meet, coming from different parts of the country, on Styhead at noon and there he was, on time, waiting for me. I remember we did the Arrowhead, the Needle and a couple of other routes in our old boots and tattered clothes and then, both in our sixties, sat on the Dress Circle and watched some schoolboys being given instruction in climbing on the Needle. They had brand new ropes, all the latest gear and clothing, and their own school bus, for we had noticed it, parked at Seathwaite. It happened to be a school from somewhere near Leslie's home in Cheshire and he remarked that he was probably paying for their climbing out of his rates. We wryly compared the facilities available to young people nowadays to the complete lack of provision in our youth, when we had to beg, borrow or steal everything ourselves. Times have certainly changed.

Our last day in the hills together, only a few weeks before he passed away in January 1976, was the round of Striding Edge and Swirrel Edge in splendid winter conditions, with ample ice and snow. As an experiment, Leslie was climbing on this occasion without crampons, cutting steps where necessary, while I used my crampons. Everything went very well, although on the icy sections Les, understandably, was a little slower. We decided that under similar conditions in future, we would both wear our crampons. But, sadly, there was to be no next time for Leslie. That was his last day, a wonderful last day, in the mountains. Yet he had looked so fit, still brown as an Arab, with no hint that his hill days would soon be over.

I sprinkled his ashes from a little rock corner on the summit of Wetherlam, one of his favourite hills. From this place, which I always visit when I'm on the hill, there is a superb view of the Scafells, with the Brathay woodlands and many scattered waters immediately below. Like so many of the Tigers Leslie died far too soon. He had always seemed so healthy with, we thought, a long lifetime ahead of him. At the funeral service someone described him as "one of nature's gentlemen". He was certainly that, and also my closest companion of all in the hills – someone I could trust implicitly in any situation. I still think of him every day.

The following year the Coniston Tigers had another very sad loss. Tommy Tyson, our first president, the friendly, happy countryman I had known from earliest days, even before we had formed our little gang, passed away at the age of seventy-five. After the death of his first wife, Debbie, he had married Mary, a member of a well-known Langdale family, and they had gone to live at Foxfield near Broughton-in-Furness. Their reason for moving to this area, I learned later, was so that Tommy could indulge in his passion for fishing the Duddon – every day, if possible. Tommy had been one of my very earliest mountain friends. He was an immensely likeable and generous man to whom I owe a great deal.

A few years later the surviving Tigers were sorrowing for the passing of another old and highly respected member: the staunch and strong George Anderson, always solid as a rock. The only original members still alive, Jim Porter, Jack Atkinson, Len Brown and myself, met again at the well-attended funeral service in Barrow, and compared memories of George and the old days. Sadly, I never came to know George as well as I did some of the other original members, but I was always aware of his sterling qualities.

The first time I met Ivan Waller, not a Coniston Tiger but certainly a "tiger", was in the late 1960s, although I had long known of his climbing and skiing exploits. We met, I remember, in Savage's Drift on Raise. I was standing near the Lake District Ski Club hut, about to set off for the tow, when he side-slipped down a steepish ice-slope, landed, with a shriek from his skis, at my feet, and introduced himself. We soon became friends, indeed, close friends, and spent scores of days together climbing, skiing, hill walking or just plain adventuring in the Lakes or Scotland and, occasionally, in the Yorkshire dales. This continued almost until his death in 1996, just before his 90th birthday.

Ivan and I didn't do much hard climbing together, mostly pottering about on amiable v. diffs. or easy severes, sharing leads. Occasionally, in more determined company, he managed to get in some quite hard routes at a fairly advanced age. We had opposing views about climbing in our sixties and seventies. I wouldn't do a climb in those days unless I could lead it, but Ivan had no such scruples, being glad to be taken up almost any climb provided he was happy with the leader. An example of this determination was his ascent of the redoubtable Mickledore Grooves on the East Buttress of Scafell, with a much younger leader, more than 40 years after he had seconded Colin Kirkus on its first ascent in 1930. Ivan's leader on his second ascent was Jim Ingham, his dentist. The older man was cheeky enough to declare his second ascent "slightly the easier of the two".

One of our first long outings together was a round of the Lake District "three-thousanders", all seven of them, to celebrate my sixtieth year. I planned to do this on my own, for many reasons, but Ivan happened to hear about it and wanted to come round with me. For some days we argued about it, but in the end I had to give in and agree to his company. I insisted, however, that I would go at my own speed, irrespective of his wishes, and would only stop when it suited me, knowing Ivan's penchant for dropping off to sleep whenever we sat down. My training for the event, the previous Sunday, was a walk up and down Skiddaw from Keswick, the drive to Thirlspot and, from there, the ascent and descent of Helvellyn.

We left Keswick at two o'clock in the morning in light drizzle and low, drifting cloud, using rather ineffective torches for the ascent. For some curious reason I was wearing an old pair of what I believe were called baseball boots – not unlike modern "trainers", but heavier and clumsier. They slid about on the wet slate below the summit and when I got back down to Keswick my feet were so badly blistered I had to change into my mountain boots for the rest of the round. I had hoped to keep on the baseball boots for the road walking so this was a bad start. My anxiety about my feet was not helped by Ivan's insistence on chanting the lugubrious verses of the Lyke Wake Dirge throughout the night hours.

The road walking to Seathwaite went well, however. The rain eased off, there was no traffic and nobody about, we enjoyed all the sounds and delights of early morning, and Stan Edmondson at the farm, an old friend, kindly gave us breakfast in the kitchen. We now had 21 miles behind us, for we had gone to the far north summit of Skiddaw – only another 27 miles or so to do. With renewed energy, after the bacon and eggs, we romped up Styhead and the Corridor Route to the Lingmell Col and then, by way of Lord's Rake and the West Wall Traverse, to the top of Scafell. Here we had a long argument about Broad Stand. Ivan was still doing quite hard climbing at this time but, surprisingly, refused to come down it unroped, saying this was irresponsible. I had no such qualms, but to avoid splitting up halfway through the round had to make the long detour with him down Lord's Rake and back up to Mickledore.

I had the same trouble with Ivan on other outings to Scafell, notably when he was accompanying me on my collection of the Lakeland two-thousanders a few years later. On this occasion he did not express his reluctance, indeed refusal, until we had actually reached the foot of Broad Stand. No pleadings from me, including an offer to lower a rucksack as a safety aid, would make him change his mind. So that time I scrambled up the route alone, while Ivan went all the way down to Lord's Rake and up to the summit where I was waiting for him. A hard man with a mind of his own was our Ivan.

There was another occasion, though, when I managed to get myself into an odd situation on Broad Stand after I had done a long round of the Scafells on my own on a very hot day. I was about to descend the little vertical pitch when I suddenly took cramp in both legs and found it quite impossible to stretch out my right leg to reach down to the hold. Both legs were curiously contracted, bent at the knees like a frog's. After several unsuccessful attempts to stretch out either leg I decided I would have to climb back up the route and go down to Fox Tarn, but then found I couldn't put my feet on to the holds. So I tried to drag myself up the easy rocks by arm strength alone, and found this, too, quite impossible. Here was a "how d'ye do". I'd been up and down Broad Stand alone on many occasions and in all weathers, and had once got my Border Collie, Sambo, down with me, but this time I was stuck and evening was coming on. I sat down on the ledge and had a think, and then searched my rucksack, unavailingly, for the salt that I knew I needed. In the search I found the remains of a rather musty cheese sandwich and ate it – and, a few minutes later, my legs miraculously straightened out and I was able to climb down without any trouble. Ever since that day I have always carried salt tablets on the fells.

But back to Ivan and me on the three-thousanders. We traversed the Pike, collected Broad Crag and Ill Crag and then pressed on to Esk Hause and Angle Tarn, where I began to scan the skyline for my brother Leslie who had promised to meet me in those parts. Sure enough, just beyond the tarn, there he was, having come up Wyth Burn and recced an easy route for us, avoiding the summit of High Raise. It was now very hot and I remember we took off our boots and sat on a rock with our feet in the delightfully-icy waters of Stake Beck while consuming a tin of mandarin oranges. Refreshed, we were soon across the shoulder of High Raise and down through the Wyth Burn bogs to the foot of Helvellyn, the last of our three-thousanders, where we were met, as arranged, by the indispensable Eric Arnison. Wet socks changed, the four of us charged up the slopes, fortified by a concoction of Eric's which he said was an egg beaten up in sherry, although it seemed a far more potent elixir.

The summit, together with Helvellyn Lower Man, was duly collected. The only problem had been that I couldn't get my leg over the gate at the foot of Helvellyn Gill without assistance. I suppose a pot of tea at the King's Head Inn, Thirlspot would have been the best thing for our dehydration but, instead, I regret to say, we consumed several pints of beer in quick succession. Eric, ever solicitous about our welfare, then announced that he would drive on ahead to Keswick, but would stop at regular intervals to provide us with the libations of malt whisky that he considered would be necessary for our completion of the course. And so, we stopped for a reviver from Eric every mile or so! This seemed to work very well for when we reached the top of the hill down into Keswick, Ivan suggested we should run the rest of the way and broke into a shambling trot. I did the same and some minutes later the two of us trooped into the County Hotel at the double and demanded drinks. Leslie, having traversed High Raise twice from Wythburn before collecting Helvellyn with us, had also done a fair day's journey.

After some time in the bar we noticed, through the alcoholic haze, that Ivan had disappeared. He was eventually discovered outside, in the street, fast asleep on a window sill of the hotel. His instructions if he should fall asleep on a walk, which he often did when we stopped for food, were to kick him awake, but this time we had to be more careful. The next day, after driving home, he did another longish walk with a friend. When I got home I went to sleep for twelve hours.

Another memorable walk with Ivan – and all walks with him were memorable in one way or another, especially when we got lost – was when we did the Cairngorm "four-thousanders". Counting all the outlying summits of Braeriach and Ben Macdhui, which we collected, I think there are ten of them. Right from the start we cheated by parking the car some way up the mountain road instead of walking from Aviemore or Coylum Bridge, which purists would have done. But, thereafter, we plodded on assiduously, ticking off the tops, and only talking when it seemed necessary. The round had been my idea, and I suppose I must have set the pace, for I arrived on top of Cairn Toul some time before Ivan. He didn't say anything about it at the time, but clearly was on the verge of taking umbrage.

We descended to the Dee by an allegedly fast route confided to me, in the Coylum Bridge Hotel a day or two earlier, by John Cunningham, the great iceman who had been with my friends George Spenceley and Tom Price in South Georgia some years earlier. We didn't think the route fast at all but it was certainly very steep. So, too, was the path up Ben Macdhui by the Tailors' Burn, but after wading across the Dee, we went up it all the way to the main summit without a stop. We really must have been fit in those days. After collecting the outlying summits we made for Cairngorm, our last four-thousander. I thought Ivan was not far behind me but we weren't wasting time in chatting, just getting on with the job. Then, just as I placed my hand on the summit cairn, Ivan mysteriously appeared from behind it, with a huge grin on his face. Somehow, he had managed to pass me, unobserved, by taking a wide sweep, thus reaching the summit first. This was his revenge for being "beaten" to the top of Cairn Toul. A very competitive mountaineer was Ivan.

We were well aware that this had been a great day in Scottish hills, but another Cairngorm day with Ivan some years later ended not quite so enjoyably for me. We were having a week's skiing holiday together and after several runs down Coire na Ciste one day, decided we would have one last run. Ivan reached the bottom first and disappeared. I finished a moment later, and was bending down in a rocky area, taking off my skis, when a stupid skier, showing off with a celebratory jump at the end of his run, crashed full tilt on to my shoulders. The sudden weight crushed me to the ground, grinding my face into the rocks, and I felt my left eye fill with blood. They took me into the nearby first aid hut to staunch the blood, assuring me, despite appearances to the contrary, that my eye was still there, and I staggered out, rather shakily, to the car.

Ivan, who had been wondering where I'd been, appeared, and I drove down to the doctor in Aviemore who knew me slightly from various broken thumbs and torn ligaments in much earlier skiing years. The injury had, miraculously, just missed my eye, but required several stitches and the doctor bound up my head with a big white bandage so that I looked like a wounded soldier from the First World War. Ivan said I needed whisky so we went into the Alt na Craig bar and had several, the bandage provoking considerable sympathy from the habitués, and many more rounds. I was staying in a bed and breakfast establishment in the village but Ivan had scorned such luxury and was living in his tiny tent on an extremely depressing patch of grass and gravel underneath a railway bridge. It was to this tent that we repaired, after the binge, for a rather miserable meal. Ivan *did* like to live rough, mostly on old sandwiches. I didn't feel like skiing the next day, not with the bandage over my left eye, so decided to go home and Ivan, since we were in my car, went with me. I must say he took his shortened holiday with commendable equanimity and humour.

When I revisited all the two-thousanders in the Lake District in the early summer of 1977, either Ivan or Ted Stacey accompanied me on some of the rounds, although most of them I did alone. Several times ten or a dozen summits were collected in one round, and one day, on the Buttermere fells around Grasmoor, my tally was thirteen. The last day was reserved, appropriately, for Pillar Rock and Ivan was with me on this occasion. We decided to go up from Ennerdale and, having obtained the key for the locked gate and driven up the dale, set off from Gillerthwaite with a rope. The idea was to reach the summit of the rock by either the North Climb or the New West but we had only walked a few yards when one of us said, "Why on earth are we taking a rope? We're supposed to be walkers, collecting summits, not climbers." It was also a very hot day, so we put the rope back in the car and wandered up the Old West and down the Slab and Notch – appropriate routes, we thought, for mere pedestrians.

On top we encountered two energetic young climbers on their first visit to the Rock who asked us to suggest a good climb. We put them on to the North-West. Later in the day, as we trotted down to the valley, we looked back at the north-west corner of the Rock, rearing up in dark silhouette against the sun, and, right on the edge, the two young men climbing up into the sunshine. As we were scrambling down Slab and Notch we had bumped into an old friend, Tony Greenbank, who insisted on taking a photograph of the two old-stagers. It was a happy finish to the two-thousanders.

With Ivan you usually had to ski down places which, with others, you would avoid. You could say that in his later years he was an old, bold skier and climber. He had been the first man, in 1951, to ski over the cornice and down the steep east face of Helvellyn to Red Tarn – a feat not repeated by the hard men of the Lake District Ski Club until 1984. Steep snow didn't bother Ivan: the steeper it was the better.

When Ivan and I were not skiing in winter we would often go snow climbing, which could mean either fairly serious stuff with two axes apiece, a few ice screws and a "dead man" belay, or just pottering about on crampons. I remember a few winter climbing days with him on ice-plastered crags on and around Helvellyn, but mostly we climbed unroped, seeking out places where we could crampon around in fairly exposed but probably not really dangerous places. One of us would spot a likely area, say Hart Crag above Deepdale, and we would go there and wander up and down the snow terraces and slopes, picking out the best lines.

Ivan had devised or perfected a "safe" method of solo winter climbing in which you were belayed from your waist-harness to both your axes. In this way, according to Ivan, you were always safe if you slipped. We both used this ploy when climbing alone although, fortunately, I never had cause to test its efficiency in an emergency. I remember using it one afternoon on a delightful solo winter round up the steep north gully of Catstycam, up and down Helvellyn Lower Man from Brown Cove and up and down the head wall of Helvellyn above Red Tarn. Straightforward work but steepish and, with the snow glinting in the sunshine and nobody about, exhilaratingly exposed.

One of my last winter-climbing memories of Ivan is of an unroped ascent of Wetherlam by its east face, plastered in snow and ice. We were traversing a steep wall of hard snow to the right of the gullies of Hen Tor and near the top I happened to look back at Ivan, plunging in his axes as he crossed the slope. Because of the angle, and the steep snow slope against the black, snow-streaked crags, it made a fantastic picture and I've always regretted I'd no camera with me. Looking back and down, the snow slope looked far steeper than it was, and Ivan seemed to be climbing up out of frightening depths. If I had managed to take a picture I could have captioned it "Crossing the Second (or Third) Icefield on the North Wall of the Eiger" and not one in a hundred people would have questioned it. And that, or a score of similar pictures, is how I remember the bold Ivan: outdoor adventuring under any conditions, in any weather, at almost any age. He was in his eighties when we had that splendid Wetherlam day together, perhaps a bit slow by then but still steady as a rock.

I remember, too, his remarkable facility with locked gates in Scotland. He would either have the key to them in his pocket, know the keeper from whom he could obtain the key, or find a way to open the gate without a key. This knowledge or expertise saved us many dreary miles of road walking, although now and again he had to buy large drams of whisky for old, weather-beaten gillies in remote Highland hostelries. All these varied skills must have stood Ivan in good stead for, having done the Cuillin ridge twice at a good age, he was able to complete all the Munros. Of course, Ivan lived for mountains, as do so many of us.

Swirl How and Great Carrs

The Little Red Robin

*Our last little walk together was five days before she passed
away. Disabled and walking with a stick, she couldn't go very far,
but she had an ambition to reach Loughrigg Terrace again. It was
a crisp, sunny afternoon with ice on the track and streaks of snow
on the tops. She struggled on bravely from the White Moss car
park, across the bridge and up the rise, stopping now and again
to look at the expanding views. At the last stop a robin alighted at
our feet, suddenly appearing out of nowhere as robins do, and
Violet talked to him. The robin, bright red, perky and friendly,
accompanied us up the track. Every time we stopped, the robin
stopped, and he and Violet would have another chat. We reached
the start of the Terrace and the first patches of snow. She had
made it! There was a chill east wind and we decided to go down –
a painful process for Violet, balancing across the icy bits with her
stick, and me chivvying and bullying her along in my usual
fashion. I pointed out the views, identifying the tops, but she
wouldn't have taken it all in. She wasn't that good at
remembering Lakeland mountain names, mixing up Caw with
Cow and talking of Stickling Pike. We reached the place where we
had last seen the robin, and there he was again. Suddenly, he
hopped on to my outstretched arm and Violet had a long chat
with him, her face barely a foot from his beak. Finally, we ambled
down to the car. It had been only a little walk, barely a mile, but
Violet said she had enjoyed it immensely. A week later,
rearranging her possessions and trying to decide which of three
large flower vases to retain, her friend told me, "She always liked
that one – the one with the red robin on it. She loved robins." So I
kept that one and it now stands half way up the stairs, full of her
favourite flowers, with the little red robin peeping out.*

February 1991

Chapter Fourteen

Beauty, Adventure and Sadness

When I had to give up rock-climbing at 78 years of age because of my funny feet and toes, and skiing, two years later, for the same reason, it wasn't the end of the world. There were still mountains and hills to be tramped, "days of fresh air in the rain and the sun", and, hopefully, even years of them. And so it has turned out – a hundred or so hill days in each of the best years, according to my mountain diary, and usually more than seventy. Of course, I sigh now and again for the old climbing days with the Tigers, the company of many other cragsmen friends who have passed on, and the comfortable feel of good, rough rock. Even today, on a fell walk, I itch to get my fingers on a bit of rock, go out of my way to scramble up little outcrops, and still find it difficult to pass a sizeable crag without devising, in my mind's eye, climbing routes to the top. Crags are always the features that first catch my eye in a mountain scene.

Looking back on my days on the crags, I have the fondest memories of many climbing partners, some of them quite well known in the mountain world. There was, for example, "Rusty" (Lt. Col. Horace) Westmorland who first introduced me to Shepherd's Crag in Borrowdale. I can picture him now, with his jaunty feathered hat and neatly trimmed moustache, patiently demonstrating the correct sequence of moves on Donkey's Ears or pointing out a harder way to finish the top pitch of Chamonix. One day before the 1953 guidebook came out, he told me that Bentley Beetham had just shown him a delightful new route of his on Raven Crag, Combe Ghyll and that we should do it together. This was my introduction, probably its third ascent, to Corvus, ever afterwards a favourite route of mine. "Rusty" and I also skied together several times, both in the Lake District and on ski club meets in the Cairngorms. This remarkable man, who had put up his first new routes as far back as 1910 and had known the very pioneers of British mountaineering, was still rock-climbing in his eighties and mountain walking in his nineties. He was always a spruce, neat, military figure and a neat, precise climber.

Then there was Lord Chorley – R.S.T. Chorley in the guidebooks – who had been involved in several Lake District first ascents and, most notably for me, had been H.S. Gross's second on the first ascent of Eliminate "B" on Dow Crag in 1922. Since then he had become a peer, a prominent figure in the national parks movement, and, among many other appointments, the chairman of Westmorland Quarter Sessions. In this last office he would travel up from London to Kendal to preside at the court, and the day before would usually ring me up to arrange a day's climbing together. Perhaps I was then the only climber in the town he knew. At that time he was quite elderly and rather short-sighted, but very enthusiastic about the crags, and still climbing to a high standard. We often climbed together on either Dow Crag or Gimmer Crag, and it was remarkable how, after his slow, rather stumbling approach to the crag, he would immediately move into top gear when he got on the climb. I especially remember a day on Murray's Route on Dow when the rough approach up the screes must have been purgatory for him, but, as soon as he could get his fingers on the rock, he was in his element. Walking up the screes he couldn't see his feet, but once on the climb he could see the holds all right, and just romped up.

Graham Macphee, a notable leader on both Lake District and Scottish crags, with whom I had climbed before the war, was another distinguished mountaineer to share a rope with me in later years. But I especially remember him for a midnight walk we once did together. I was going to bed one June evening when he telephoned to ask whether I was aware it was a wonderful moonlit night, and what on earth was I doing wasting my time in bed. "Get your boots," he said, "and meet me at your garden gate in half an hour. We're going up Helvellyn."

And so we drove into Grisedale and walked up Striding Edge in the moonlight to the top of Helvellyn. As we went along the Edge – naturally, with Graham, over the top of all the towers – we could see its shadow clearly outlined in the moonlight, beyond the black pool of Red Tarn. On top, in our sleeping bags, we dozed off for an hour or two, and then waited for the dawn. It came at precisely ten minutes to five. There was a gradual lightening of the sky in the east and then, suddenly, the sun peeping over the Northern Pennines, and a new day. We watched the first golden rim swell into a great ball of fire, lighting up the whole of Lakeland with new, friendly colours. The distant views were remarkable: mountains and sea and, over in the north-west, the Lowland hills of Scotland.

We finished off the coffee, rolled up the sleeping bags, and rattled down Swirrel Edge to the dale. There was not a sign of life as we motored back over Kirkstone, and we were back home before seven for breakfast, with the feeling that, somehow, we had stolen an extra day.

I had the pleasure of the company of David Sproson, a much younger friend and a good cragsman, for my last rock-climbs. We went to Grey Crag in Birkness Combe, Buttermere, a favourite corner of mine for many years, but, surprisingly, new to David. Sharing leads, we did three modest routes of about v. diff. standard. I didn't find any particular difficulty with the familiar climbs, apart from discomfort with my feet, but descending the screes between climbs proved excruciating and I realised my climbing days were really over. Since then there has been further deterioration, but with assorted appliances in my boots I can, thankfully, still cope with fell walking.

Writing of Birkness Combe reminds me of once being shamed into climbing there, on a nasty, wet day, by two elderly climbers. My brother Leslie and I had been intending to climb on Grey Crag but decided to abandon our plans when we saw the streaming rock. But then two ancient climbers, in rickety nailed boots and old tattered clothing, appeared out of the mist and told us they had just repeated some climbs on the crag they had first put up generations earlier. One of them was Claude Elliott, the distinguished former headmaster and provost of Eton, who had a house in Buttermere, and whom I happened to know slightly, but I can't now remember his partner's name. Elliott had been involved in first ascents in Buttermere as early as 1912. When they had tottered down the screes we just had to do something, and managed to crawl, with difficulty, up a couple of the old gents' routes.

An occasional mountain companion, but certainly never on the crags, was the eminent guidebook writer, Alf Wainwright. I had known him, as the borough treasurer of Kendal, before he started on his guidebooks, and we went into the fells together on two or three occasions. Once he asked me to take him to Dove's Nest caves above Combe Ghyll in Borrowdale, but on our arrival below the caves – now said to be dangerous because of rockfalls – he refused to scramble up the easy rocky slope to reach the entrance. Anticipating this, I had secreted a rope in my rucksack, but A.W. wouldn't have anything to do with this, either, so he never saw the caves.

Alfred Wainwright was a remarkable man in many ways, but not a very agile walker and would go miles to avoid climbing drystone walls. Once, coming down Troutbeck Tongue together, I had to wait twenty minutes for him while he took a roundabout route to avoid a wall. In view of this complete lack of dexterity, his lone ascent, for guidebook purposes, of places like Jack's Rake or the direct scramble up Grasmoor End were quite courageous enterprises. Indeed, since he had no idea how to use a compass, many of his walks (alone and often in bad weather) must have been minor adventures. And the real story behind his Lakeland guidebooks – how he covered all the fells of Lakeland, in considerable detail, relying entirely on public transport – has still to be written.

He and I always remained friends although I blamed him, to his face and in print, for taking away some of the adventure by almost leading people by the hand up the fells, and also for causing much of the erosion of the popular paths. Far better, I thought, to work out your own route from the map and then read up your Wainwright afterwards – to see what you'd missed out.

But, despite his lack of agility, Alf was a sound mountain man with a splendid sense of direction and a real love of the hills. He was also a gifted cartographer and artist, a sensitive and often witty writer, and one of the most single-minded and industrious people I have ever known. In private, he was also, quietly, a friendly and generous person. More than forty years ago, before the great financial success of his guides, he offered to finance a book culled from some of my early writings. I had to decline the offer, but there were other instances of his liberality and it is well known that most of his money went to animal rescue. He kindly dedicated one of his books of Scottish mountain drawings to me, and on the wall of my study there is a splendid pen and ink drawing of Dow Crag that he once did for me. It is a completely unique drawing, not one that was used in any of his books. And, to illustrate one of my books, he drew, at my request, an outstandingly original map of the Lake District. Alfred Wainwright might have been a difficult man to know

My last rock climb on Grey Crag, Buttermere in 1989, aged 78. *(David Sproson)*

Josie on the summit of Ben Nevis in June, 1993 (she had insisted on taking her Union Jack tea towel).

Robin, aged 5½, on the summit of Coniston Old Man. 1945.

Josie on the way up Red Pike, Buttermere

My wonderful son Robin, on Catstycam, shortly before his passing.

Myself, on the fell behind my home in 1991. *(This photograph, by Denis Thorpe, is reproduced by kind permission of The Guardian)*

but there were more things about him, good things, than met the eye. I'm very honoured to have known him fairly well. Perhaps he was some sort of a genius, who knows?

For more than twenty years, Ted Stacey of Levens, Cumbria has been a constant mountain companion. Indeed, since his retirement most Wednesdays have been set aside for our outings together or, when the weather has been too foul, for chats about our adventures in the hills, or plans for future walks. We must have spent hundreds of mountain days together in the Lake District, Scotland or the Yorkshire Dales, occasionally with our wives, and I hope there will be many more of them.

I first met Ted in 1976, when Mollie and I were on holiday in Glencoe, staying in a large caravan we often used. One day Ivan Waller called on us for a chat and a drink and introduced us to Ted. They were on their way, I seem to remember, to Glen Shiel in the Highlands, collecting Munros from a tent. Thereafter, the three of us met frequently, and Ted and I became regular partners. Ted isn't a rock-climber, although he'd done a little in younger days, but is usually game for a scramble and is a very strong and knowledgeable mountain walker. He is also something of an amateur meteorologist, a useful attribute in a mountain man, and adept at retaining masses of facts and figures, not all of them important, in his head. He can tell you, for instance, the exact height of any Lake District mountain and many other British hills. He once told me he could tell me the day of the week on which I was born if I gave him the date and the year. He did this in about one minute, but whether he was correct or not, I can't say.

In Scotland we were often together in the "Arrochar Alps" and were always considerably impressed by the luxurious, almost sybaritic, excellence of the Arrochar public toilets which, I seem to recall, ran to potted palm trees. Amusingly, too, there was also a first-aid room. Certainly, we decided, these were the finest public conveniences in Scotland – in dramatic contrast to the toilets, many years ago, at Ullapool where you performed in a windswept, rusty tin shelter on the beach, completely open to the sea. One year Ted and I were trotting down the steep slope of Ben Vorlich in the Arrochar hills, after having first climbed Ben Vane, when the sole of one of my boots came loose and I went sprawling. I was supposed to be "testing" the first version of Chris Brasher's new "magic", lightweight boots and this was my first outing in them. We tied up the boot with string and I limped back to the car, but rang up Chris when I got home. Naturally, he was concerned – it could have been bad publicity – but he arranged for me to pick up another pair at the Kendal factory and to be taken on a tour showing the making of the boot. Apparently, they could tell by various markings exactly who had been responsible for the minor mistake in production, although they promised me that he or she would not be punished. Bad luck that the one complaint they had had should have been on a boot being "tested".

Memories of scores of happy Lakeland days with Ted are triggered off by glances at my mountain diary. I have noted long ridge walks collecting summits, sometimes as many as a dozen in a day, winter days kicking our way up snow-filled gullies or, when I was collecting "scrambles", minor epics with loose rock on remote crags. There were days on the High Street tops, one of them, doing them from either end and meeting in the middle; an evening scamper round the Fairfield Horseshoe, just making it to the Golden Rule in Ambleside before closing time; and long Buttermere and Mallerstang rounds with our ladies. But three wonderful mountain days seemed especially memorable.

We had decided one bright autumn morning to make a scrambling route of perhaps 1600 feet up the precipitous face of Ill Crag, overlooking the wilderness of upper Eskdale. It was an almost unknown mountain wall, without tracks or recorded climbs. Near the head of Mosedale on our way up we came upon W. Heaton Cooper, the artist, seated at his easel painting, by a remarkable coincidence, the very crag we had decided to climb. It was clear in the sunshine, about three miles away. Heaton, an old friend, was then approaching his eighties but bronzed, alert and very interested in our project. He wished us well.

By linking three or four crags together we climbed the cliff up easy slabs, pleasant walls of sound, rough rock and shattered outcrops, finding little real difficulty, and decided that other routes would probably be equally feasible. Just across the ravine of Little Narrowcove was the bold, little peak of Pen, a favourite summit of mine, and we watched it slowly sink beneath us as we clambered to the top of Ill Crag to look down the winding shoals of the Esk reaching to the sea. This area is among the steepest and roughest in the district, and that day it had all the magic of high, lonely places: silence, solitude, exciting depths and sunlit views to far horizons. We wandered back, down to the Esk and along Mosedale to the car, happy with a mission successfully accomplished and virtually a new route up a Lakeland "three-thousander".

Another memorable day with Ted was a winter trip to Wetherlam when the fog was so thick that, doing a snow climb up the east face, we had to use the compass to work out the direction of the summit. Probably more by luck than skill we managed to hit the right line and cramponned up on to Wetherlam Edge, just below the summit. Recognising the place, we made for the top, still in the thickest gloom. And then, just before the cairn, we suddenly stepped up out of the dense fog into dazzling sunshine and bright blue skies. Immediately below and all around us was a white sea of cotton-wool mist, reaching to the horizon and, apparently, covering the whole of Lakeland. But just sticking above the fleecy-white clouds, seven miles away to the north-west, were the topmost rocks of the Scafells, the highest land in England, so clear they looked within throwing distance.

For a while we basked in the sunshine, marvelling at the fantastic scene, and then, turning round, were surprised and delighted to see something perhaps even more fantastic: a gigantic Brocken Spectre, with two concentric rainbows, or "glories", apparently straddling a rock ridge 200 yards away. Over the years I've seen several of these giant apparitions in the mountains, caused by the shadow of the observer being thrown on to a curtain of thin mist by sunlight. However, this was the first, and only time, I had seen a "double glory". For some time we studied the huge spectre on the ridge, making him wave his arms by waving ours, and then, after memorable revelations that had made our day, we stepped down out of the sunlight into the almost impenetrable fog. Feeling our way, we crept carefully down the snow to the car.

A last memory of another excellent day with Ted Stacey, although I hope and believe there will be many more, is also of a winter outing. In alpine picture-postcard conditions of sunlit snows and a cloudless blue sky we went up Fairfield from Tongue Gill. To avoid possible processions on the tourist track, we went straight for the summit from the source of the gill – about 1400 feet of steep, deep powder snow, compacted wind slab, crusted snow-ice and straightforward black ice. For added flavour we deliberately left our crampons on our rucksacks and kicked and cut our way up the steepening snow dome with our axes – the old way.

It was quite a challenging ascent, and from the summit the view had the clarity and perfection you might enjoy on the high fells, if you were very fortunate, perhaps once or twice each winter. Dazzling sunlight glistened on waves of snow-bound summits reaching to the horizon, with all the greens and browns hidden away in unseen depths, and nothing to be seen except snow and ice, blinding white or faintly blue in the shadows. All the way down the Stone Arthur ridge, as we picked our way through the ice, it was freezing hard, but the blazing sunshine, reflected off the snow, was strong enough to burn our faces. Down again at the foot of Tongue Gill, well satisfied with our good day, we happened to look back at the great snow dome of Fairfield, all aglow in the late afternoon sunlight. And there, nearly two miles away but clear as ink blobs on a map, was the long line of our steps, arrow-straight to the summit – our step-ladder to the skies.

Certainly I owe my good friend Ted a great deal for his many years of mountain companionship, his reliability under difficult conditions, his ready acceptance of my many failings and his sense of humour. During the past seven years or so, since the passing in 1988 of Mollie, my dear wife for 51 years and, later, of Violet, my second wife, I have also had the pleasure of the company in the hills of my partner and constant companion, Josie. But whereas with Ted, we are usually in country familiar to both of us, with Josie, I have had to teach her everything from the start. Before we met she had had no experience of the fells. It has been a happy time for me, passing on knowledge of hills I have loved all my life. After these first few years she has now been up all the Lake District "two-thousanders", except two or three around Pillar, collected all the forty Yorkshire summits, most of the thirty or so in the Northern Pennines, and several other mountains in England and Scotland. Uphill, she goes very strongly, often shaming me, but in descent, especially on rough ground, is rather slow. But, then, she's a great-grandmother. Josie is rather proud of a fairly recent photograph of herself, draped in a Union Jack for some reason, in snow and thick mist on the top of Ben Nevis.

And so, as I approached my nineties, life seemed pleasant enough, despite minor afflictions. I could still get into the hills and wonderful mountain companions were readily available. True, there were no longer any excitements but at my age I could do without these. And then, right out of the blue, just before my 85th birthday, there was a delightful surprise when the 1996 New Year's Honours List announced my appointment to MBE "for services to literature and the Lake District". As a former scribbler and hack I was greatly flattered that someone in high places must have considered some of my writings to be literature.

Close companions in the hills, especially in later years, included my wonderful son Robin, who, forty years earlier, had accompanied me on our memorable traverse of the Cuillin Ridge in Skye and, increasingly, had been drawn back to his boyhood hills in Lakeland. Robin had married again and first took his new wife, Mary, then unaccustomed to mountains, up all the Lake District "two-thousanders" in a remarkably short time. They then carried on, using my Kendal home as a sort of climbing hut, and collected all the two-thousanders in England, including the Cheviots and the couple of summits down in Devon. Meanwhile, Robin took a first-aid course, so that he might help people in distress on the hills, qualified as a mountain leader and, in the spring of 1998, went on an expedition to the Himalayas. Out of the party of ten only four people made it to the summit of Mera Peak (over 21,000 feet), Robin leading three others to the top after the professional leader had collapsed with altitude sickness. At 58 he had been the oldest in the team – and the fittest.

But then, in early August 1998, my whole world collapsed about me with shattering finality when I heard that Robin, in his home in Northampton, had suddenly and inexplicably passed away from a heart attack. Just before his death he and Mary had spent the weekend with us in Kendal, and on the Saturday had had a wonderful day together on the Coniston fells, wandering along the Old Man and Dow Crag, a round that Robin had known for most of his life. The Old Man had been Robin's first mountain at four years of age and, tragically, was to be his last. I have a treasured photograph of him on the summit at five and a half years of age. The picture was taken by my father, Robin's grandfather, making his first ascent of the mountain. Robin, however, was already well acquainted with the way up and had acted as the leader.

Robin was a natural leader, both in the mountains and on the rugger field. He read maps as other people read books or newspapers and always knew exactly where he was, both on the hill and on the map. You never got lost in the mountains with Robin. Sadly, he and Mary had planned to retire to Kendal in about a month's time so that they could devote the rest of their lives to Robin's homeland hills. They were building a new house in the town and many plans for the future were afoot. The memorial service was held in the Sedbergh chapel, looking out to hills that he knew so well, where Robin and Mary had been married only three years earlier. It will be difficult picking up the threads of my life again for

Robin was everything I could have wished a son to be – kind, gentle, thoughtful and quiet and a splendid mountain man. Both of us, quietly, were working on ideas for future trips in the hills together. Sadly, these are not to be. God, indeed, works in a mysterious way, His wonders to perform.

And so, hoping that time will ease my sorrow, I potter about on the fells with Josie or Ted or some other friend, once or twice a week if the weather's reasonable. There's an easy six-mile round over Scout Scar and Cunswick Scar I do regularly from the house, without needing to use the car, and other modest, local opportunities are available. We avoid the Lake District at weekends and holiday times, sometimes driving into Yorkshire or the Northern Pennines. The lovely Howgills are a favourite corner where we're more likely to find quietude. Having to contribute the Lake District "Country Diary" to *The Guardian* every other Monday is an excellent discipline, propelling me outdoors into the hills on a regular basis, instead of wasting my time watching television. Once or twice a year we go into Scotland for some hill walking but I don't go abroad any more. Ted Stacey, though, still goes walking in the Swiss Alps every year besides at least one good long trip to the Highlands, where we often meet up.

Now and again I bump into my old Coniston Tigers pal, Jim Porter, and we enjoy a chat together about the old days. Perhaps, too, the other two surviving Tigers, Jack Atkinson and Len Brown, both still living in Barrow, meet up occasionally to talk about those exciting years when we were young and fit. As we always say, "the best years of our lives". I am immensely grateful that I have all these wonderful memories of a long mountain life to hearten me, that I am still able to get into the hills, and that I can see some of them from my windows every day.

There they are, due east, behind the town hall clock, the shapely hump of Benson Knott appearing to fill the sky – I was up there three days ago. To the north is the long line of the Whinfell range, from Grayrigg Common to Ashstead Fell, with the dark shadow of the recent afforestation plain to see, and, moving westwards, the ridge leading to Grey Crag, the most easterly two-thousander in Lakeland. They are only little hills really, and not especially exciting ones. However, if I walk up to the golf course, just behind my house, or on to Scout Scar, a little further on, I can see most of the Lakeland hills, from Black Combe to Mardale's Harter Fell, stretched across the horizon. The Scafells, Bowfell and Great Gable can be seen sticking up in the middle.

And if I turn round and look to the east, there's the unmistakable flat top of Ingleborough, just peeping up behind the dark mountain wall of Gragareth.

I hope there'll always be mountains to see and, even when I can only manage hummocks, little hills to climb. The house is full of mountain paintings, photographs and drawings – many by mountain friends like Heaton Cooper, Geoffrey Pooley, Jill Aldersley, Geoffrey Berry or Alf Wainwright – and store rooms and cupboards crammed with skis, crampons, ice axes, rucksacks and boots that I can't bring myself to discard. I still keep my mountain diary up to date, although the outings are a little shorter nowadays, and not nearly so exciting.

But I can still, closing my eyes, remember every move on Eagle's Nest Direct or Tophet Wall on Gable, Murray's on Dow, White Ghyll Wall in Langdale or, even, Great Gully on The Screes and a score of other climbs. When I walk up the hill behind the house I subconsciously list the names of the fifty or more hills crowding the horizon, every one of them with a dozen memories of great days in all sorts of weather. Not to mention memories of hundreds of Scottish hills, mountains in the Alps or the Rockies, or even just the lovely Howgills. Altogether, hundreds of rock-climbs, hundreds of mountains, maybe hundreds of days in the snow and, over the years, a thousand adventures, every one of them worthwhile. It started with Stickle Pike in schoolboy short trousers and then, a few years later, Dow Crag with dear old George Basterfield. Then came the Coniston Tigers, grand lads every one of them, the happy years with the hut before and after the war and, later, climbing partnerships with wonderful companions. And the love affair with hills and all their delights hasn't quite finished yet – a long lifetime of beauty and adventure sadly clouded with heart-rending sorrow towards the end. But, as the pain, hopefully, eases a little, so very much for which to be grateful and, wonderfully, I can still lift up my eyes to the hills – every day.

Epilogue

"The Other Side of Eden"

Northwards from Morecambe Bay to the heart of mountain Lakeland and west to east from Wordsworth's Duddon to the Yorkshire moors lies perhaps the fairest land in England. Here, with its feet in the sea and its head on the mountain tops, is a glorious, almost 40 miles sweep of our second largest county – a green, rolling countryside of fells and dales, lakes and woodlands, hard-won farmlands reaching to the heights and ancient market towns. With its thousand years of history from the Vikings to the smugglers and the coaching days it was the chosen home of the Lake Poets and today is the cherished sanctuary of all those who seek the fresh air and quietude of the hills. More than 90,000 people live and work within these 600 square miles of beautiful countryside. Nowadays we call this area the district of South Lakeland but the poet sang of "The roots of Heaven".

...   .

There is no corner of England more crowded with history and legend, perhaps no stretch of countryside better known to the holiday-maker, with the country's largest lake, some of our most notable mountains and a literary tradition built on man's search for natural beauty and contentment, and no area in greater need of constant vigilance and safeguarding if its treasures are to remain unspoiled. Those of us who have the good fortune to live and work in the district of South Lakeland will always be proud of our heritage for, as the poet said: "I dream that heaven is very like this land, mountains and lakes and rivers undecaying, and simple woodlands and wild cherry flowers . . ."

– *Extracts from a text by Harry Griffin read out at a thanksgiving service in Kendal Parish Church on Sunday, May 18 1983 to mark the emergence of South Lakeland District Council.*

Index

Also from Sigma Leisure:

SPACE BELOW MY FEET

This is a republication of a classic book about "mountains, men and love". It tells how Gwen Moffat, an army deserter, made her uninhibited, unconventional way to become Britain's leading female climber, and the first woman to qualify as a mountain guide. "As a story of climbing and compulsive love of mountains, Space Below my Feet is magnificent." – *The Observer* £9.95

LAKELAND ROCKY RAMBLES: GEOLOGY BENEATH YOUR FEET

This is the companion book to Snowdonia Rocky Rambles: the perfect way to learn about why things look the way they do in our most beautiful National Parks. "Refreshing ... Ambitious ... Informative ... Inspiring" – *New Scientist.* £9.95

100 LAKE DISTRICT WALKS

If you plan to buy just one book of Lakeland walks, this is the one you need: "A useful addition to any walker's library" – *West Cumberland Gazette.* £7.95

IN SEARCH OF SWALLOWS & AMAZONS: Arthur Ransome's Lakeland

This is a new edition of a popular book originally published in 1986. Additional material has been added to satisfy even the most avid reader of "Swallows & Amazons" – three decades of Ransome hunting with text and photographs to identify the locations of the ever-popular series of books. There's a two fold pleasure in this book – enjoying the original stories and discovering the farms, rivers, islands, towns and hills that formed their backdrop. £7.95

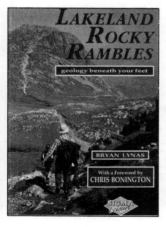

TEA SHOP WALKS IN THE LAKE DISTRICT

The original – now in its second edition! Do not confuse with any other book of the sameor similar title! Scones with strawberry jam and other delights await weary walkers. A leisurely introduction to the Lake District. *£6.95*

MORE TEA SHOP WALKS IN THE LAKE DISTRICT

Norman and June Buckley have planned more leisurely rambles in this companion volume to the first tea shop book on the region. Crossing both the central regions

and the lesser-known fringe areas, their 25 easy-going, circular walks range from 2 to 9 miles. £6.95

WALKS IN MYSTERIOUS NORTH LAKELAND

An unusual collection of 30 walks which provide a unique opportunity to visit places with a strange and mythical history.
"Each walk features remarkable hand-drawn maps and stylish, entertaining writing that is almost as good to read before a roaring open fire as on the open fells" LAKELAND WALKER.
'Graham writes with robust enthusiasm...colourful excursions' KESWICK REMINDER. £6.95

WALKS IN MYSTERIOUS SOUTH LAKELAND

Old Nick, witches, wizards, monsters, fairies, and grizzly monsters! Graham Dugdale intertwines intriguing tales of these dark beings with his 30 skilfully chosen gentle walks in south Cumbria. "This is a well-researched guide book, well written, with a welcome thread of humour." THE GREAT OUTDOORS. £6.95

BEST PUB WALKS IN THE LAKE DISTRICT

This, the longest-established (and best-researched) pub walks book for the Lakes, is amazingly wide-ranging, with an emphasis on quality of walks and the real ale rewards that follow! £6.95

BEST PUB WALKS ON THE LAKELAND FRINGES

The fringes of the Lake District have a great atmosphere of peace - a quality which has almost vanished from the crowded central areas of England's favourite National Park. In this collection of 25 walks, Neil Coates takes a fresh approach to the area, urging ramblers to discover the tranquility of the mountain paths, wild woodland, waterfalls and local heritage of the Lake District Fringes. Walks range from 4 to 11 miles and each one features a refreshing stop at a quiet village pub or country inn, personally selected by the author. £6.95

All of our books are available through booksellers. In case of difficulty, or for a free catalogue, please contact: SIGMA LEISURE, 1 SOUTH OAK LANE, WILMSLOW, CHESHIRE SK9 6AR.
Phone: 01625-531035
Fax: 01625-536800.
E-mail: info@sigmapress.co.uk
Web site: http//www.sigmapress.co.uk

MASTERCARD and VISA orders welcome.